Pruning

by Christopher Brickell
Published in Cooperation with the Royal Horticultural Society

A Fireside Book
Published by Simon & Schuster Inc.
New York London Toronto Sydney Tokyo

Editor-in-chief Christopher Brickell
Technical editor Kenneth A. Beckett
Editor Michael A. Janson
Art editor Leonard Roberts
Designers Tony Spalding, Celia Welcomme
Editorial assistant Margaret Little

FIRST FIRESIDE EDITION, 1988
Published by Simon & Schuster Inc.
Simon & Schuster Building
Rockefeller Center
1230 Avenue of the Americas
New York, New York 10020
FIRESIDE and colophon are registered trademarks of Simon & Schuster Inc.

Published in Great Britain by Mitchell Beazley Publishers Limited under the title *The Royal Horticultural Society's Encyclopedia of Practical Gardening: Pruning*
Edited and designed by Mitchell Beazley International Ltd.
Artists House, 14–15 Manette Street, London W1V 5LB

Typesetting by Servis Filmsetting Ltd.
Origination by Culver Graphics Ltd.

Printed in Portugal by Printer Portuguesa

10 9 8 7 6 5 4 3 2

Library of Congress Catalog Card Number 79-1717
ISBN: 0-671-65841-7

Contents

Introduction

Much of the success in the cultivation of plants is due to correct pruning and this book is designed to explain the subtleties of this gardening art in a practical way. Each stage of pruning is shown, indicating which branch or stem should be removed and how the plant will look after the operation.

When using the step-by-step diagrams remember that your own plant of the species concerned will not be exactly like that shown. The diagrams are designed to show the basic principles and methods. You must adapt these basic rules to your own situation and your own plant. The different tones of green have been used to designate each year of growth. This enables the gardener to see how the framework of the plant is built up and to identify parts of the plant to be pruned.

Many of the points made in this introduction are mentioned again in various sections of the book. This repetition is intentional and it is done to emphasize the specific points so that as experience is gained these rules will become automatic.

There may sometimes be many equally acceptable methods which can be used to do the same job. The method described may be one which I prefer personally, but other methods will, in some instances, produce similar results.

Pruning can be defined as the removal of any part of a plant to encourage it to grow, flower and fruit in the way the gardener wants. The degree of pruning will vary greatly from the removal of a large tree limb to dead-heading roses or pinching back growths on young pot plants, such as fuchsias, to make them branch. Even the cutting down of old growth on herbaceous plants in autumn or winter is a form of pruning, but in this book we are mainly concerned with trees and shrubs grown as ornamentals or for their fruit. The basic principles described will apply, however, for any pruning of garden plants.

Why prune at all—wild plants are not pruned and they grow and flower perfectly well? This is a question often asked, but in fact nature has her own method of pruning. Small branches are shed naturally, twigs, leaves and flowers die and fall off. All plants are slowly but continuously undergoing a process of renewal in nature, so by pruning we are, in part, accelerating a normal process.

Many plants will thrive with only very limited pruning and it is almost always better not to prune at all than to resort to the "slasher" or "haircut" techniques. These involve the merciless chopping down of all new growth annually to keep the plants "tidy" or because the plant concerned has grown too large for its position in the garden.

Pruning is sometimes necessary for specific reasons, but should never be used merely to keep plants tidy or under control.

Basic aims and principles

When we train and prune plants the main purpose is to obtain the maximum decorative effect or the best crop possible. At the same time it is important to maintain an attractive shape and appearance, with a balance between growth, flowering and fruiting, while keeping the plant vigorous and in good health.

Many trees and shrubs do not need rigorous annual pruning to fulfill these aims and after their initial training may need no more than minor "cosmetic pruning"; that is a gentle control of nature involving the removal of spent flowers and cutting out of thin, weak or crossing shoots to maintain an overall balanced shape.

On the other hand formally clipped hedges or topiary work involve not only firm early training but careful, continuous pruning if they are to be kept in a well-tailored condition.

Before beginning to prune any plant it is vital to know a few facts about its growth and flowering habit. Simple examination will show that most woody plants have at the end of each shoot a terminal or apical bud. Below this bud, on the stem, lateral or axillary buds are arranged in a characteristic pattern which varies with the species concerned. They may be alternate, opposite, whorled or arranged spirally and their position will determine where the future branches will form.

The terminal bud exerts what is known as apical dominance over lateral buds, that is it grows more rapidly and can assert its dominance by producing a chemical which inhibits the growth of lateral buds. If the terminal bud is cut away or broken off the lateral buds or shoots below will grow more rapidly. So what we are doing when we pinch out the soft tip of a young fuchsia or prune back a woody shoot on a shrub is breaking this apical dominance by removing the source of the lateral bud inhibitor. This process is known to gardeners as "stopping" and the lateral shoots which develop as a result of stopping are said to be "breaking."

This fact is basic to all pruning. The degree of apical dominance varies from species to species and sometimes seasonally within a species, each of which has a characteristic growth cycle. Generally trees, particularly in the first few years of growth, exhibit strong apical dominance, while shrubs that are intricately branched show it much less.

In plants such as *Syringa vulgaris*, the common lilac, which have opposite pairs of buds, the dominance is shared by the uppermost pair, which will usually grow at approximately the same rate and produce a typically forked pattern of growth. Sometimes one of the pair will gain dominance over the other and the growth becomes one-sided as can frequently be seen with *Deutzia*.

When pruning any plant it is important to cut back to a selected bud which will produce a shoot in the required direction. If the cut is above a bud facing outward the bud will break to produce a shoot that grows away from the center of the plant. The terminal bud of this shoot then asserts itself and controls the lateral growth below.

Similarly, when it is necessary to restrict the growth of a tree or shrub it is important to thin out the shoots or branches, removing some completely and, if needed, shortening each of those remaining back to an appropriately placed bud or main shoot.

The importance of correctly positioning pruning cuts is emphasized throughout this book. Cuts should always be made just above a healthy bud and sloping away from it so that the resulting shoots will grow in the direction required. Bad cuts will frequently contribute to "die-back" of the shoot and the selected growth bud.

There are no visible growth buds on the woody branches of trees and shrubs although dormant or adventitious buds are normally present underlying the bark. If dead wood or weak branches need to be removed the position of the cut must be chosen carefully. The cut should be made close to a healthy branch so that the minimum surface of the wound is exposed without leaving a snag of wood where disease might enter. All pruning of cuts or wounds more than $\frac{1}{2}$ inch in diameter should be treated with a wound paint to combat possible infection.

Early training and pruning

The majority of trees and shrubs benefit from a certain amount of early training, although some will develop naturally into well-shaped specimens with only gentle guidance and the removal of a few surplus or poorly placed shoots. Others need much firmer control, particularly if they are to be grown formally and trained to grow against a wall or fence. It is very important to make certain that the training given is timely and correct, even if it only involves the removal of one or two weak shoots. Allowing a double leader to develop on a tree at this stage or an awkwardly placed branch to grow can cause considerable problems in years to come.

There is always a natural reluctance to cut back vigorous growths on young plants even when they are obviously in the wrong position, but sometimes this must be done if the basic, balanced framework which will support the plant all its life is to be formed correctly.

Throughout this book considerable emphasis is placed on the development of a "framework" of branches which will act as the strong skeleton on which the foliage, flowers and fruit are carried.

Trees, unless they are pollarded, and many large shrubs and evergreens will retain this main framework throughout their lives and it is vital that it is strong and that the branches are fairly regularly spaced so that it is balanced with the weight of the smaller branches evenly distributed over the entire framework.

With shrubs which undergo periodic renewal pruning the framework is not permanent but it is still important to build up an evenly balanced, well-shaped plant. Shrubs such as *Deutzia*, black currants and some roses all depend on a regular supply of vigorous basal or near-basal shoots to replace worn-out growths.

Introduction

Pruning to maintain a healthy plant
Plants are most susceptible to diseases and pests when they are in poor condition. It is essential to make sure that adequate food and water are available so that healthy vigorous growth is produced regularly. This particularly applies to plants that are hard pruned annually. It is useless to cut their growth back severely if the plants are short of the food and water needed to produce new shoots. Feeding and watering, therefore, are directly relevant to pruning.

It is important also to remove and burn all dead, damaged and diseased shoots or wood—the "3 D's"—as soon as any are seen. In all cases the shoots or branches concerned should be cut back cleanly into healthy wood, where possible to a growth bud (or pair of buds) which will provide replacement shoots in due course. Dead or damaged growths always invite diseases and it is important to prevent infection by cutting these out to prevent any further deterioration. Pruning to maintain health also includes the removal of all crossing, immature, thin and weak shoots which frequently develop in the center of unpruned trees and shrubs due to the lack of light and air. This eliminates possible disease reservoirs and allows the vigorous shoots to develop unhindered and to produce healthy foliage and fine flowers.

Maintaining shape or habit
A number of trees and shrubs are best allowed to develop naturally after their initial pruning, apart from cosmetic pruning and the removal of dead, damaged or diseased growth. Occasionally vigorous, awkwardly placed shoots will upset the balanced symmetry of a mature tree or shrub and such shoots should be cut out completely.

With many shrubs, and less frequently with small trees, one section may be more vigorous than the others so that the plant is asymmetrical. When this happens remember the principle that the strong shoots should be lightly pruned while the weak shoots require hard pruning. The reason is that hard pruning stimulates vigorous growth, so pruning back strong growths will simply encourage more vigorous shoots to be produced, which encourages the uneven shape further. The maxim *"weak growth, hard prune; strong growth, light prune"* should always be kept in mind when remedial pruning is needed.

Decorative effect or the most crops
It is essential to know the growth, and the flowering and fruiting characteristics of the plant to be pruned. These factors will govern the technique needed to obtain the maximum decorative effect or the highest crop capacity.

The gardener needs to know whether the plant flowers on the current year's growth, such as *Buddleia davidii*, or whether it produces blooms from shoots one or more years old, such as *B. alternifolia*. It would be useless to prune the latter species hard each spring, because the one-year-old flowering shoots for the season would be removed.

With red currants the fruit is borne on short spurs growing from a permanent framework of old wood. Black currants, however, fruit from one-year-old shoots and a renewal system of pruning is needed.

Some plants may be pruned in two ways to provide different garden effects. An example is the purple-leaved forms of the smoke bush (*Cotinus coggygria*), which is usually grown as a large shrub bearing attractive foliage and flowers, and requires only minor cosmetic pruning. The growths can be cut hard back each spring to provide handsome large foliage on the current season's growth but no flower.

Knowledge of growth characteristics will help to determine when pruning should be carried out, but as a general rule the best time of year to prune is when the maximum growing period to produce either flowering shoots or growth which will flower the following season can be encouraged.

Pruning tools
The basic tools most gardeners will need for pruning are a good pair of shears, hand or power shears for hedge-cutting, and if heavier work is necessary a pair of long-handled pruners and a pruning saw. Pruning knives (a), the kind with a slightly curved blade and handle (b), are available but they are not easy to use without considerable practice. Inexpert use of pruning knives often results in ragged cuts and heavy shears are easier to use.

Three main kinds of shears are available but a number of variations on these themes can be bought. One has a straight-edged blade which cuts down onto a bar of softer metal (c). The second has a convexly curved blade which cuts against, but not directly on to, a fixed bar (d). The third has two convexly curved blades which cut in a scissorlike fashion (e). Any of these styles, if used correctly, can give excellent results. Always position the stem to be cut close to the base of the blade where it can be held firmly. If the cut is made with the tip, the blades are liable to be strained or forced apart.

Long-handled pruners are basically strong shears with long handles which give extra leverage when cutting fairly thick stems or branches (f). They are extremely useful for dealing with old stems on such vigorous shrubs as *Philadelphus* and for cutting out the old stumps which gradually build up at the base of rose bushes. They are also known as 'loppers" or occasionally as "parrots."

Pruning saws will be required for cutting larger branches. Several designs are available which are especially suitable for use in small spaces and narrow angles between branches.

A pruning saw with a tapering blade with teeth on both sides, one set producing a smoother finished cut than the other (g) is very useful. Care has to be taken not to damage nearby branches with the set of teeth not in use and for this reason some gardeners prefer a tapered version of the normal carpenter's saw. A saw with a curved blade tapered to a sharp point that has sloping teeth designed to cut on the return stroke is also very useful in confined spaces (h).

Hand shears are available in several designs (i). Whichever style is chosen, it should be well-balanced, light and comfortable to use, with an efficient, sharp cutting edge.

It is important to use good-quality tools and to keep your tools in good condition. This means cleaning and oiling them after each use to keep them free of rust, and making sure they are sharp before use. Never attempt to cut through wood that is too thick or large for the tool. This will only strain the tool and make it less effective. Twisting the tool while cutting through a branch will also strain it and cause a ragged cut.

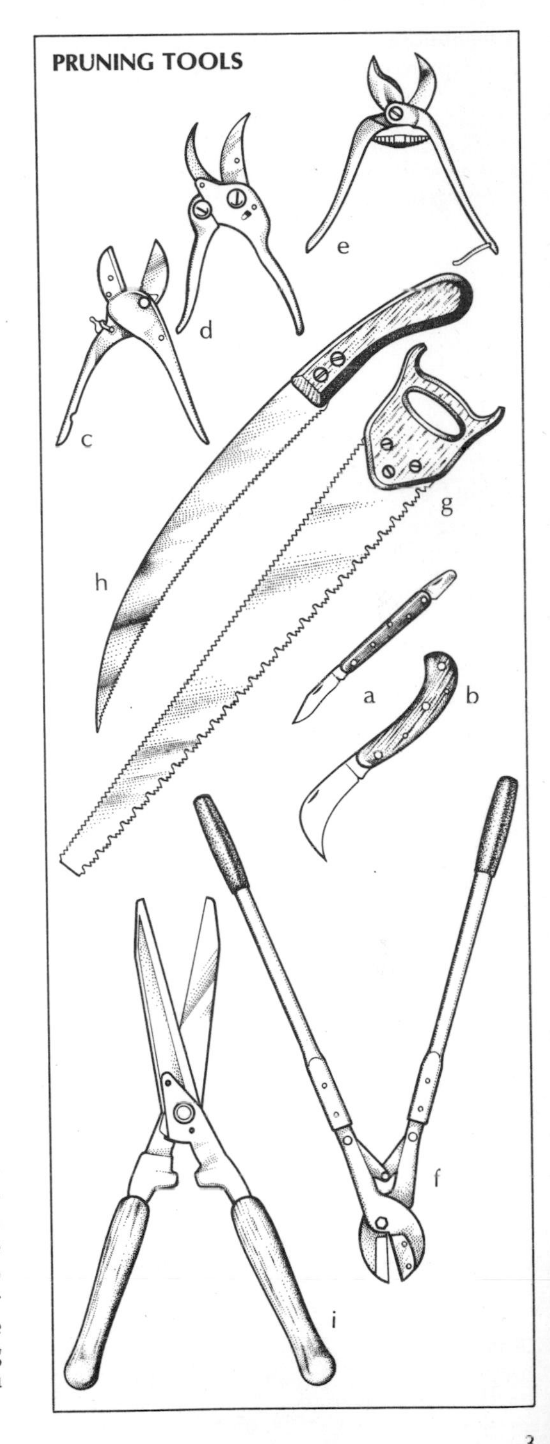

Glossary

Adventitious buds Normally growth buds develop between leaf and stem in a definite order. Adventitious buds are growth buds that arise without any relation to the leaves, usually in response to a wound. The shoots that arise from cut-back stems of a pollarded willow grow from adventitious buds.

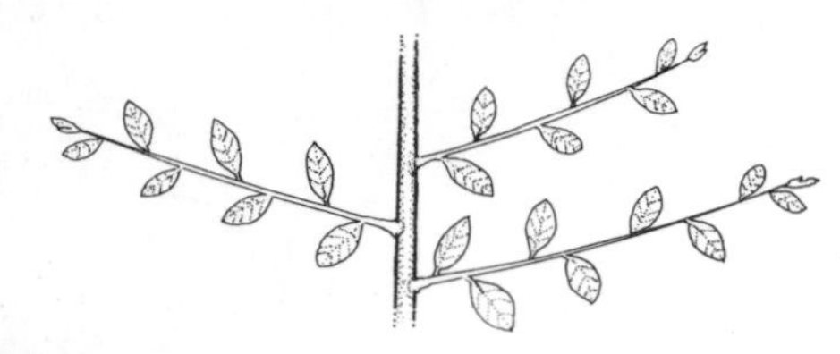

Alternate leaves, buds, shoots These occur singly on stems at different heights, alternating from one side to the other.

Apex The tip of a stem, hence **apical bud**, the uppermost bud on the stem, and **apical shoot**, the uppermost stem on a system of branches.

Apical dominance Said of a terminal or apical bud which inhibits the growth of lateral buds and grows more rapidly than they do.

Axil The angle between a leaf and the stem on which it is growing. Hence **axillary bud**, the bud between leaf and stem, and **axillary shoot**, the shoot which arises between leaf and stem.

Bark-ringing The removal of a ring of bark from the trunk of an unfruitful tree to check shoot growth.

Basal At the lowest part of the plant or of a stem, hence **basal growth, basal shoots** and **basal leaves**.

Blind shoot A shoot which does not develop fully, in which the apical bud aborts and no further growth is made.

Branched head A branch system on a tree in which there is no central leader shoot.

Break The development of lateral shoots as a result of pruning (stopping or pinching back) a shoot to an axillary bud.

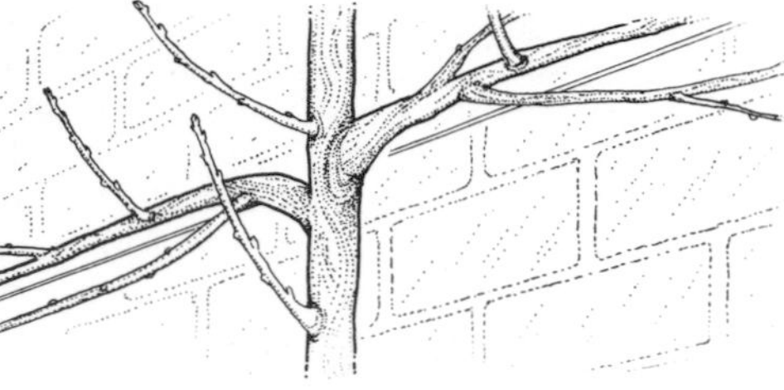

Breastwood Shoots which grow forward from trees or shrubs trained against walls, fences or other support structures.

Bud The embryo shoot, flower or flower cluster hence **growth bud, flower bud**.

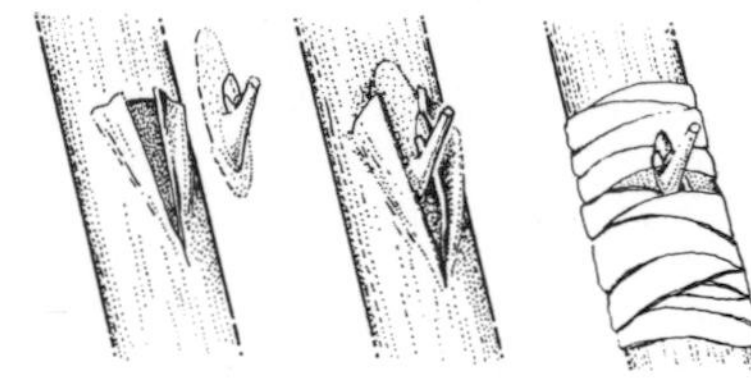

Budding A method of grafting using a single growth bud rather than part of a stem with several buds.

Callus The growth of corky tissue which forms naturally over a wound as a protective layer.

Central leader The central, vertical, dominant stem of a tree.

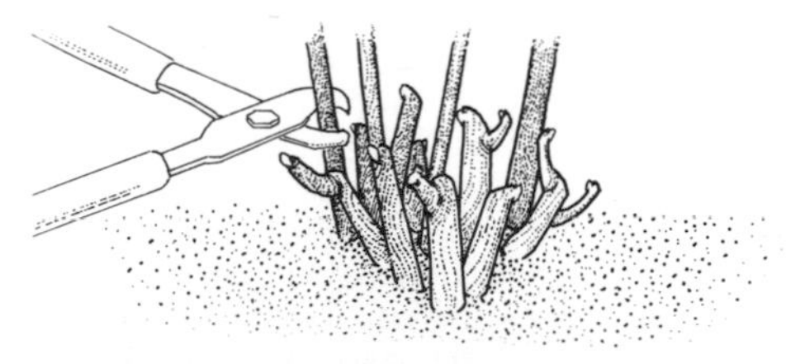

Coppicing The regular pruning of a tree or shrub close to ground level resulting in the production of a quantity of vigorous basal shoots. (See also pollarding.)

Cordon A normally branched tree or shrub restricted by spur pruning to a single stem.

Cosmetic pruning Minor pruning of dead or spent flowers and thin, weak or crossing shoots to keep a plant tidy and balanced in its overall shape.

Crown The upper part of a tree, the main branch system.

Current year's growth/wood The shoots which have grown from buds during the present growing season.

Dead-head To prune the spent flowers or the unripe seedpods from a plant.

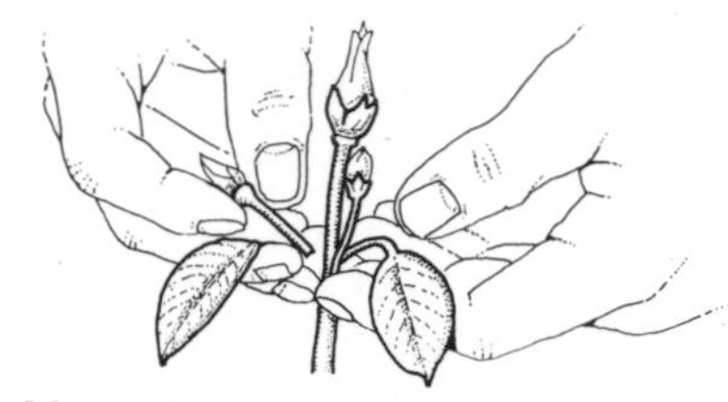

Disbudding The removal of surplus buds or shoots that are just beginning growth.

Dormant buds Buds which are formed in leaf axils but do not become active unless stimulated to form shoots though injury to the shoot or branch system. For practical purposes synonymous with adventitious buds.

Double leader Two shoots competing as leaders on a tree, each trying to assert apical dominance.

Epicormic shoots A cluster of shoots, derived from adventitious or dormant buds, on a main stem or branch after a wound or cut has been made. (See also water shoots.)

Espalier Trees trained with a vertical main stem with horizontally trained branches in tiers usually about 15in apart. Four or five tiers are usual. In effect each branch is a horizontally trained cordon. (See page 60.)

Extension growth Shoots which develop as a result of the growth of the apical or terminal bud of a stem or branch. Used normally in reference to the current season's shoots.

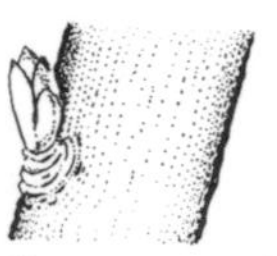

Eye Used to describe a growth bud, particularly of roses and vines.

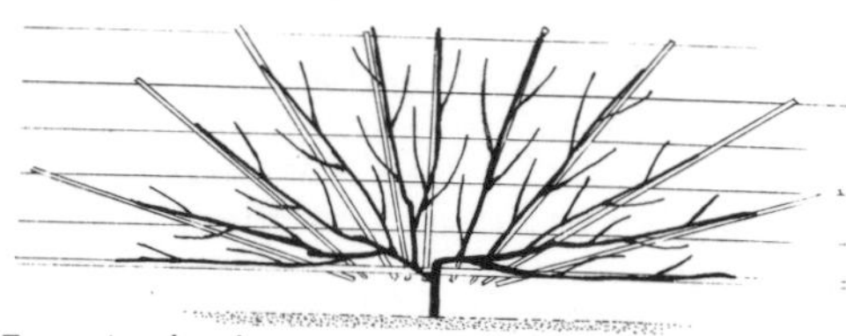

Fan A shrub or tree in which the main branches are trained like the ribs of a fan against a wall, fence or other support system.

Feathers The lateral growths on a one-year-old (maiden) tree.

First-(one-) year wood Growth or shoots that are up to one year old.

Framework The "skeleton" of main branches of a tree or shrub.

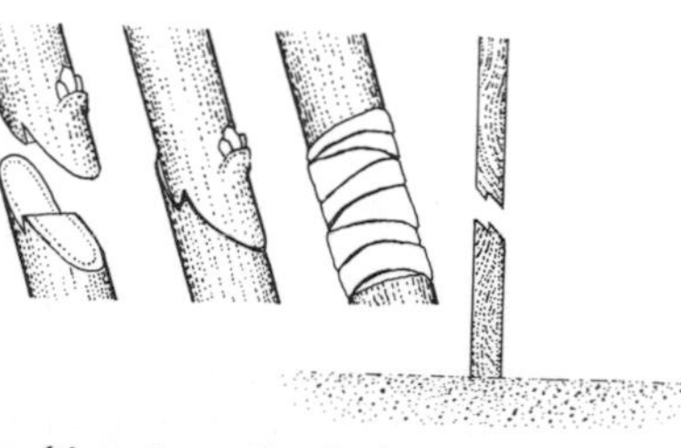

Grafting A method of propagation to unite a shoot (or single bud) of one plant—the **scion**—with the root system and stem of another—the **stock** (**rootstock**).

Glossary

Growth bud A bud that gives rise to a shoot.

Half-standard A tree or shrub grown with 3–4ft clear stem.

Internode The section of stem between two nodes or joints.

Joint see node.

Lateral A side growth which develops at an angle from the main axis. **Lateral shoots** are side-shoots which grow from **lateral buds** on a main or leading stem.

Leader The shoot that terminates a branch and is actively growing and extending year by year. (See also apex, central leader and terminal bud.)

Leaf Axil see axil.

Maiden A term used to describe a one-year-old tree or shrub or, occasionally, with fruit trees to describe one-year-old growth.

Mulch A topdressing of organic material on the soil around a plant.

Node The point on a stem where a leaf or leaves arise.

Open center A tree or shrub in which the branch system is pruned and trained so that the center of the framework is fairly open and free of main branches.

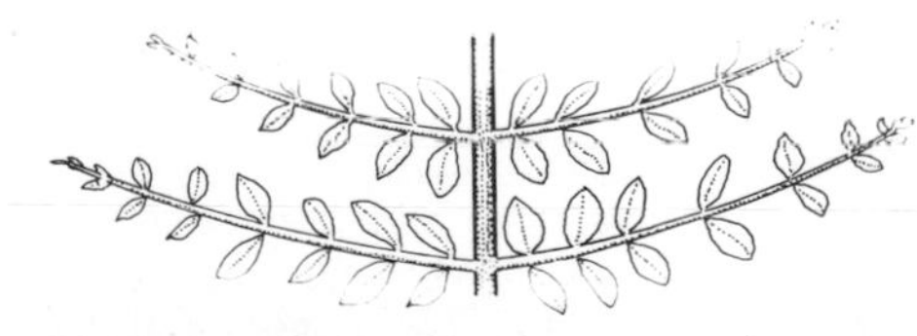

Opposite A term applied to buds, leaves or shoots that are opposite to one another on a stem or branch.

Ornamentals Plants grown for their aesthetic value rather than for their commercial usefulness or food value.

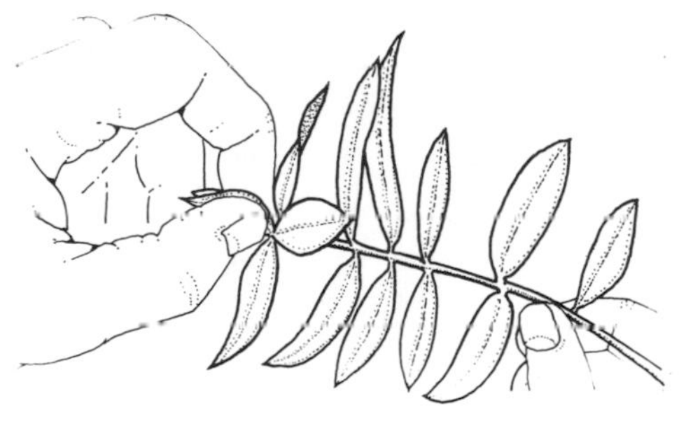

Pinch back To prune soft growth, by cutting or nipping out with fingers the growing tip of a shoot. (Also known as stopping.)

Pith The central, cylindrical, often soft, region of young stems.

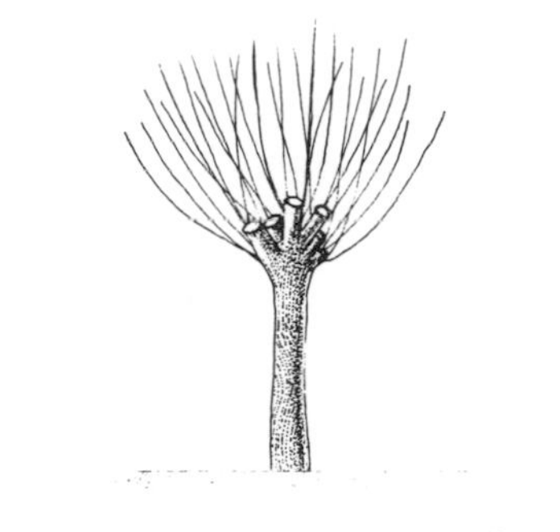

Pollarding The regular pruning of a tree or shrub back to the main stem or trunk. (See also coppicing.)

Recurrent flowering The production of several crops of flowers during one season more or less in succession.

Renewal pruning Pruning to obtain a constant supply of young shoots on a tree or shrub so that vigor and freedom of flowering are maintained.

Rod The main, woody stem of a vine.

Rootstock see grafting.

Scion see grafting.

Second-year wood Growth or shoots that are between one and two years old.

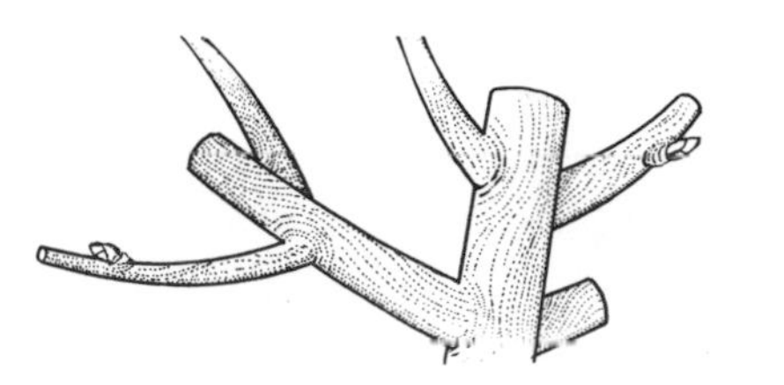

Snag A short stump of a branch left after incorrect pruning.

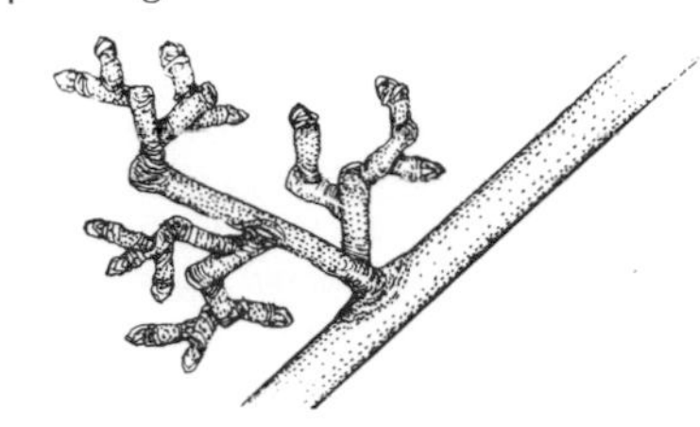

Spur A slow-growing short branch system that usually carries clusters of flower buds.

Standard A tree (or shrub) grown with 5–6ft of clear stem.

Stock see grafting.

Stopping see pinch back.

Sublateral A side-shoot growing from a lateral shoot.

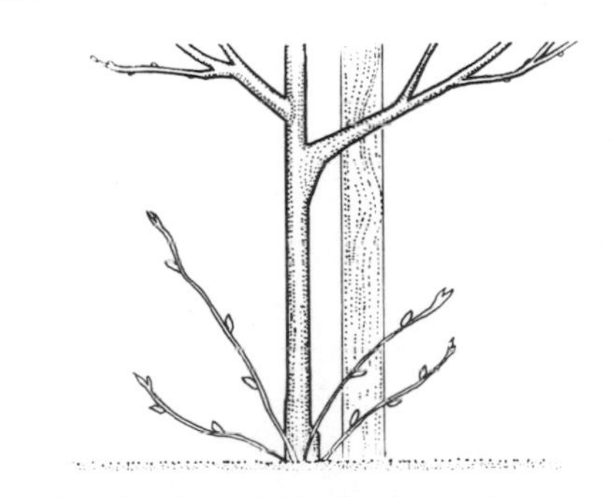

Sucker A shoot arising from a root system (or occasionally another shoot) below or just at ground level. The term usually refers to unwanted growths from the rootstock of grafted or budded plants.

Terminal bud, shoot, flower The uppermost usually central, growth on a stem. (See apex.)

Thinning Reducing the number of shoots in an overcrowded branch system so that the remaining shoots are evenly spaced to allow free air circulation and to let light reach the foliage in the center of the plant.

Tip bearer Usually applied to fruit trees which bear most of their fruits at the tips of one-year-old shoots.

Topping Applied occasionally to the stopping of shoots but more frequently to the removal of the top of a tree leaving only a skeleton of the main branches.

Top-worked A standard or half-standard tree or shrub which has been grafted or budded at the top of the stem of the stock.

Truss A cluster of flowers or fruit.

Water shoots Vigorous, often fairly soft, shoots that arise from adventitious buds on old wood when trees are growing very vigorously or have been damaged.

Whorl Three or more flowers, buds, leaves or shoots arising at the same node.

Wind-rock The loosening of the root system of a shrub or tree by strong winds. Usually indicates a lack of balance between the root and shoot systems and can be avoided by firm staking and reduction of the branch system of top-heavy plants in autumn.

Roses: introduction

Most people grow at least a few roses in their garden or against the walls of their house, but to many gardeners the correct way to prune roses remains a complicated and mysterious process.

In the wild, roses produce strong new shoots from near the base of the plant each season. In the following years the secondary, or lateral, growth from these shoots becomes progressively weaker. When strong new shoots appear, the food taken in by the roots is directed to this new growth and the original shoots are gradually starved out. Eventually the old shoots die and remain as dead wood before falling to the ground—a natural but long-winded method of pruning. The purpose of pruning is to short-circuit nature by cutting away the old worn-out shoots and so encourage the production of vigorous, disease-free new growth and the largest number of flowers for the rose gardener.

Pruning is a simple operation, but because roses range in size from miniatures, which are less than 1ft tall, to vigorous climbers, which may reach 30–40ft, they require a variety of pruning techniques to keep them healthy, flowering, and within control.

Rose "eyes" or growth buds are located in the axils of the leaves. If the leaf has fallen they can be seen just above a leaf scar. Always cut close to a bud.

There are certain general principles that apply to pruning all kinds of roses.

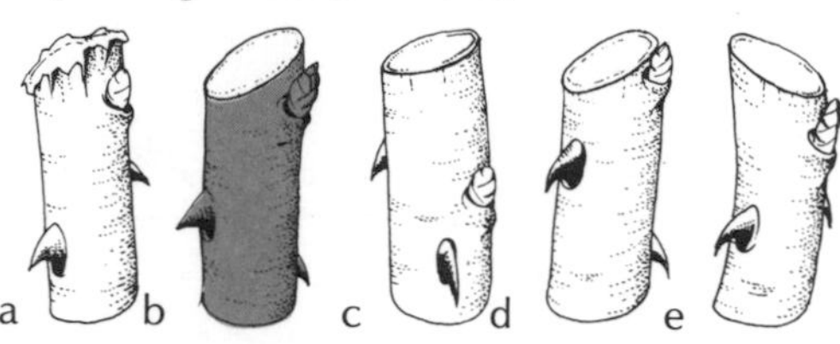

1 Always use sharp shears and a knife; a ragged cut caused by blunt tools may cause the shoot to die back (a). The cut must not be more than $\frac{1}{4}$in above the eye and must slope gently away from it (b). If you cut too high the snag will die back (c); a cut that is too low may damage the eye or allow disease spores to enter the wound (d). A cut in the wrong direction allows moisture to gather by the eye (e).

2 Cut back into healthy wood. If the pith is brown or discolored cut the shoot back until healthy white pith is reached.

3 Cut to an outward pointing eye to encourage an open-center habit. With roses of spreading habit it is sometimes useful to prune some branches to inward-pointing eyes to obtain more upright growth.

4 Vigorous modern roses often produce two or three shoots from one eye after pruning. As soon as possible reduce these to one shoot by pinching out the young growth. Never allow more than one shoot to grow from a pruning cut.

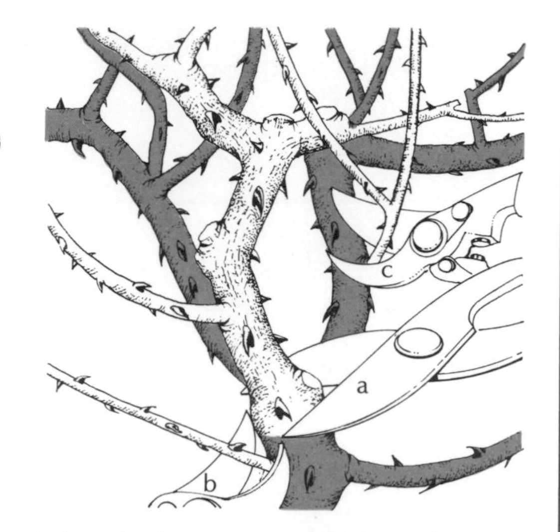

5 Completely cut out any dead and diseased stems (a) and weak, spindly growth (b). This may mean cutting it out to ground level or, with a lateral growth, to the junction with a healthy stem. Where two branches cross, cut one back below the point where they cross (c). With shrub and climbing roses this is not always easy, but wherever possible at least prevent branches rubbing against each other or on their supports.

6 Keep all branches well spaced to allow free air-flow through the plant and to allow light to reach the leaves. This lessens the likelihood of such diseases as black spot, rose mildew and rose-rust, which all thrive under stagnant air conditions.

7 Burn prunings to reduce the possibility of spreading disease.

You may not know to which group the roses in your garden belong, particularly if you moved into your house in late autumn or winter and there are no labels on the plants. If you are not sure how to deal with them, confine your winter pruning to the points made in the section on general principles. Next summer you can see from the way they flower to which group they belong and prune accordingly. Pruning techniques may vary slightly in different conditions, and with experience you will quickly learn how to deal with them to suit your soil and climate.

SUCKERS

Most roses are budded on to the selected rootstock of a wild rose species. During the growing season shoots may arise from below the budding point. These are sucker growths from the rootstock, which can quickly weaken, and eventually replace, the rose variety concerned. They must be removed as soon as they are seen.

Trace the sucker back to the root from which it springs and pull it off at the point of origin. Never cut it off at ground level; this only encourages basal buds to produce several more suckers.

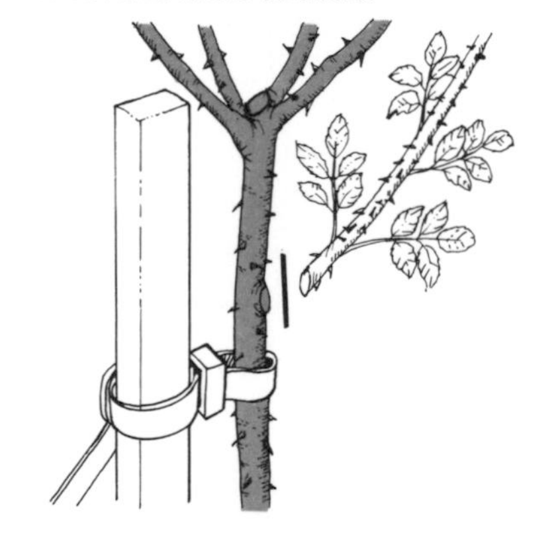

With standard roses, which are budded at the tops of stems of wild rose rootstocks, shoots may arise from below the budding point on the stem. These are treated as suckers and carefully pulled off, or pared away with a sharp knife.

Time of Pruning

Time of pruning differs to some extent with the group of roses concerned and further details are given in each section.

Winter pruning
Winter pruning is best carried out between mid-February and mid-March, depending on locality, season, and prevailing weather conditions. Earlier pruning from December to January can lead to precocious growth and this is often damaged in severe weather. Later pruning in April often involves wasting the plant's energy by cutting off young growth already produced. The best guide is to prune —weather permitting—when the growth buds about halfway up the most vigorous stems are beginning to swell.

After winter pruning put a good mulch of well-rotted compost or manure around the bases of your roses. Pruning encourages a constant supply of young, vigorous shoots and these will only be produced if sufficient food is available for the new growth.

Frost damage may occur in some seasons, particularly with fluctuating spring weather of warm spells followed by frosty periods. If new shoots are damaged by frost the main shoots must be cut back to dormant eyes.

EXHIBITION PRUNING

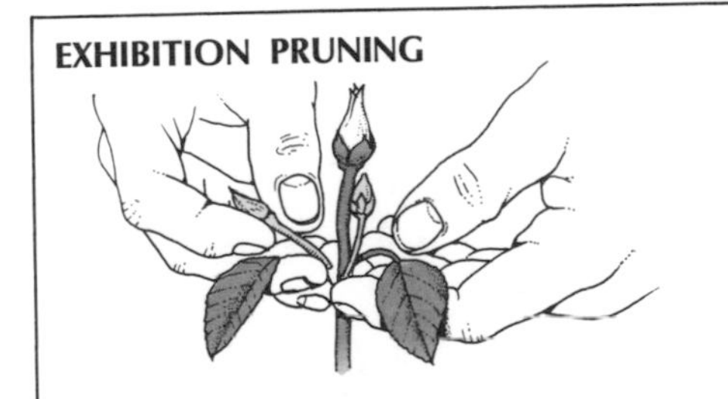

Rose-growers who exhibit at national and local shows aim to provide high-quality blooms for a given date. This involves considerable experience and an intimate knowledge of individual rose varieties. It is not the purpose of this book to attempt to provide a guide for would-be exhibitors. Suffice it to say that it usually involves harder initial winter pruning to limit the number of shoots produced and, for Hybrid Tea roses, disbudding to only one flower per stem.

Summer pruning
Summer pruning is confined to the removal of flowers or flower clusters and is carried out through the flowering season.

Some roses, such as 'Scarlet Fire' and *Rosa moyesii* are grown for their autumn display of brightly colored hips as well as their flowers. With these roses the flowers should be left on the bush, but with most roses it is best to remove all flower clusters as soon as they fade. This prevents the plant wasting food on unnecessary seed production, and it removes a possible source of disease—the decaying petals (particularly in wet weather). Removing the roses also encourages fresh growth and bloom in repeat-flowering roses.

Cut back to the first convenient strong eye or young shoot below the flower stem or flower truss. Normally this should be an outward-pointing eye, but occasionally it may be inward-pointing to maintain a well-shaped plant. If only the flower and its stalk are removed weak stem buds just below the inflorescence will grow and produce thin, straggly shoots.

Never cut a flower stem longer than is really required and never take more than one or two long stems from a single bush. Leaves manufacture much of the plant's food so cutting off too many leaves when it is in active growth will weaken the plant.

In late summer the removal of faded flower clusters should be discontinued or kept to a minimum to avoid stimulating further growth shoots, which may be damaged in winter.

Hybrid Tea

Correctly cut Hybrid Tea inflorescence
Cut back to a strong outward-facing shoot or eye below the inflorescence.

Incorrectly cut Hybrid Tea inflorescence
The stems are cut too long and will weaken the plant.

Floribunda

Correctly cut Floribunda Inflorescence
Remove the whole truss by cutting back to the first strong outward-pointing eye or shoot.

Incorrectly cut Floribunda inflorescence
The individual flowers in the truss have been cut off leaving weak stems.

BLIND SHOOTS

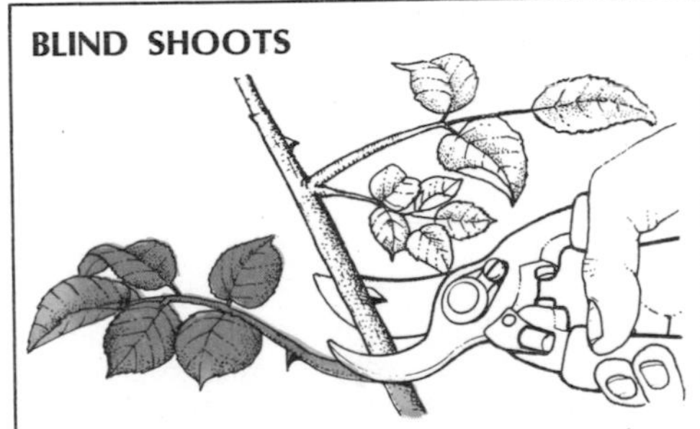

Some varieties of Hybrid Teas and Floribundas and climbers produce a few shoots that are "blind" and do not flower. These blind shoots should be cut hard back as soon as they are seen, to encourage vigorous growth from buds lower down on the shoot, otherwise the flowering potential of the plant is diminished.

Autumn pruning
In very windy areas it is worth shortening any very long growths by 6–12 in during November. This reduces the risk of damage by windrock to the roots.

Hybrid Teas and Hybrid Perpetuals

Hybrid Teas and Hybrid Perpetuals are pruned in the same way. The aim is to encourage the production of strong basal growths to form an open-centered, cup-shaped plant with an evenly spaced framework of shoots.

Hybrid Teas and Hybrid Perpetuals flower on the new (current) season's growth and most benefit from a moderate to fairly severe annual pruning. This keeps the plants bushy and ensures a constant supply of strong young shoots. Annual pruning is from mid-February to mid- to late March. Some variation will occur depending on local soil conditions and the prevailing weather.

Very vigorous roses, 'Peace' for example, should be pruned only lightly as hard pruning stimulates very robust but often flowerless shoots. Other vigorous cultivars, such as 'Chinatown' and 'Uncle Walter,' produce their flowers on tall, 5–6ft stems. An alternative method of growing these cultivars is to peg down the stems horizontally. A different pruning technique is required (see page 9). This method is also suitable for many rambler roses.

The first year

First-year, or newly planted, Hybrid Teas or Hybrid Perpetuals are usually bought in autumn from the nursery with 3–4 strong shoots. Cut back main shoots slightly if not already done, and then prune long, coarse or damaged roots before planting. In late February to mid-March cut back each shoot to 2–4 eyes or 6in from ground level. This encourages strong basal growths to be produced. If the soil is very sandy and lacking nutrients, more moderate first-year pruning to 4–6 eyes or 9in is advisable. This first pruning is followed by more severe pruning in the second year.

Second and following years

In the second and following years Hybrid Teas and Hybrid Perpetuals should be moderately pruned. Cut back the strongest (thickest) shoots to 4–6 eyes or 9in and the less vigorous shoots to 2–4 eyes or 6in. This method of pruning gives the best all-round results. As the plant becomes older, one or two old stems should be cut out to the base.

The first year

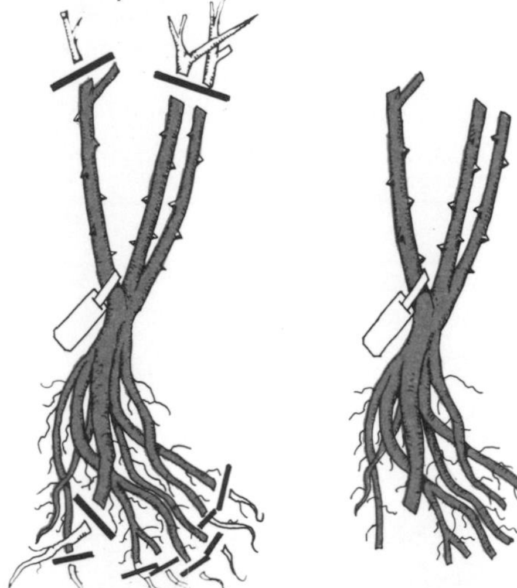

1 Autumn. Open ground bush as received. Cut back the main shoots slightly, if it is not already done. Prune long, coarse or damaged roots before planting.

2 Mid-February to mid- to late March. Cut back each shoot to 2–4 eyes or 6in from ground level. By June or July new shoots will have grown.

3 September to October. At the end of first season's growth, tip back flowered stems and cut out any soft, unripe shoots.

Second and following years

4 Mid-February to mid- to late March. Cut out dead or diseased wood. Cut out weak stems. Cut out crossing stems. Cut out inward-growing stems.

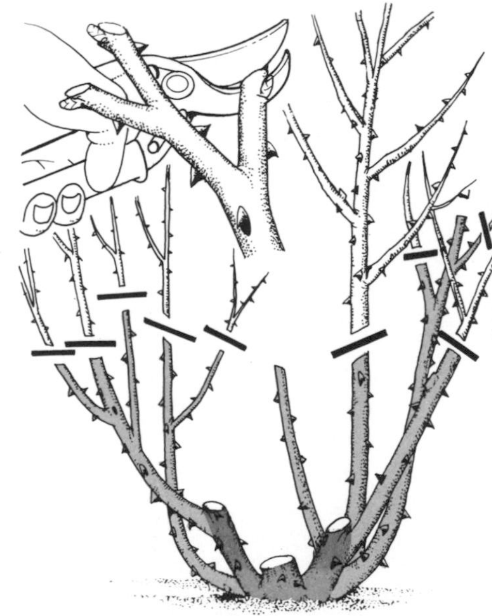

5 At the same time, cut back strong stems to 4–6 eyes or 9in and less vigorous stems and remaining laterals to 2–4 eyes or 6in.

6 September to October. At the end of the season's growth, tip back flowered stems and cut out any soft, unripe shoots.

Hybrid Teas and Hybrid Perpetuals

Pegging down. Several modern Hybrid Teas and Hybrid Perpetual cultivars, such as 'Chinatown' and 'Uncle Walter,' are very vigorous and produce their flowers at the top of 5–6ft stems. These stems can be trained horizontally on a framework or pegged down.

The first year
Newly planted roses of this kind are treated as normal Hybrid Teas or Hybrid Perpetuals.

Second, third and subsequent years
At the end of the first flowering season the strong new basal growths are pegged down. Half of the old shoots and any unsuitable weak, dead or diseased growths are cut away. Remaining lateral growths are shortened to 2–3 eyes or 4–6in. This method stimulates lateral growth along the pegged-down shoots the following summer. These lateral branches flower freely, creating a wonderful display.

In the third and subsequent years remove all the old pegged-down shoots, provided the plant remains vigorous.

The first year

1 October. At the end of the first season's growth cut out the old flowered stems to base. Leave vigorous basal shoots that have developed during the summer.

2 At the same time, tip back these vigorous shoots and remove any flowers and weak side-shoots.

3 Peg down shoots to within 6in of ground level. Cut back any laterals to 2–3 eyes or 4–6in. Cut out any unsuitably placed laterals.

The second year

4 July. Bush flowers on laterals of the pegged-down shoots. Strong nonflowering shoots appear in the center.

5 September to October. Cut away half of the pegged-down shoots that have flowered. Peg down vigorous shoots from the center of the bush. Cut out any weak growth and shorten remaining laterals to 2–3 eyes or 4–6in. Cut out any unsuitably placed laterals.

Third and following years

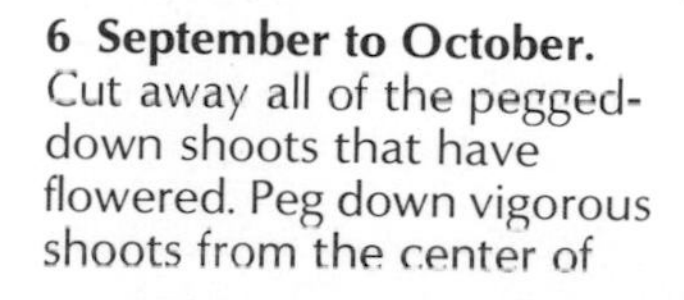

6 September to October. Cut away all of the pegged-down shoots that have flowered. Peg down vigorous shoots from the center of the bush. Cut out any weak growth and shorten remaining laterals to 2–3 eyes or 4–6in. Cut out any unsuitably placed laterals.

Floribundas

Floribunda roses are more vigorous than most Hybrid Teas and Hybrid Perpetuals and produce a succession of large clusters of moderate-sized flowers. It is sometimes difficult to prune Floribundas to obtain the optimum number of blooms. Severe annual pruning, as used for Hybrid Teas and Hybrid Perpetuals, can weaken Floribundas within a few years, but light pruning creates large bushes filled with weak, spindly growth.

Moderate pruning of each shoot to 6–8 eyes or 12–18in is often recommended and proves reasonably successful, particularly in windy areas. It does not, however, always produce the almost continuous summer display which can sometimes be achieved, and some of the older wood tends to die away without replacement basal shoots forming.

A combination of light pruning of some shoots to produce early flowers and harder pruning of other shoots can encourage renewal of basal growths and provide later flowers. This has proved the most satisfactory method. Annual pruning is from mid-February to mid-March, depending on local soil and weather conditions.

The first year
First-year Floribundas are usually received with 3–5 strong shoots and often weak, spindly laterals. Between mid-February and mid-March cut back each strong shoot to 3–5 eyes or 6–9in and remove all weak shoots.

The second year
In mid-February to mid-March of the second year all the main one-year-old basal, or near-basal, shoots must be shortened by approximately one-third of their length and any remaining laterals should be cut back to 2–3 eyes or 4–6 in. Strong shoots from older wood (pruned back at planting to 3–5 eyes) must be cut back to 3–5 eyes or removed completely to keep the center of the bush open.

Third and subsequent years
In the third and subsequent years this renewal program is continued between mid-February and mid-March. Prune back strong one-year-old shoots lightly by one-third and cut back two-year-old wood to 3–5 eyes or 6–9in from ground level. If the bush is crowded cut out some old growths to base.

The first year

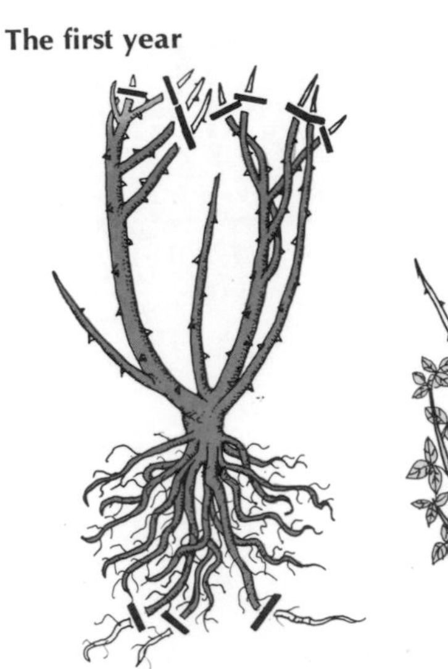

1 Autumn. Open-ground bush as received. Cut back main shoots slightly if not already done. Prune long, coarse or damaged roots before planting.

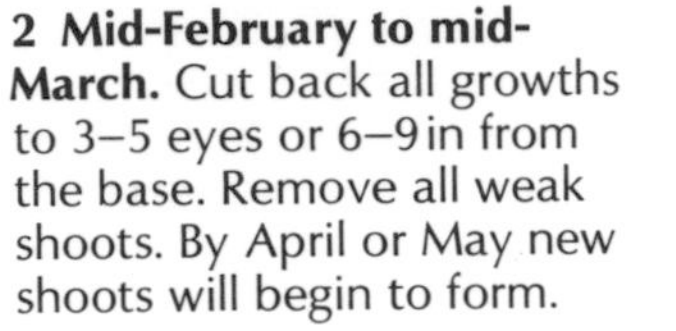

2 Mid-February to mid-March. Cut back all growths to 3–5 eyes or 6–9in from the base. Remove all weak shoots. By April or May new shoots will begin to form.

3 October. Growth at end of first season. Tip back main growths and cut out any soft, unripe shoots.

The second year

4 Mid-February to mid-March. Cut out dead or diseased wood, weak stems, crossing and inward-growing stems. Prune back one-year-old basal shoots by one-third. Cut back older wood to 3–5 eyes or 6–9in and remaining laterals to 2–3 eyes or 4–6in.

5 October. Growth at end of second season. Tip back main growths and cut out any soft unripe shoots.

Third and following years

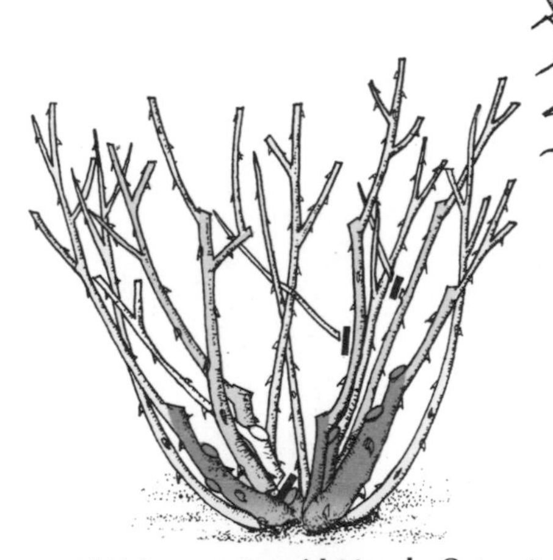

6 Mid-February to mid-March. Cut out dead or diseased wood. Cut out weak stems. Cut out crossing stems. Cut out inward-growing stems.

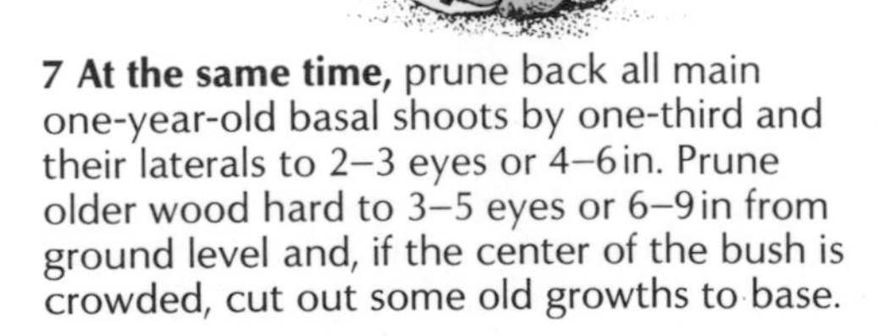

7 At the same time, prune back all main one-year-old basal shoots by one-third and their laterals to 2–3 eyes or 4–6in. Prune older wood hard to 3–5 eyes or 6–9in from ground level and, if the center of the bush is crowded, cut out some old growths to base.

Miniatures and Polyantha Pompons

Miniature roses are a popular group of low-growing roses that reach 1–2ft in height. The blooms are similar in shape to those of Hybrid Teas and Floribundas and are produced on the current season's growth.

Pruning for miniature roses is basically similar to that recommended for Hybrid Teas and Hybrid Perpetuals, although it is best not to cut back newly planted miniatures too severely.

If very strong vigorous shoots are occasionally produced which alter the overall symmetry of the plant, remove these entirely when pruning in early spring so that balanced growth can be maintained. If a miniature continually produces vigorous shoots which unbalance the plant, then it is best treated as a Floribunda for pruning purposes. A number of so-called miniatures are of this kind and are sometimes known as "patio" roses. (See page 10 for the correct pruning technique).

The first year

1 Mid-February to Mid-March. Bush as received. Trim roots. Cut back strong shoots to 3–5 eyes or 4–6in. Remove weak growth.

2 June to July. Vigorous shoots forming at base. Flowers are produced in clusters on thinner, twiggy growth. Summer prune to maintain flower production.

Second and following years

3 February to March. Cut out weak shoots entirely. Prune well-spaced stronger growths to 3–4 eyes or 4–6in.

Polyantha pompon roses are a group of low, bushy, often repeat-flowering roses which are the forerunners of modern Floribundas. They seldom exceed 2–3ft in height and produce a large amount of rather twiggy, thin growth.

The first year newly planted roses in this group should be lightly pruned in February or March, strong shoots being tipped back by one-third and weak, thin, twiggy growth removed completely.

During the second and following years, remove old, weak, diseased and dead wood in February or March. Little pruning is required other than to maintain an open center and to tip back strong stems by one-third. Summer prune to maintain blooms.

The first year

1 February to March. Trim roots before planting. Cut back strong shoots by one-third and remove completely any weak growth.

2 June to September. Bush in flower, with new growth. Faded flowers are pruned to maintain a succession of blooms.

The second year

3 February to March. Cut back strong stems by one-third and maintain an open-center bush by cutting out old, weak, diseased and dead wood.

Third and following years

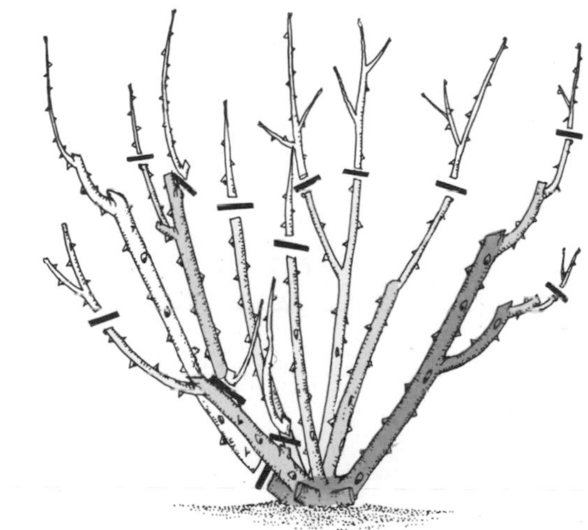

4 February to March. Tip back strong stems by one-third, remove twiggy growth and maintain an open-center bush by cutting out very old, weak, diseased or dead wood.

Climbers and Ramblers

Climbing and rambling roses either bloom freely in glorious unruly tangles or produce only a few poor-quality flowers. However, with pruning and training they will provide a regular supply of good-quality blooms each year.

For convenience, the ramblers and climbers have been divided into five groups, but these are not rigid divisions and some overlap of pruning techniques occurs.

Wherever sufficient space is available it is always a good idea to train new extension shoots of climbing roses as near to the horizontal as possible. But be sure to provide allowance to create a balanced plant. Vertically placed shoots frequently form on only a few flowering laterals, at the tips. Horizontally placed shoots will produce flowering laterals along most of their length and create a far better display.

The provision for new shoots depends on adequate feeding, particularly in Group 1, where virtually all the old wood is removed annually. To avoid wind breakage and make training into a balanced framework easier, make sure that all new long growths are tied in as they develop.

Group 1 includes the true ramblers, varieties such as 'Dorothy Perkins' and 'Excelsa,' derived from *Rosa wichuraiana*. They flower in June and July on laterals of long, flexible, basal shoots (canes) produced the previous season.

The first year
Prune all vigorous shoots back to 9–15in from the base at planting and remove completely any weak growth. This hard initial pruning encourages vigorous, balanced growth during the first season, but no flowers are produced until the following year.

Second and following years
Pruning of established plants consists of cutting to the base all the shoots that have bloomed. This should be done soon after flowering, usually between August and September. The developing young basal growths are tied in to replace the old shoots, and the young shoots will produce flowering laterals the following summer. Where the site allows, train most of the new shoots as near to the horizontal as possible to encourage maximum development of flowering laterals.

Sometimes only a few basal growths are produced. if this happens, retain some of the strongest old shoots and cut back their laterals to 2–3 eyes or 4–6in from the main stem after flowering.

The first year

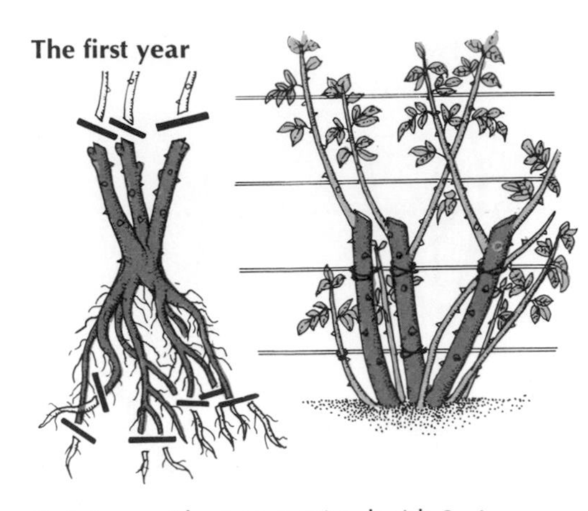

1 Autumn. Plant as received with 3–4 shoots about 4–5ft long. Prune back shoots to 9–15in and trim uneven and coarse roots before planting. **Spring.** New shoots begin to develop.

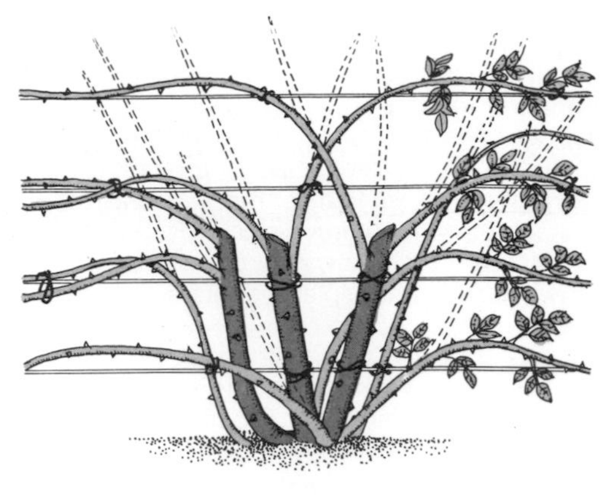

2 June to September. Strong shoots have developed from the pruned growth and from the base of the plant. Train them into place.

Second and following years

3 June to July. Plant flowers on lateral shoots produced on previous year's growth. Young basal shoots develop; train these more or less horizontally and tie in.

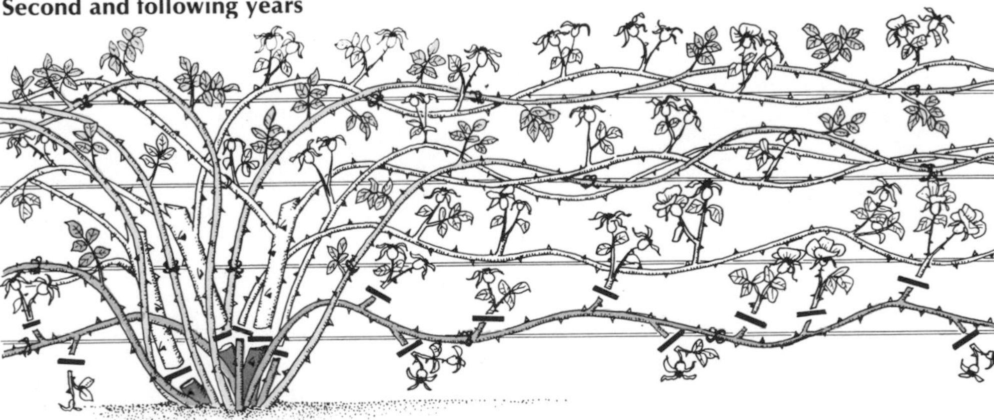

4 August to September. Cut out flowered shoots to base leaving one or two to fill in framework if required. Cut back laterals to 2–3 eyes or 4–6in. Tie in all new growth.

5 October. Shoots fully trained in at end of the second season's growth.

Climbers and Ramblers

Group 2 includes many well-known vigorous rose varieties such as 'Albertine' and 'Chaplin's Pink.' They flower once in summer on the laterals of long shoots produced the previous year. They differ from true ramblers in producing very few basal shoots each season, most of the new growth coming from higher up on the old stems. The aim of pruning is to remove old wood in proportion to the new.

The first year
Newly planted varieties in this group are treated in the same way as those in Group 1.

Second, third and following years
Pruning of established plants takes place soon after flowering. Completely cut away one or two old growths and train any basal shoots that have started to develop in their place. If no basal shoots are forming cut back one or two old stems to 12–18 in from base.

Cut back old wood higher up on the plant to a point where a vigorous new leading shoot has started to grow. Keep leading shoots at full length and train them as near to the horizontal as possible. Any shorter laterals should be cut back to 2–3 eyes or 6 in.

The second year

1 June to July. Plant flowers on lateral shoots produced on previous year's growth. Allow one or two basal growths to develop and some leader shoots develop higher up.

2 August to September. Cut back old growth to main replacement leaders. Cut back flowering laterals to 2–3 eyes or 6 in. Train replacement leaders as near to the horizontal as possible. Cut back weak leaders to 2–3 eyes or 6 in.

Third and following years

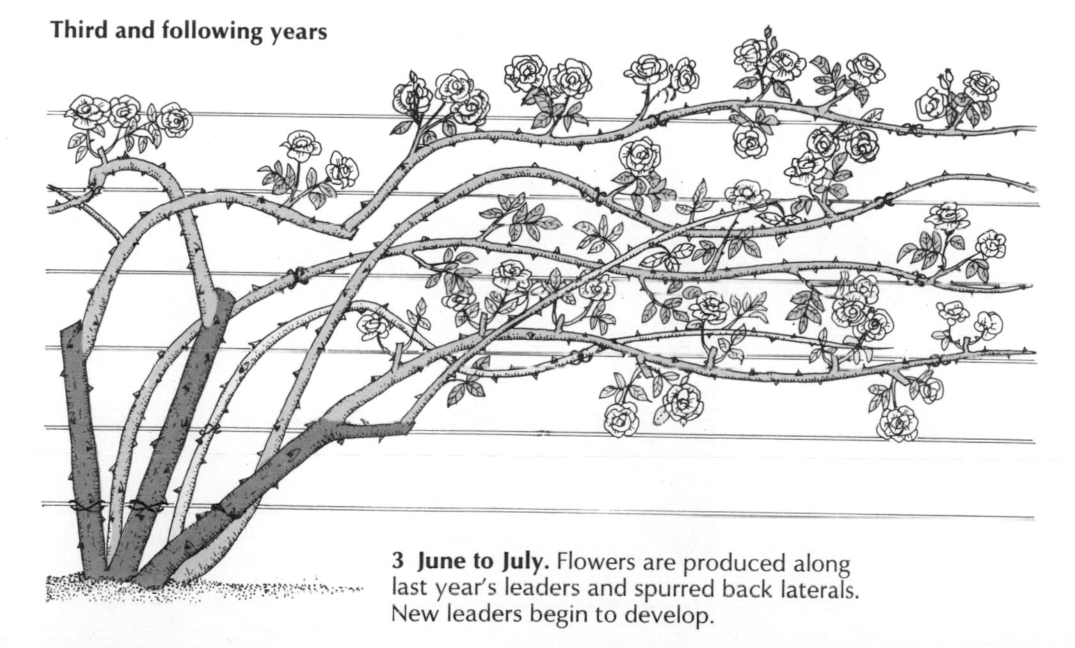

3 June to July. Flowers are produced along last year's leaders and spurred back laterals. New leaders begin to develop.

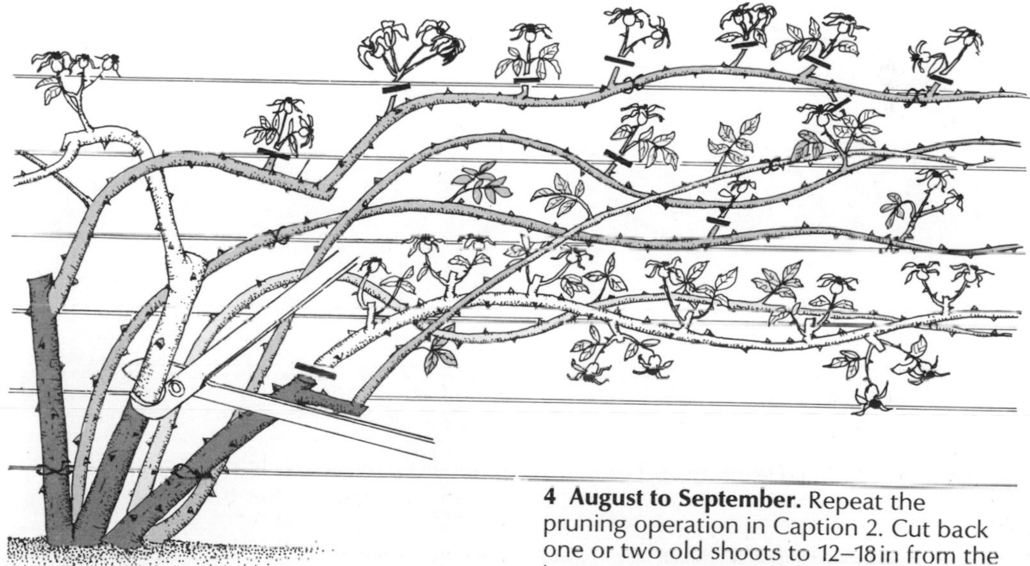

4 August to September. Repeat the pruning operation in Caption 2. Cut back one or two old shoots to 12–18 in from the base to encourage replacement basal growth.

Climbers and Ramblers

Group 3 contains the ramblers and climbers that produce their blooms on the current season's growth, and includes climbers of Hybrid Tea style and climbing sports of Hybrid Teas and Floribundas. Most, although by no means all, of the roses in this group are repeat-flowering. Their long, flexible shoots make them ideal for training against walls and fences and on pergolas.

The first year

Newly planted roses in this group should not be pruned back at planting, although the roots should be trimmed and any damaged tips and very weak growth removed. This is because many are climbing sports from bush varieties and hard pruning at planting may cause them to revert to bush form.

It is essential to build up a strong, evenly spaced framework of branches, as roses in this group do not readily produce vigorous basal growths once established, but they develop most of their young shoots higher up on existing main stems. Horizontal or angled training of new leader shoots at an early stage will help to prevent the base of the plant becoming too bare.

Second and following years

Apart from maintaining the plant within its allotted space, pruning and training of mature roses in this group is restricted to summer pruning flowering laterals during the growing season as the flowers fade. Diseased, dead and weak wood should be cut out in late autumn or winter before any growth begins. At the same time train new growths into gaps in the framework and trim all flowered laterals back to 3–4 eyes or 6in.

With old plants it will occasionally be necessary to cut back weak and exhausted shoots to a few inches from the base. This should encourage one or two vigorous basal shoots to be produced.

The first year

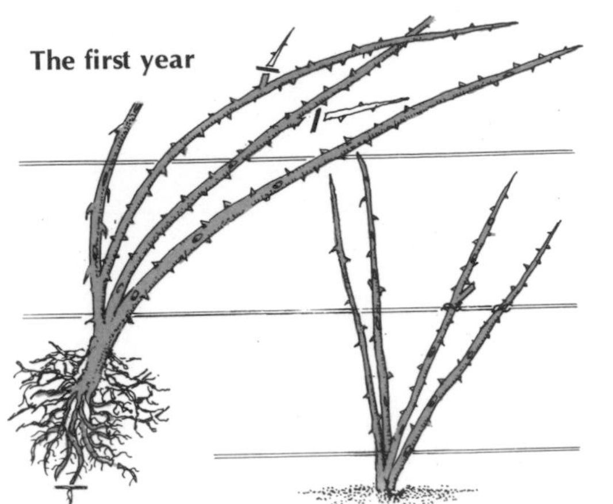

1 Autumn or early spring. Plant as received with 3–4 shoots 4–5ft long. Trim any uneven and coarse roots. Slightly tip back any unripe or damaged growths. Do not prune except to cut out any weak side shoots. Begin to train shoots.

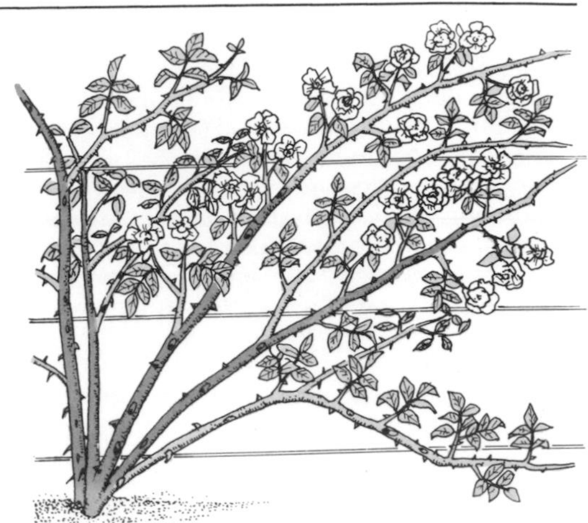

2 July to August. Tie in framework of new shoots as they develop. Some flowers are produced at the tips of new growths and on laterals. New shoots develop and should be tied in. Summer prune.

Second and following years

3 October to March. Prune back flowered laterals to 3–4 eyes or 6in. Cut out weak wood and tie in leading shoots.

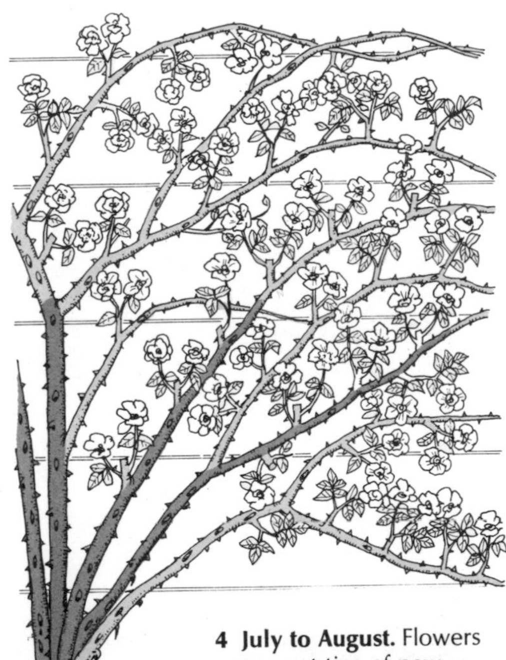

4 July to August. Flowers appear at tips of new growths and on laterals. Summer prune. Tie in new shoots as they develop.

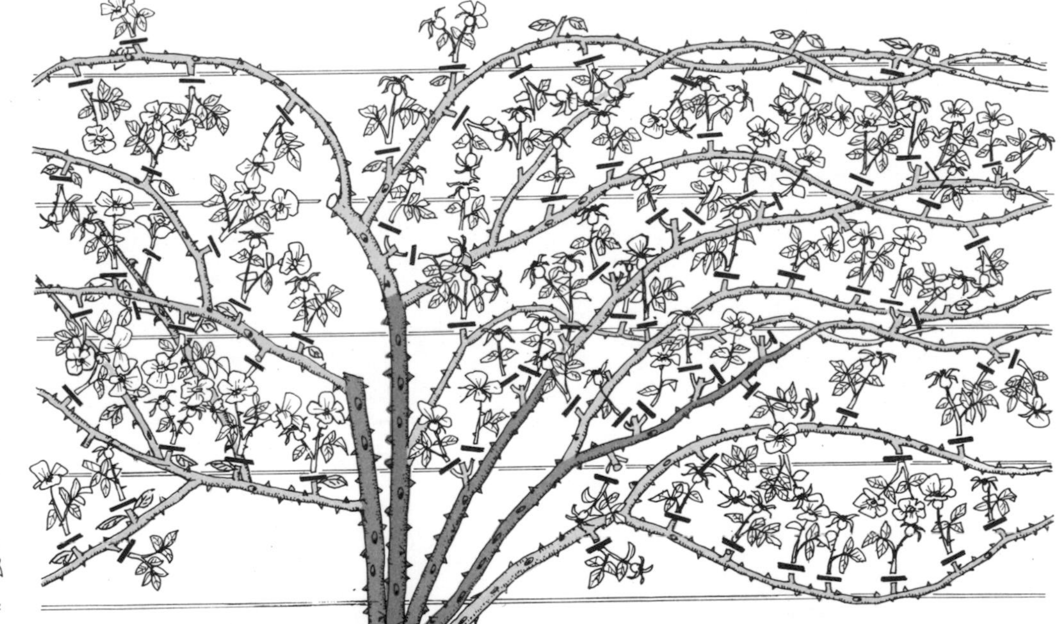

5 October to March. Prune back flowered laterals to 3–4 eyes or 6in. Cut out weak wood. Tie in leading shoots from main stems of framework.

Climbers and Ramblers

Group 4 includes pillar roses, which are repeat-flowering and produce their blooms on the current season's wood. They differ from roses in Group 3 because they are more moderate, usually upright in growth and seldom exceed 8–10ft in height. Their shoots are generally less flexible than in Group 3 and, as their name indicates, they are suitable for growing against pillars or for training in positions where horizontal space is limited.

The first year
Newly planted varieties in this group are treated in the same way as Group 3. Before planting, trim the roots and remove any damaged tips and weak growth. In view of their naturally upright habit do not train the leader shoots at an angle as in Group 3.

Second and subsequent years
Pruning of mature pillar roses involves routine removal of all flower trusses as they fade in summer. In late autumn or early winter, cut away weak, diseased and dead wood and shorten some leaders and laterals on main growths just enough to maintain a symmetrical shape. To stimulate growth at the base of the plant, cut back the lower leaders by two-thirds of their length. In old plants where growth is crowded, cut out one or two of the oldest stems to ground level.

The degree of trimming differs with the rose variety and the space available. Some of the more vigorous varieties of pillar rose, which have flexible growth, particularly of the lateral shoots, may require more severe restrictions.

VIGOROUS CLIMBERS

Group 5 includes climbing species, or near-species, and hybrids of tremendous vigor. These often produce flexible 20ft growths each season. These roses are typified by the exuberant *Rosa filipes* 'Kiftsgate' and the Banksian roses. If grown unrestricted in trees it is impractical and quite unnecessary to prune or train them at all, except for the removal of dead, diseased and weak wood where this is possible.

When they become too overwhelming the renovation procedure as illustrated on page 20 should be employed.

Initial planting and training is as for Group 3, but laterals need only very light pruning.

HORIZONTAL TRAINING

Many climbing roses can be trained to grow horizontally along the ground, instead of on a wall or other support.

A similar method is used with vigorous Hybrid Tea, Hybrid Perpetual and shrub roses (see page 9). The flexible trailing shoots of several varieties derived from *Rosa wichuraiana* are admirably suited for this kind of training. They can be used to cover banks and other areas where fairly dense ground cover is required.

The shoots are pegged down close to ground level and the same pruning methods are used as when these rose varieties are grown more conventionally as climbers.

The first year

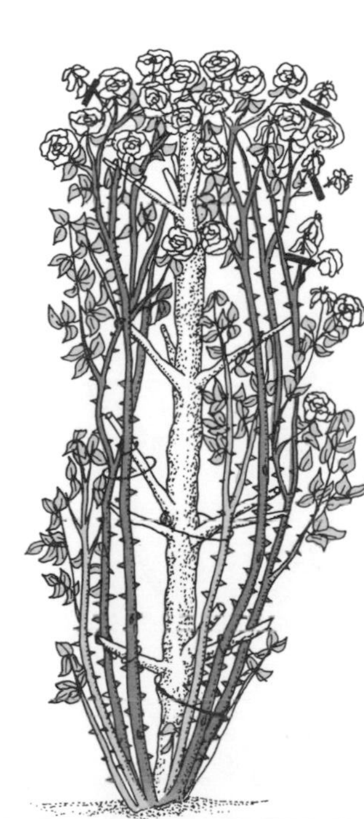

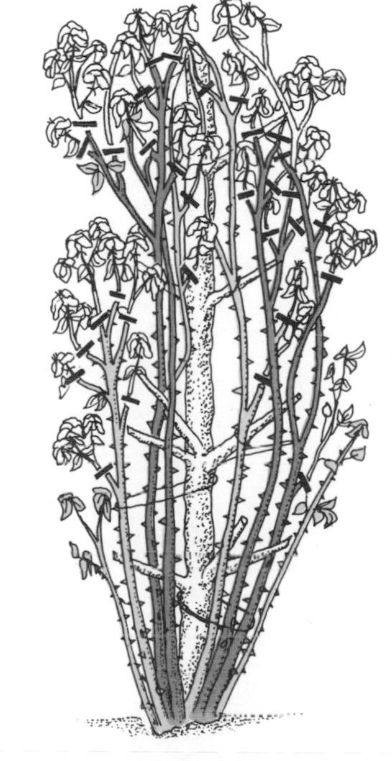

The second year

1 Autumn to early spring. Plant with shoots tied into a post or pillar.

2 June to August. Plants flower on laterals of the old growth. New growth has developed from previous year's stems and from the base. Summer prune.

3 November. Cut back flowered laterals and some new leaders sufficiently to maintain the symmetry of the plant.

4 At the same time, cut out weak, diseased and dead wood. Tie in new shoots.

5 June to August. Plants flower on laterals of the old growth. New growth has developed from previous year's stems and from the base. Summer prune.

6 November. Cut back flowered laterals and some new leaders sufficiently to maintain the symmetry of the plant.

Species and Shrub Roses

Shrub and species roses are grown less often than Hybrid Teas and Floribundas, but are increasing in popularity. Grouped together or planted singly in shrub or mixed borders, shrub roses are extremely rewarding during summer and autumn, particularly in informal settings, where modern bedding roses may look out of place.

It is often recommended to leave shrub roses entirely unpruned, "to grow naturally," or suggested that only very minor trimming is necessary. Generally shrub and species roses left to their own devices will grow and flower well for a few years, but this *laissez-faire* approach, although appealing, will not always provide the best display of roses.

To obtain the best results it is necessary to carry out a certain amount of pruning annually, even though it may be no more than a gentle manicure.

In order to simplify the process, as much as possible, three groups have been identified. The divisions are arbitrary and not rigid, and inevitably overlap occurs and slight modifications of pruning techniques may be needed for a few individual roses that do not fit neatly into the groups defined here.

Pruning shrub and species roses involves exactly the same general principles that apply to other roses (see page 6): that is, to encourage strong basal, or near-basal growths and to replace older stems that have lost their vigor and flower sparsely.

It is important also to take into account that the flowers of some varieties may be produced on the current season's growth late in the year as well as on laterals and sublaterals from older growth. Flowers of some varieties are produced mainly during June and July in one flush, but other varieties may be repeat-flowering and produce bloom until the autumn. Attractive fruits (hips) are a feature of some varieties and therefore do not need their spent flowers removed.

The following general points always apply:

1 No initial pruning is required when planting, beside the removal of coarse and damaged roots and the shortening of unripe or damaged shoots.
2 A sturdy framework of well-spaced shoots should be built up and thin weak growth should be removed after flowering. Dead and diseased wood should be cut out.
3 Regular pruning to remove spent flowers is desirable unless dealing with varieties grown for their fruits. Repeat-flowering shrub roses, such as the hybrid musks, benefit considerably from this manicuring because their growth energy is put into producing new flowering laterals rather than into fruits.
4 Slight tipping back by a few inches of all vigorous shoots in winter will encourage flowering laterals and sublaterals the following summer. It also helps to remove a possible source of disease.

Group 1 brings together the following kinds of roses, which require only minimal pruning for many years:

Species roses (other than climbers) and their close hybrids

Rosa spinosissima, the Burnet rose, and hybrids derived from it

Rosa rugosa, the Japanese rose, and hybrids derived from it

Gallica roses

Hybrid musk roses.

Almost all of these roses are of a fairly dense, bushy habit and flower mainly on short lateral and sublateral shoots produced from second-year or older wood. They do not regularly produce vigorous basal growths once established.

The first and second year

In the first year and second year after planting, pruning is more or less confined to points 1 to 4 mentioned in the introduction to this section. Occasionally a badly placed shoot may need to be cut out to the base.

Third and following years

In the third and following years one or two older main growths, which only flower sparsely, may be cut out in winter. This will encourage basal replacement shoots and maintain a sturdy vigorous framework. More drastic treatment may occasionally be necessary with very old bushes. In winter cut out several old and poorly placed main branches to leave a well-spaced framework.

The second year

1 February to March. Tip back all vigorous shoots. Cut out to the base any badly placed shoots. Basal shoots have developed.

2 June to August. Plant flowers on laterals of old wood, new basal shoots develop.

3 September. Summer prune. After flowering cut out thin, weak growth. Cut out dead and diseased wood.

Third and following years

4 February to March. Tip back all vigorous shoots and laterals if required. Cut out one or two older main shoots that have flowered sparsely.

5 July to August. Plant flowers on laterals of old wood, new basal shoots develop.

6 September. Summer prune. After flowering cut out thin, weak growth to maintain a well-spaced framework. Cut out dead and diseased wood.

Species and Shrub Roses

Group 2 consists of roses that flower mainly on short lateral and sublateral shoots produced from second-year or older wood. This group includes "old roses" such as the Albas, Centifolias, Moss roses and most Damasks. A large number of modern shrub roses, which do not repeat-flower but have one main flush of bloom in midsummer, are also included.

The first year

First-year roses are treated in the same way as those in Group 1. Tip back unripe or damaged shoots and remove coarse or damaged roots.

Second and following years

Mature roses in Group 2 differ from those in Group 1 by their regular production of vigorous basal, or near-basal, shoots, which may grow to 5–8ft in one season. In the second year these long shoots produce an abundance of flowering laterals, which often weigh them down so that the shoots are almost resting on the ground and in danger of breaking.

This growth habit necessitates a different pruning technique from Group 1 so that the natural habit is maintained while preventing the top-heavy flowering shoots from snapping or dragging their blooms in the mud.

In addition to the general points 1–4 of the introduction to this section all the vigorous, long shoots of the current year are pruned back by up to one-third of their length and the laterals on older main growths are cut back to 2–3 eyes or 6in from the stems during the winter. Care must be taken not to shorten these long shoots too much or the elegant arched habit can be lost and the potential of producing an abundance of flowering laterals is diminished.

This annual pruning with the removal each year of one or two old spent growths, should keep all roses in this group flowering profusely and growing strongly and healthily for many years ahead.

The second year

1 February to March. Cut back long new basal growths by up to one-third. Cut back laterals on flowered shoots to 2–3 eyes or 4–6in. Cut out any badly placed shoots.

2 June to August. Plant flowers on cut-back laterals of old wood. New basal shoots develop. Summer prune.

Third and following years

3 September to November. Tip back extra-long growths to minimize wind-rock. No other pruning is required.

4 February to March. Cut back long new basal growths by up to one-third. Cut back laterals on flowered shoots to 2–3 eyes or 4–6in. Cut out to base any badly placed and old shoots that flower sparsely.

5 June to August. Plant flowers on cut-back laterals of old wood. New basal shoots develop. Summer prune.

6 September to November. Tip back extra-long growths to minimize wind-rock. No other pruning is required.

Species and Shrub Roses

Group 3 can be regarded as a variant of Group 2. It includes most of the China roses and a number of modern shrub roses such as 'Fountain.' Of the "old roses" many Bourbons, such as the well-known 'Zephirine Drouhin' and 'Mme Isaac Pereire' are also part of this group. Certain very robust Hybrid Teas and Hybrid Perpetuals can be included in this group and treated as border shrubs.

The first year
First-year plants in this group are treated in the same way as those in Group 1.

Second and following years
Mature roses in Group 3 differ from those in Group 2, because they flower more or less recurrently throughout summer and autumn on both the current season's shoots and on laterals and sublaterals from second-year or older wood. Many also produce long, flexuous or robust growths. These come from either the base or higher up the plant on strong, established stems. These new shoots often develop sprays of flowers at their tips during the current season, unlike roses in Group 2.

Severe, or moderately severe, winter pruning of all these roses produces vigorous but sometimes sparsely flowering—or even non flowering–shoots. The blooms are often delayed and intermittent rather than continuous. Light pruning is needed to achieve the best results.

Group 3 roses tend to produce fresh flowering laterals and sublaterals all summer and they quickly build up into dense twiggy tangles. Dead-head and slightly thin during the flowering period. This treatment helps to encourage continuity of flower. Otherwise winter pruning is similar to that of Group 2 with more emphasis on removing twiggy growths that have lost their vigor.

The second year

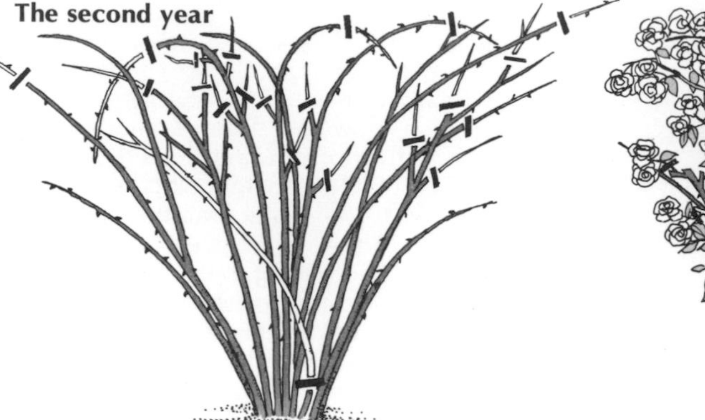

1 February to March. Cut back very long, new basal or near-basal one-year shoots by up to one-third. Take care to maintain the arching habit. Cut back laterals on shoots which flowered last season to 2–3 eyes (3–6 in). Cut out weak or badly placed shoots.

2 June to July. Plant flowers on laterals from previous season's wood. Basal and near-basal shoots are developing. Summer prune.

3 August to September. Flowers are produced on laterals from current season's growth. Twiggy sublaterals have developed from summer-pruned growth.

4 October. Tip back extra-long growths to minimize wind rock.

Third and following years

5 February to March. Cut back very long, new basal or near-basal one-year-old shoots by up to one-third. Take care to maintain the arching habit. Cut back laterals on shoots that flowered last season to 2–3 eyes (3–6 in). Cut out to base any old, badly placed or weak shoots. Mulch well.

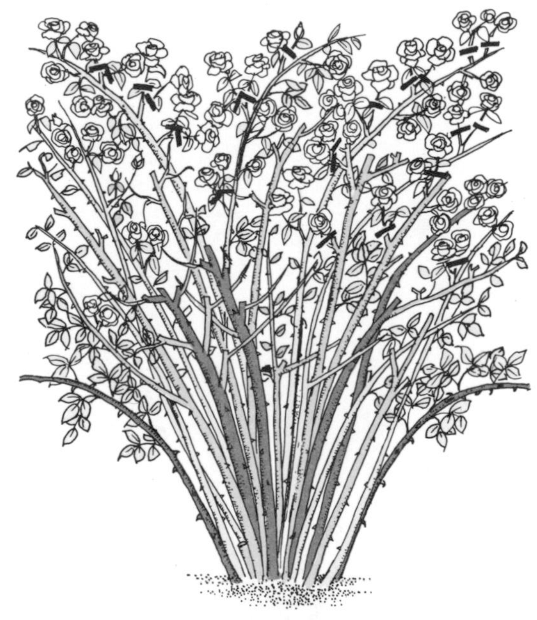

6 June to July. Plant in flower on laterals from previous season's wood. Basal and near-basal shoots are developing. Summer prune.

Standard Roses

Hybrid Tea and Floribunda roses are frequently grown as standards, or half-standards among bedding roses. They give height in the garden, where they can be extremely effective, particularly if used in a formal context. They are usually budded on stems of *Rosa rugosa* or common briar, but have become less popular in recent years as the head is often frequently top-heavy and the slender stem requires careful staking to maintain the formal habit. Initial pruning, and subsequent treatment, is similar to that given to the same varieties when grown as bushes.

Light pruning leaves a fairly large head on a standard which is vulnerable to wind damage, particularly in exposed gardens. Moderately severe pruning appropriate to the variety should be practiced.

With Hybrid Teas cut back strong shoots to 3–5 eyes or 6 in. With Floribundas cut back one-year-old growth to 6–8 eyes or 10 in and two-year-old shoots to 3–6 eyes or 6 in.

BUDDING STANDARD ROSES

Standard roses are best propagated by inserting growth buds each side of the stem in order to obtain an even head; if only one bud is used one-sided growth normally occurs, so before you buy a standard make sure it is double-budded.

Weeping standards

Climbing roses are budded on tall stems of *Rosa rugosa* or common briar so that the long trailing growths hang down.

Weeping standards of rose varieties in Group 1 of ramblers and climbers (page 12) can be most attractive when correctly grown. Pruning is quite simple. In August to September cut out all of the two-year-old shoots that have flowered and leave the vigorous young shoots to flower the following season. If insufficient young growths are produced leave a few of the two-year-old shoots in appropriate positions and cut back their laterals to 2–3 eyes or 6 in.

Varieties in Group 2 of ramblers and climbers (page 13) are less satisfactory when grown in this way, and are seldom seen. Pruning should be confined to cutting out surplus older wood and cutting back laterals to 2–3 eyes or 6 in after flowering. Tie down any vigorous young growths as they appear.

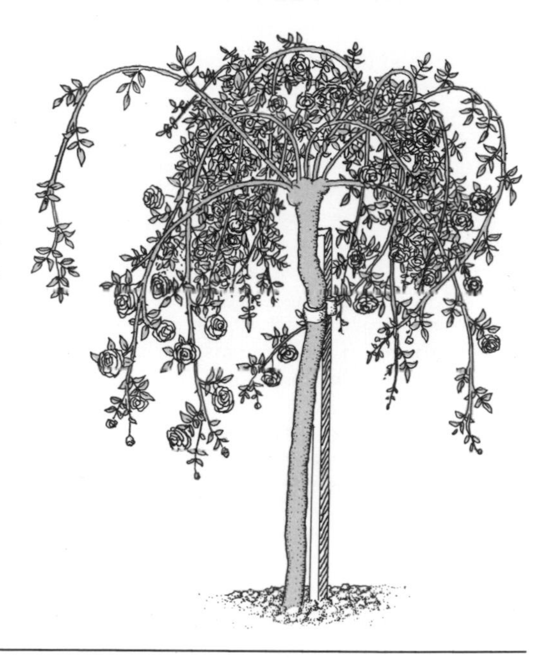

The first year

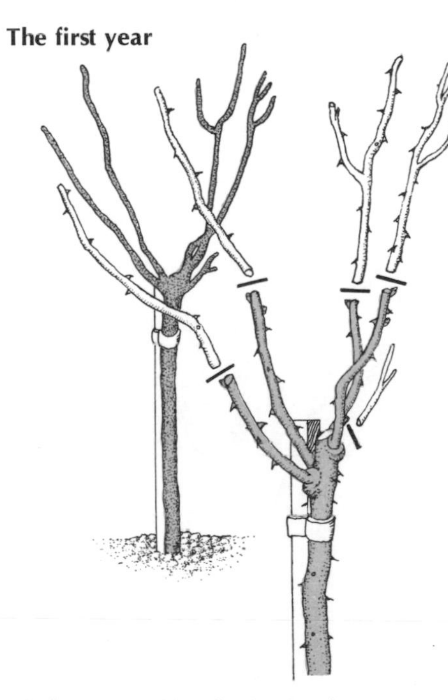

1 February to March. Cut back strong stems to 3–5 eyes or 6 in.

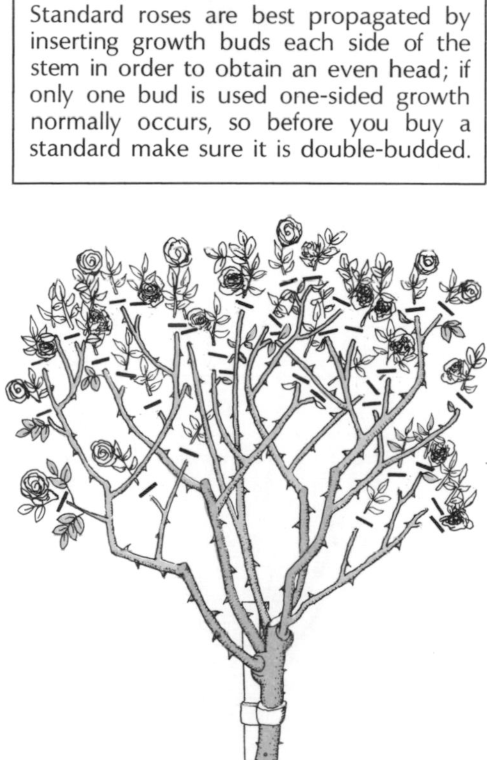

2 October to November. At the end of the season's growth, tip back main stems and cut out any soft, unripe shoots.

Second and following years

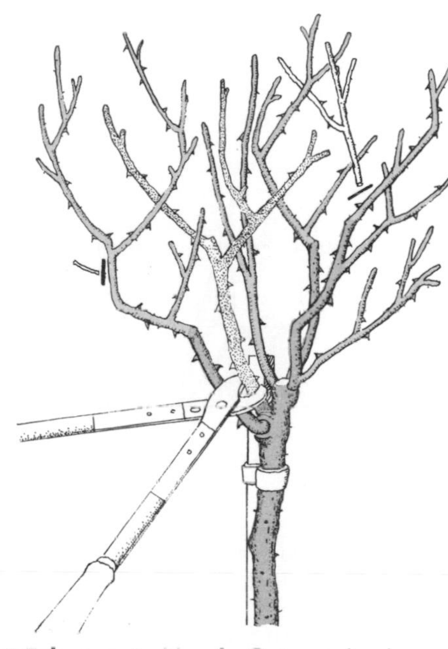

3 February to March. Cut out dead, diseased, weak and crossing stems.

4 At the same time, cut back new shoots to 3–5 eyes or 6 in and remaining laterals to 2–4 eyes or 4–6 in.

Renovation

Unpruned and neglected roses may continue to flower for many years but they are usually a sorry sight and it becomes difficult to ignore the tangled mass of dead, thin, and sometimes disease-ridden shoots, except when the plants are in bloom. Even then a close look will show that the flowers are often poorly shaped, small, and less numerous than the blooms of the same variety treated a little more kindly. A few roses, particularly vigorous climbers such as *Rosa filipes*, will thrive without any attention for 20 years or more, but these are exceptions and most roses require some form of pruning to remain vigorous, healthy and free flowering.

What does the gardener do when faced with an overgrown and neglected rose? The initial reaction is usually to turn away and forget it or to pull out the plant and replace it with a young one. Most roses, however, are extremely tenacious of life and will stand being cut to ground level, provided that aftercare, in the form of plenty of manure and water, is provided. Although this treatment may appear horrifying to some gardeners, in many instances it works well and has the merit of simplicity. This extreme treatment can rejuvenate apparently hopeless cases of neglect, although it is not recommended for wholesale use.

For most roses a somewhat gentler approach which will give equally good results can be adopted. Even neglected roses will usually have a few fairly vigorous shoots within the plant's framework and the first aim is to preserve these.

The first year

In winter cut out all the dead, thin, tangled and diseased shoots around the vigorous shoots and remove any suckers, which will certainly be present on a budded plant. Remove up to half of the main growths to the base, leaving only those on which there are any young vigorous shoots. The remaining shoots will also need to have weak twigs cut out and any strong laterals cut back to 2–3 eyes or 6 in. A heavy top dressing of well-rotted manure or compost should be applied around the base of the plant in spring. If possible, feed regularly at two- or three-week intervals during the growing season. Strong replacement shoots from the base will then be encouraged to grow.

The second year

In winter cut out to the base the remaining old growths. Cut back any laterals on the new growths to 2–3 eyes or 6 in and undertake any pruning necessary for the particular variety. Manuring is again necessary to maintain vigor. By the following summer the entire framework of the neglected plant should have been replaced. The pruning routine appropriate to the variety can then be established. The renovation can take place over a three-year period, but most roses will recover within two years.

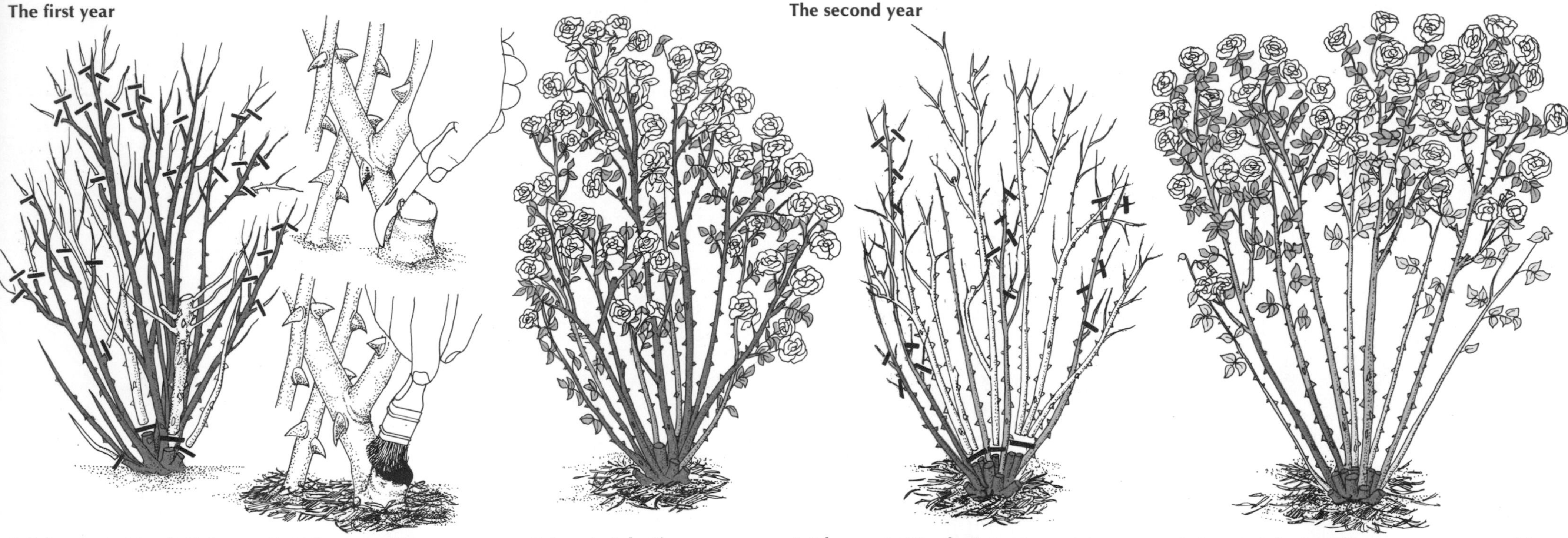

1 February to March. Cut out dead, weak and diseased shoots. Cut out half of main stems to base, leaving those with vigorous young growth. Cut back laterals to 2–3 eyes or 6 in.

2 At the same time, pare over cuts on the main stems with a sharp knife and paint with a wound paint. Add a good mulch of manure.

3 June to July. Flowers present on laterals of older wood. Vigorous new basal shoots appear.

4 February to March. Cut out remaining old growths to base. Prune any laterals on new growths to 2–3 eyes or 6 in. Repeat the procedure given in caption 2.

5 June to July. Bush flowers on one-year-old shoots and new vigorous shoots fill in the framework of the plant.

Shrubs: introduction

There is a commonly held, but quite incorrect, belief that all shrubs should be pruned, and pruned hard, each year. This often takes the form of a "haircut" or involves slaughtering the branches to keep the plant within bounds. Both treatments result in a misshapen ugly specimen with few or no flowers.

The other extreme of leaving the shrub entirely unpruned is preferable. Many deciduous and most evergreen shrubs will grow well enough by themselves and give adequate flowers without being pruned at all, if there is enough room for the plants to develop and the soil is reasonably fertile.

There are several groups of shrubs where correct pruning is beneficial to producing regular and abundant flowers together with healthy, vigorous growth and foliage. These same species, left unpruned, may still flower fairly well, but the quality and quantity of bloom and growth is poor compared with correctly pruned specimens.

An understanding of the basic principles behind pruning and knowledge of the growth habit and the method of flowering of the plant concerned is important, particularly the age of the wood on which flowers are borne.

Placing of the shrub in the garden also has an effect on pruning. Never try to fit a shrub which naturally grows to a large size into an area where limited room is available and constant pruning will be necessary. This may seem obvious, but frequently one sees large shrubs cut back several times a year, just to fit a particular space. The result is an ugly plant with a mass of growth and virtually no flowers. So, if you want to grow a *Philadelphus* in a site where only a 4ft spread is possible choose 'Manteau d'Hermine' (3ft × 3ft) or 'Erectus' (5ft × 3ft) which will fit, not 'Burfordensis' (12ft × 6ft) which is far too large.

Feeding and watering are also important if the shrub is to be pruned so that it produces healthy vigorous growth over a number of years.

When pruning any shrub try to obtain the best decorative effect whether it is grown for the flowers, fruit, foliage or the beauty of its winter stems. The pruning techniques will vary from shrub to shrub, depending on the plant and the effect required.

In some circumstances shrubs may be pruned by different methods to obtain different effects. The purple-leaved varieties of the smoke bush, *Continus coggygria*, are an example. If left virtually unpruned, this plant will form a large 10–12ft shrub, valued for the colored foliage and smokelike plumes of flowers. But the young plants may also be cut back hard each spring to form smaller shrubs with masses of long unbranched stems with large bright purple leaves.

Also try to create and maintain a well-balanced and attractive overall shape and

appearance for the plant. Many shrubs are naturally neat and symmetrical in outline and require no more than the removal of the occasional awkwardly placed shoot that destroys this symmetry.

Others are unruly and may grow unevenly, presenting a lop-sided shape with weak, twiggy growth on one side and strong healthy branches on the other. These plants require pruning to restore them to a reasonable shape. Strong shoots should be lightly pruned (a), which will result in moderate growth, while the weak wood (b) should be cut back hard to stimulate vigorous shoots, which will help to balance the shape (c). Do not cut back the strong shoots hard (d) and leave the weak unpruned (e) so that the overall height is the same. This will result in further strong growths being produced from the hard-pruned side but not from the unpruned growth, which will accentuate rather than correct the lack of balance (f).

In many, but not all, shrubs pruning will encourage the production of vigorous, basal or near-basal shoots. These will maintain the vitality of the plant and provide replacement growth for the older, worn-out branches. Pruning will also ensure an even distribution of flowers. The exceptions are such shrubs as the Japanese maple, witch hazel, and most evergreens.

Shrubs: introduction

To keep shrubs in a healthy condition involves the three "D's" mentioned on page 3—the removal and burning of all dead, diseased and damaged growth as soon as possible. It is obligatory in the case of all plants.

Pruning cuts. All pruning cuts should be made correctly as shown. Incorrect cuts can result in die-back and disease problems. Cuts should be made just above an outward-pointing bud or shoot or above a strong pair of opposite buds so that the resulting shoots will be well placed in relation to the other new growths on the plants.

Reversion. Occasionally branches of shrubs with variegated foliage may revert to the original green-leaved form of the species. If this occurs it is most important to completely remove the nonvariegated branches as soon as they are seen. They are frequently more robust than the variegated shoots, and if allowed to remain they will—like suckers—gradually become dominant, and eventually the shrub almost reverts to its green-leaved form. Examples include *Elaeagnus pungens* 'Maculata' and *Kerria japonica* 'Picta.'

Newly planted shrubs. When plants are taken from the nursery or garden center any shrub should be well shaped and bushy with a strong root system (a), and not one-sided (b). Most evergreens should need no pruning at planting, besides removing damaged shoots or tipping back a wayward branch.

With such deciduous shrubs as *Deutzia* there may be some weak growth present and to encourage strong basal growth this should be cut out completely. Terminal growth should also be shortened slightly to a strong bud, or strong pair of buds. Sometimes more drastic initial pruning is required. Details are given in the appropriate group.

Suckers. Although most modern shrubs are propagated vegetatively from cuttings and are on their own roots, a few are still budded or grafted on to stocks. These may occasionally produce sucker growths from the rootstocks and it is important to remove these as soon as they are seen. The sucker shoots should be traced back to their point of origin and carefully cut or pulled off. The dormant buds at the base of each sucker should be removed at the same time. Cutting them off at ground level merely results in a further cluster of suckers from these dormant buds. If the suckers are left they will gradually take over and replace the grafted plant.

Early training. Most shrubs produce a number of vigorous basal shoots during the first year or two after planting. These shoots will form the basic framework of the shrub and it is important to make sure that they are evenly spaced. Often they are too close, or cross, and if left unpruned they will spoil the balance and overall symmetry of the shrub (c). If shoots are ill-placed cut them out (d).

It is particularly important to do this with shrubs that do not naturally renew their growth from basal replacement shoots when they are older. When these shoots form a permanent, woody framework on which both extension growth and flowers are borne. Examples of shrubs in this category are

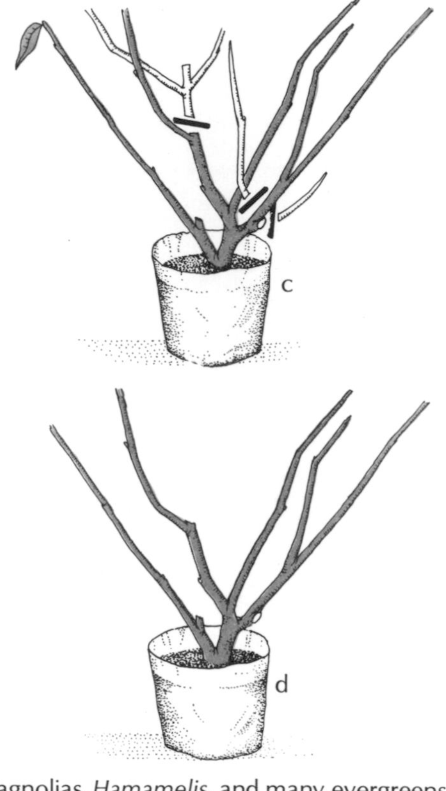

magnolias, *Hamamelis*, and many evergreens, including rhododendrons and camellias.

In many cases it is desirable to keep deciduous shrubs open in the center to allow free air circulation. This avoids stagnant conditions, which invite the spread of disease.

A number of deciduous shrubs such as the Japanese maple, *Acer palmatum*, naturally form an intricate network of crossing branchlets. Pruning, after the initial year or two, is unnecessary and undesirable except the removal of dead or diseased wood. Overpruning may ruin the natural habit of the plant. Pruning of crossing branches should be confined to early training with shrubs of this habit.

Root pruning. This is seldom practiced with ornamental shrubs, but is occasionally useful to check excessive top growth. It is sometimes used in preparing large shrubs for transplanting. The method described on page 65 can be used on all shrubs.

Deciduous Shrubs

Group 1 includes
Acer palmatum (Japanese maple)
Acer japonicum (Japanese maple)
Amelanchier
Buddleia globosa
Clethra
Colutea
Cornus florida
Cornus kousa
Corylopsis
Cotinus (unless treated as in group 4)
Cotoneaster (deciduous species)
Daphne (deciduous species)
Euonymus (deciduous species)
Fothergilla
Hamamelis
Hibiscus syriacus
Magnolia (deciduous species and hybrids)
Potentilla fruticosa
Rhus
Stachyurus
Styrax
Syringa (Lilac)
Viburnum (deciduous species and hybrids)

Group 1 consists of a number of deciduous shrubs that do not regularly produce vigorous replacement growths from the base or lower branches of the plant. The extension growth of these plants is produced on the perimeter of a permanent framework of older branches. The growth habit can be thought of as the crown of an oak tree without its trunk.

These plants require the minimum of pruning once they are established, but for the first few years after planting it is important to build up a framework of sturdy branches, removing the weak, crossing and misplaced shoots in the dormant season so that a symmetrical and balanced plant results. Open-center plants in this group, such as *Hamamelis* and *Magnolia × soulangiana,* may need removal of only the occasional misplaced shoot or shoots or branches that cross.

Pruning of the mature shrub is restricted to removing any dead, damaged or diseased growth as seen and to maintaining the overall symmetry of the shrub by pruning back weak and wayward growths.

Occasionally vigorous shoots will be produced from near the base or on the framework of mature plants. These may be used as replacement growths for old branches in the framework if they are suitably placed. But more usually, these growths are produced in an awkward position and should be cut out completely.

When old branches are removed always use a wound paint on the cut surfaces to protect the plant from such diseases as coral spot, which can be troublesome.

JAPANESE MAPLE

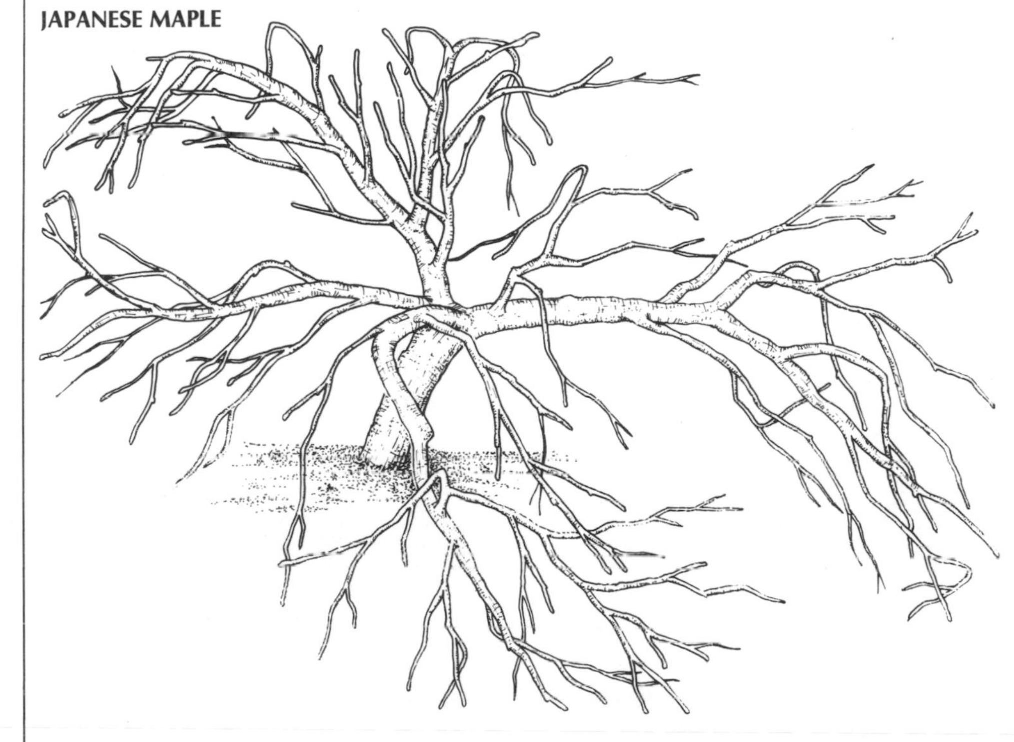

An intricately branched form of *Acer palmatum* (Japanese maple). Note the basic framework branches. After the initial framework is formed no further pruning is needed except for the removal of dead, diseased and damaged shoots as seen. The normal habit should be maintained and the crossing branches left unpruned.

The first year

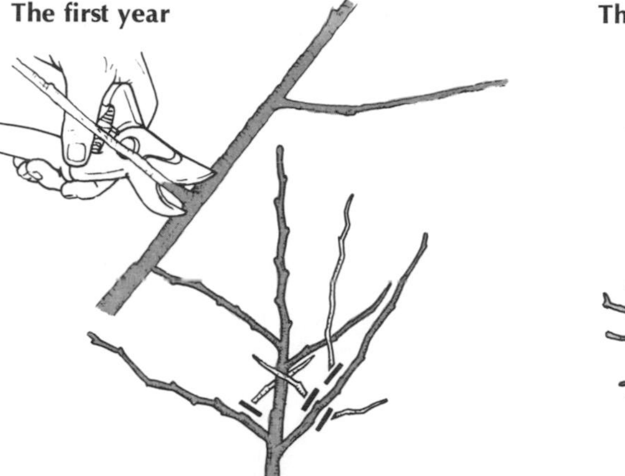

1 November to April. *Magnolia stellata* at planting. Remove weak shoots and crossing branches. Create a balanced framework by removing any unruly growths.

The second year

2 March to April. Cut out any badly spaced extension growth and laterals produced during the first growing season. If growths are well-spaced leave them alone.

Third and following years

3 March to April. Minimum pruning is now required. Allow the plant to develop its natural habit, but always remove the dead, diseased and damaged wood.

4 April. The mature plant in flower.

Deciduous Shrubs

Group 2 includes
Buddleia alternifolia
Cytisus scoparius and its hybrids
Deutzia
Dipelta
Forsythia
Hydrangea × macrophylla
Kerria
Kolkwitzia
Neillia
Philadelphus
Ribes sanguineum
Spiraea × arguta
Spiraea thunbergii
Stephanandra
Tamarix (spring-flowering)
Weigela

Group 2 includes deciduous shrubs that flower on shoots that are produced during the previous growing season. The flowers are formed either on short laterals produced from this one-year-old wood as in *Deutzia, Philadelphus, Ribes sanguineum* or directly from the one-year-old branches as in *Forsythia*. Many spring and early summer-flowering shrubs belong to this group. They require renewal pruning to maintain them at a reasonable height and to ensure that there will be each season a regular supply of strong young shoots from low down on the plant. Unpruned shrubs in this group quickly form many twiggy branchlets, often becoming ungainly with fewer flowers of poor quality.

The first year

The plant will usually be two to three years old when you buy it at the nursery. Pruning when planting is limited to cutting out weak and damaged growth and cutting back main shoots a few inches to a strong bud or pair of buds. This ensures that during the first growing season the plant's energy is concentrated on producing a strong basic framework of branches. Little flower is produced the first year. Immediately after flowering cut back any flowering laterals to a strong developing shoot and remove thin weak branch growth.

The second year

Flowers will be borne either on short lateral branchlets or direct from the stem. One or more strong growths will develop below the flowering branchlets. Once the flowers have faded remove all the one-year-old wood that has produced flowers. Cut back the branches to the lowest (usually also the strongest) of the developing new shoots, provided this does not spoil the balance and shape of the plant. If the flowered wood is not pruned away immediately after flowering, many weaker shoots develop from lateral buds.

Third and following years

During the second year branchlets that have borne flowers should be cut out immediately after flowering, in the same way. In addition completely cut out one-quarter to one-fifth of the old stems to the base, taking care to balance the shape of the plant.

Deutzia provides a typical example of a shrub in Group 2. The time of pruning will differ slightly, depending on the flowering period of the shrub. Prune immediately after flowering.

The first year

1 Autumn or early spring. Young *Deutzia* at planting. Cut out all weak growth and tip back the main shoots to a strong pair of buds (or an outward-pointing bud for shrubs with alternate buds). Add a good mulch of manure.

2 October to November. A few strong basal growths and many laterals from the main branches have developed during the first season. Cut out any weak or misplaced shoots to maintain a symmetrical framework. Mulch well in early spring.

The second year

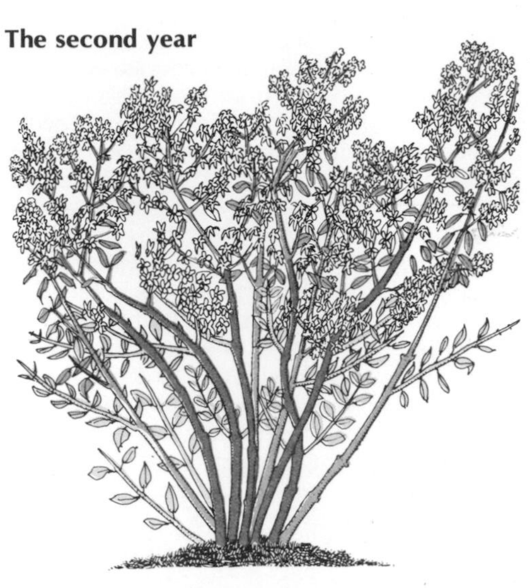

3 June to July. Flowers are produced from short laterals along many of the upper shoots which grew last season. As the flowers fade strong shoots will grow from the base of the plant and from low down on the main stems.

4 July. Immediately after flowering cut back the stems that have flowered to vigorous young growths developing lower down on the main stems. Remove any weak growth. Make sure the overall balance and symmetry of the shrub is maintained.

5 October to November. The vigorous young shoots have grown several feet and produced laterals on which the following season's blooms will be borne. Mulch well in early spring.

Third and following years

6 July. Immediately after flowering cut back the stems that have flowered to vigorous young growths developing lower down on the main stems. Remove any weak growth. If the main stems are becoming crowded cut out one-quarter or one-fifth of the oldest stems to the base. Mulch well.

Deciduous Shrubs

Kerria

Group 2 also includes a few shrubs such as *Kerria*, which produce almost all of their new growth from ground level. They flower on one-year-old wood, but require a slightly different pruning technique. Immediately after flowering the shoots that have flowered should be cut out to the base or occasionally to a point low down on the shoot where vigorous young growth is appearing. If flowering wood is left most of it will die back naturally by the following winter, but it is unsightly.

The first year

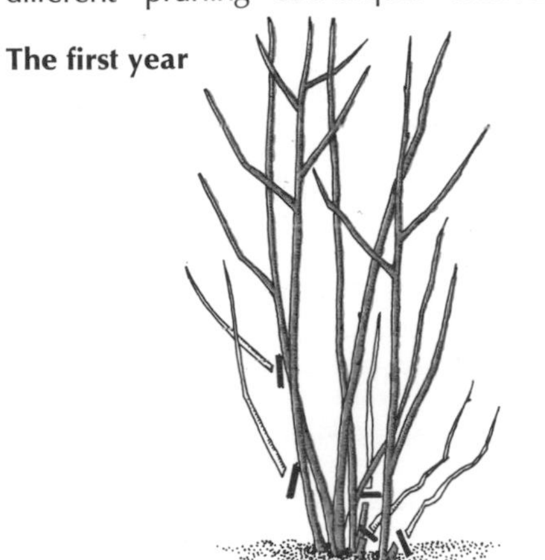

1 Autumn or early spring. Young *Kerria* at planting. Cut out any thin weak growth. Leave the vigorous stems and their laterals as these should flower this season.

2 May. Cut out the flowered shoots to the base or, with very strong stems, to points low down where vigorous young shoots are forming. Basal growths develop. Mulch well.

Second and following years

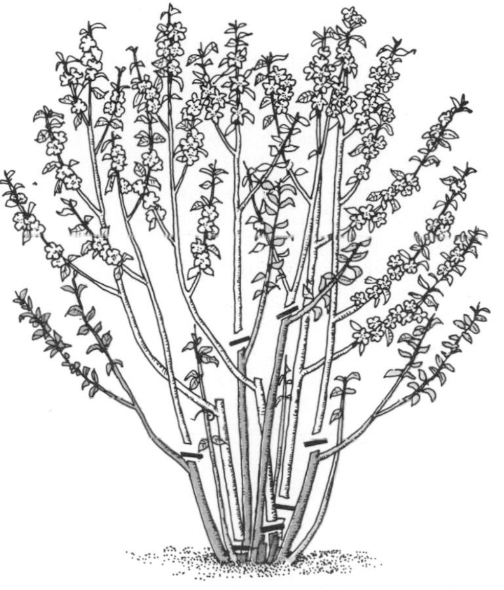

3 May. Cut out the flowered shoots to the base or, with very strong stems, to points low down where vigorous young shoots are forming. Basal growths develop. Mulch well.

Hydrangeas

Hydrangeas are included in Group 2. Pruning the Hortensia hydrangea (*H.* × *macrophylla*), which includes the familiar Mop-head and Lace-cap kinds, frequently causes difficulties. They flower late in the season and there is a tendency to prune them hard each spring in the belief that the resultant strong growths will flower in late summer or autumn. Unfortunately this does not occur.

Only cosmetic pruning is needed for young plants. And plants left unpruned will usually flower quite freely. They tend to produce a good deal of twiggy growth if left entirely unpruned, and, with plants three or more years old, a proportion of the older wood should be cut out to the base in early spring to encourage a constant supply of vigorous young replacement shoots each season. Do not remove the previous year's flower heads in winter as these provide some protection to the growth and flower buds, which may be damaged in severe weather. Remove them in early spring.

1 Late March to April. Cut out one-third to one-quarter of the older exhausted shoots to the base. Cut out any weak thin shoots still remaining. Cut back the old flower heads to leave only a strong pair of buds.

2 September. The upper growth buds on the pruned shoots have grown and the strongest have produced flower heads. New vigorous basal shoots have developed but will not flower until next season.

BROOMS

Many brooms (*Cytisus scoparius* and its hybrids) are included in Group 2. They are deciduous shrubs, although the bright green young stems make them appear evergreen. They flower in May and June along the entire length of the previous season's wood.

No pruning is required at planting. Once the blooms have faded cut back the flowered wood by two-thirds of its length to where young growths are developing. The pruning principle is the same as for *Deutzia* and similar shrubs, but brooms should not be cut back hard because shoots do not grow very well from old wood. It is essential to prune even one-year-old plants after flowering to prevent them becoming leggy and top heavy.

1 June to July. In second and subsequent years, immediately after flowering, cut back the flowered wood by two-thirds to vigorous young growths developing near the base of the previous season's wood.

Deciduous Shrubs

Group 3 includes
Buddleia davidii
Caryopteris
Ceanothus (deciduous)
Ceratostigma
Fuchsia (hardy)
Hydrangea paniculata
Perovskia
Prunus glandulosa
Prunus triloba
Romneya
Spiraea × bumalda
Spiraea douglasii
Spiraea japonica

Group 3 includes those deciduous shrubs that bear their flowers on the current year's growth. When pruned back hard in early spring they produce vigorous shoots that flower in summer or early autumn. If left without pruning they soon develop into unkempt, twiggy bushes that gradually deteriorate in the quality and quantity of flowers that they produce.

It is convenient also to include in Group 3 a small number of deciduous shrubs, typified by *Prunus triloba*, which flower early each year on the previous season's wood. They also respond to hard pruning in March or April, by which time they will have flowered already, producing long, wandlike shoots which bloom the following spring. The pruning technique is exactly the same.

The basic requirement is to prune early in the year so that there is a maximum amount of time for the flowering wood to develop. This may simply mean cutting out all growth to ground level between March and April of each year for small subshrubby plants, such as hardy fuchsias, *Leycesteria* and *Perovskia* or allowing a framework of woody branches to develop to the required height and then cutting back the growths close to the framework each spring, as with *Buddleia davidii*. Variation in the height of the growth and flowers on a single plant can be achieved quite simply by pruning a few of the basic framework shoots higher or lower than the remainder. This is useful in a place where the plant is only being seen from one side and allows a greater surface area of flower to be presented to the viewer. This hard pruning is carried out in March to early April each year just as the growth buds begin to swell and the position of the new shoots can be seen.

In windy areas it may be necessary to trim back the flowered growths in late autumn to minimize wind-rock, but normally only the spring cut-back is required.

It is most important to feed shrubs pruned by this method to ensure that adequate healthy growth is produced each season.

The first year
Initial pruning is aimed at building up a strong well-spaced framework of branches. in the first season pruning is usually less severe than in subsequent years so that the root system is able to become well established. Remove all weak and damaged growth at planting. Cut back the remaining growths by one-quarter to three-quarters of their length in March to April, the more vigorous shrubs such as *Buddleia davidii* being pruned more severely than less robust species, such as *Perovskia* and the deciduous *Ceanothus*.

The second year
In March to April cut back hard the previous year's growth to developing buds just above the older wood. With fuchsias, *Leycesteria* and similar subshrubs which may not develop a woody basal framework cut back almost to ground level. In mild areas these subshrubs may become woody and are than treated using the framework principle. Apply a good mulch of compost or manure around the plant to encourage vigorous new growth.

Third and following years
The pruning sequence is exactly the same as in the second season. After a number of years the basic woody framework may become congested and slight thinning of the old woody stumps may be needed. Always apply an annual basal mulch to ensure continued vigorous growth.

Because of the slight variations in the degree of pruning needed to form the initial framework three examples which require marginally different techniques are provided of shrubs in this group. Failure to feed regularly may result in weak spindly growth.

This method is suitable for deciduous shrubs such as *Ceanothus, Caryopteris, Spartium junceum* and other shrubs in Group 3 which are less vigorous than *Buddleia davidii* (see page 28.) It is important to let them grow unchecked during the first season, and only remove the weak growth and badly placed shoots that will spoil the symmetry of the plant, so that a sturdy natural branching system is developed. If they are cut back hard at planting they may produce only weak growths or die back completely.

The first year

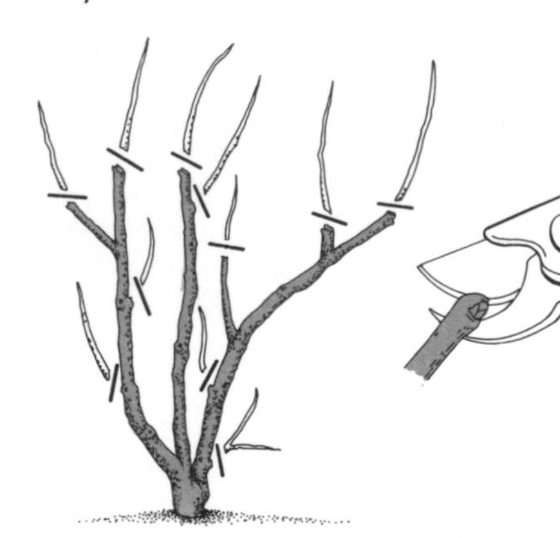

1 March to early April. Cut out any damaged or very weak growths. Tip back main shoots by 1–2in to strong outward-pointing buds. Cut out entirely any badly placed shoot.

2 August to September. Strong shoots have grown from upper buds on last season's growths and these will flower during late summer.

The second year

3 March to early April. Cut back all last season's growths by one-half to strong outward-pointing buds. Remove entirely any weak straggly shoots.

Third and following years

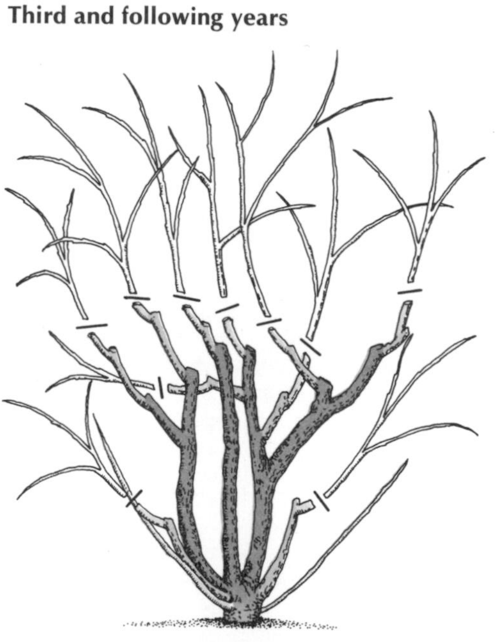

4 March to early April. Cut back all last season's shoots to within one or two buds of the previous season's growth. The basic framework of woody stems is formed.

Deciduous Shrubs

Group 3 includes such shrubs as *Perovskia* (Russian sage), *Leycesteria formosa*, hardy fuchsias and *Ceratostigma*, which may not develop a woody framework and are cut back almost to ground level.

The first year

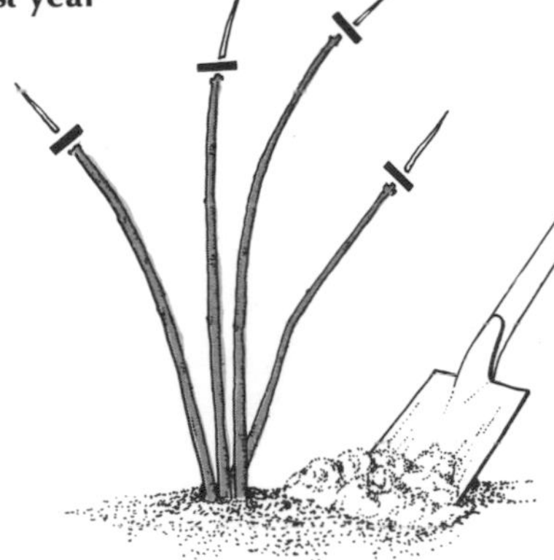

1 March to April. *Perovskia* as planted. Cut back any weak, thin tips by a few inches to a pair of strong buds. Add a good mulch to the base of the plant.

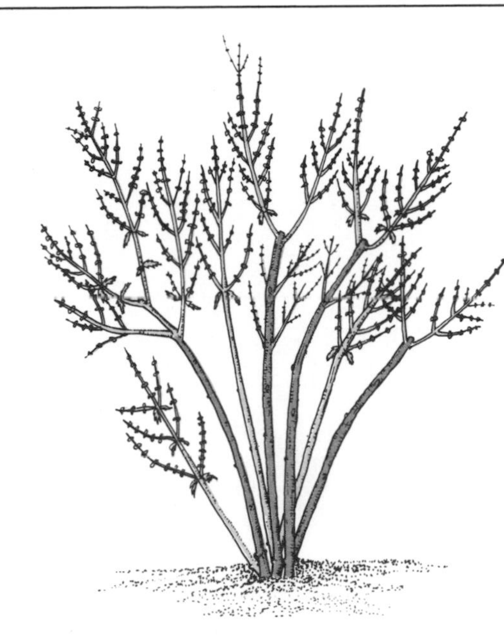

2 November. Basal shoots have developed during the summer and last year's shoots have produced lateral growths. The grey stems remain attractive in winter.

The second year

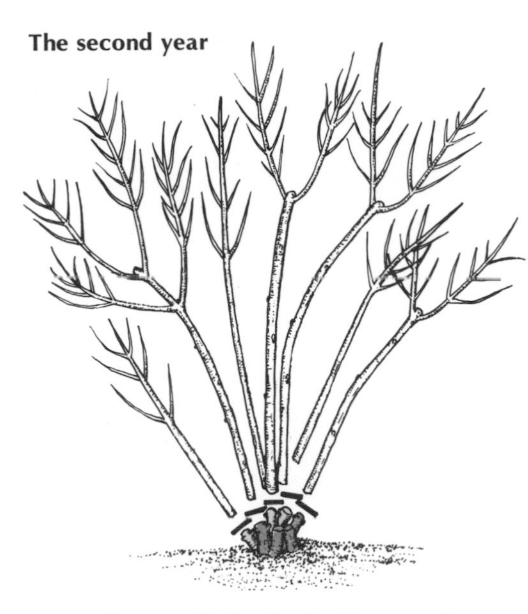

3 March to April. Cut back all stems almost to ground level, above strong pairs of buds.

CREATING A FRAMEWORK

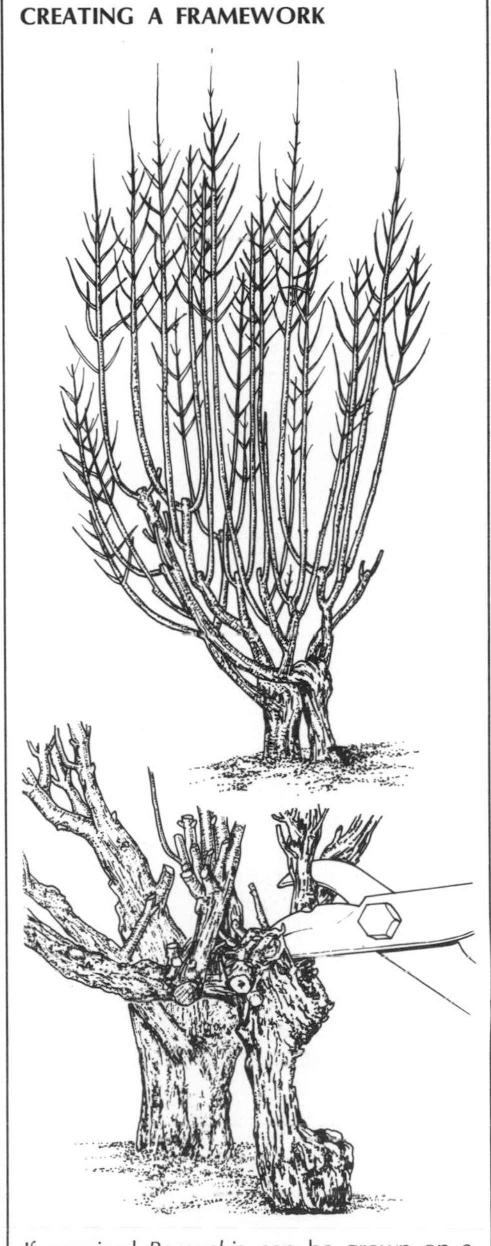

If required *Perovskia* can be grown on a framework of woody basal shoots. Early training and subsequent pruning is exactly as shown under deciduous *Ceanothus*.

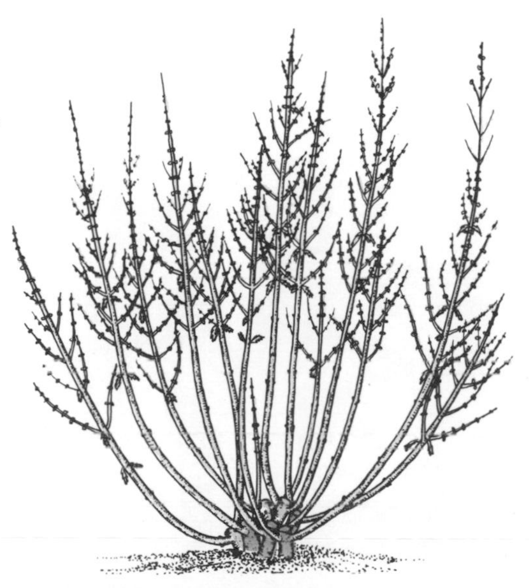

4 September. Strong growths have developed to a height of 2–3ft. Laterals are produced towards the top of each shoot. Flowers are borne on laterals and shoot tips.

Third and following years

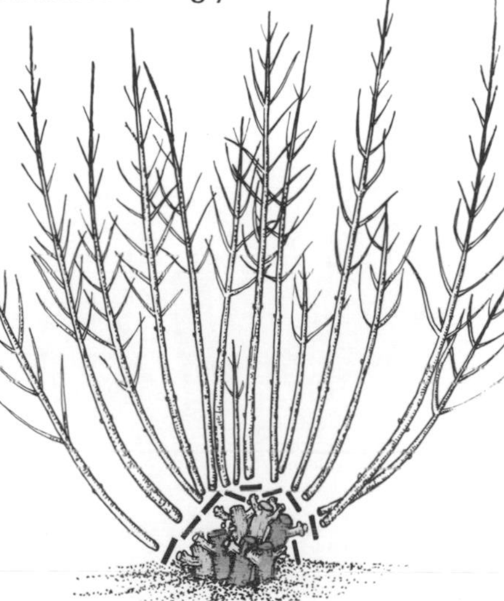

5 March to April. Cut back all stems almost to ground level, above strong pairs of buds.

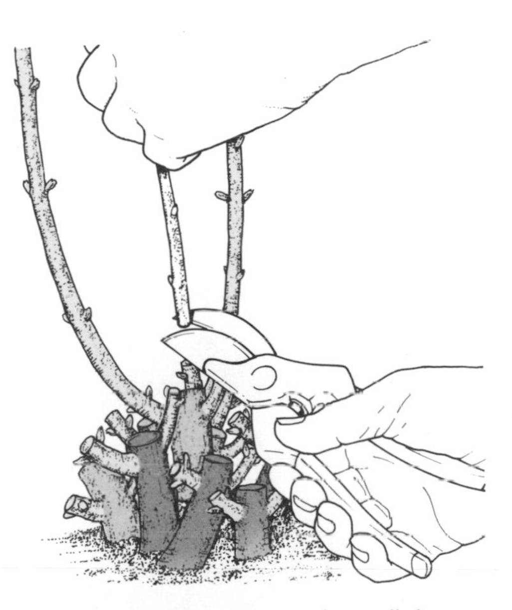

Take care not to leave snags that will die back during the year.

Deciduous Shrubs

Group 3 includes vigorous shrubs such as *Buddleia davidii* that should grow on a framework of woody branches, which is allowed to develop to the required height.

The first year

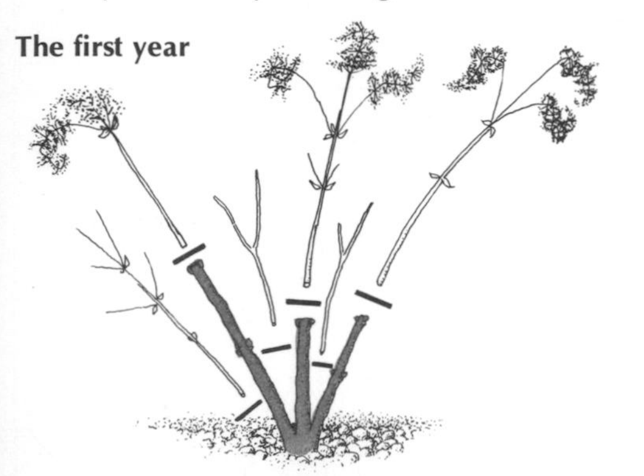

1 March to early April. *Buddleia davidii* as planted. Cut back all main shoots by one-half to three-quarters of their length to points where vigorous shoots are developing or the buds are swelling. Cut out remaining weak growth entirely. Mulch well.

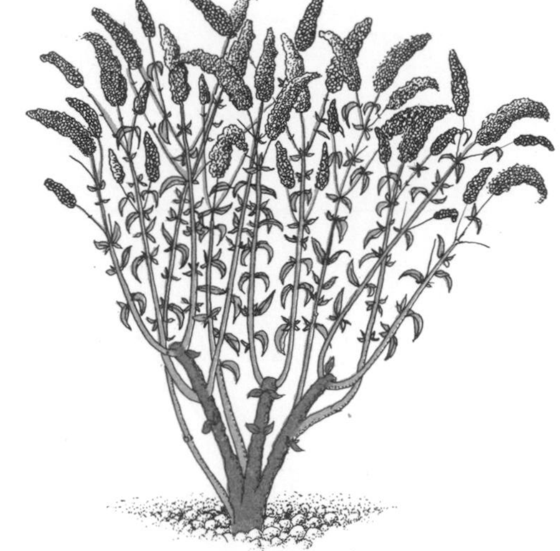

2 July to August. Long wandlike growths have been produced from the pruned branches and also from the base. These will flower near the tips in late summer.

The second year

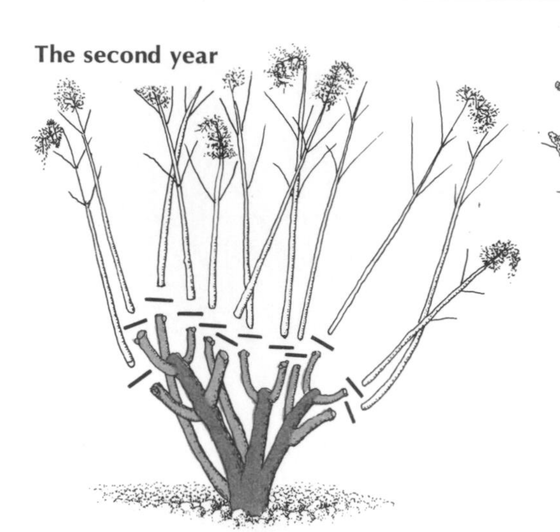

3 March to early April. Cut back new shoots hard to within one or two pairs of buds of the previous year's growth. Cut back any basal or near-basal growths that have developed the previous season to the required height. Mulch well.

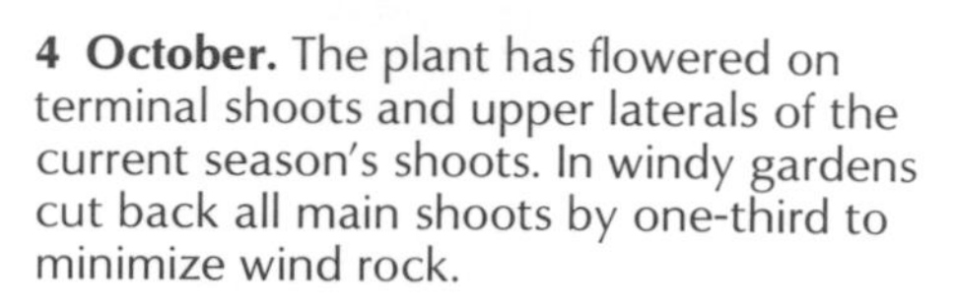

4 October. The plant has flowered on terminal shoots and upper laterals of the current season's shoots. In windy gardens cut back all main shoots by one-third to minimize wind rock.

The third year

5 March to early April. Cut back as in caption 3. The main framework is now formed. Any basal or near-basal shoots that develop in future years may be used to fill gaps in the framework or cut out if not required. Mulch well.

Fourth and following years

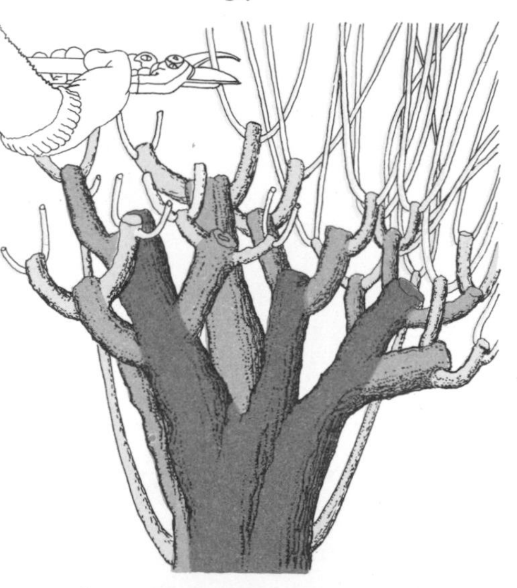

6 March to early April. Carry out normal pruning. When the framework becomes very woody and congested remove any badly placed "stumps," leaving the remainder as well spaced as possible. Train in any new shoots as required to replace the old framework wood that has been cut out.

Group 4 includes
Cornus alba
Cornus stolonifera
many Salix species
Rubus cockburnianus
Cotinus coggygria
Corylus maxima 'Purpurea'
Sambucus (Golden-leaved and purple-leaved forms)

Deciduous Shrubs

Group 4 includes shrubs that are pruned hard in early spring each year so that the most attractive decorative effect is obtained from their foliage or the bark of their stems during the winter. The technique is very similar to the one described in Group 3. Most of the shrubs included here would flower on wood produced the previous year, but pruned by this method, they do not bloom at all. With the right feeding the foliage of variegated or purple-leaved variants of such shrubs as *Cotinus coggygria* and *Cornus alba*, or of those such as *Rhus typhina*, grown for autumn color, will be two or three times larger.

Many shrubs with beautifully colored bark, such as the red- and green-stemmed dogwoods, some willows and the white-stemmed brambles, also react well to this drastic pruning, producing vigorous, unbranched new growth. They also show more pronounced color than unpruned specimens.

As with Group 3 the basic framework can usually be varied in height to suit the position of the shrub. The exceptions are species such as the white-stemmed brambles, which do not build up a woody framework but sucker to produce canelike growths from the base of the plant.

Cotinus coggygria
This method is used to increase the decorative value of the shrubs in Group 3 that have colored or variegated foliage, such as the purple-leaved smoke bush, *Cotinus coggygria* 'Foliis Purpureis'. It is also very effective with the golden elder and purple hazel, and useful in small gardens, where the same plants if left unpruned would be too large.

The technique is very similar to the method of pruning *Cornus alba* (see page 30), but the plant is allowed to develop a woody stem or group of stems to the required height before being pollarded.

The first year

1 March to early April. *Cotinus coggygria* 'Foliis Purpureis' at planting. Cut back all main growths to 12–18 in to create the base framework. Cut out any weak basal growths. Mulch the plant well.

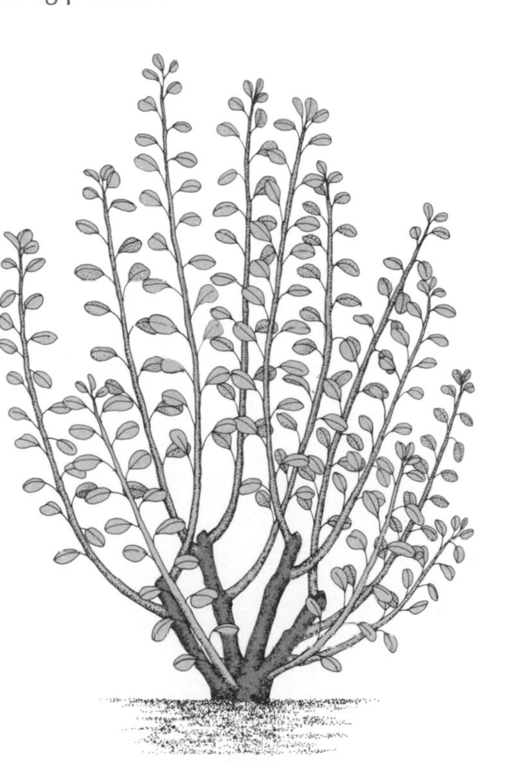

2 July to August. Vigorous unbranched shoots have developed with larger and more handsome foliage than that of an unpruned bush.

The second year

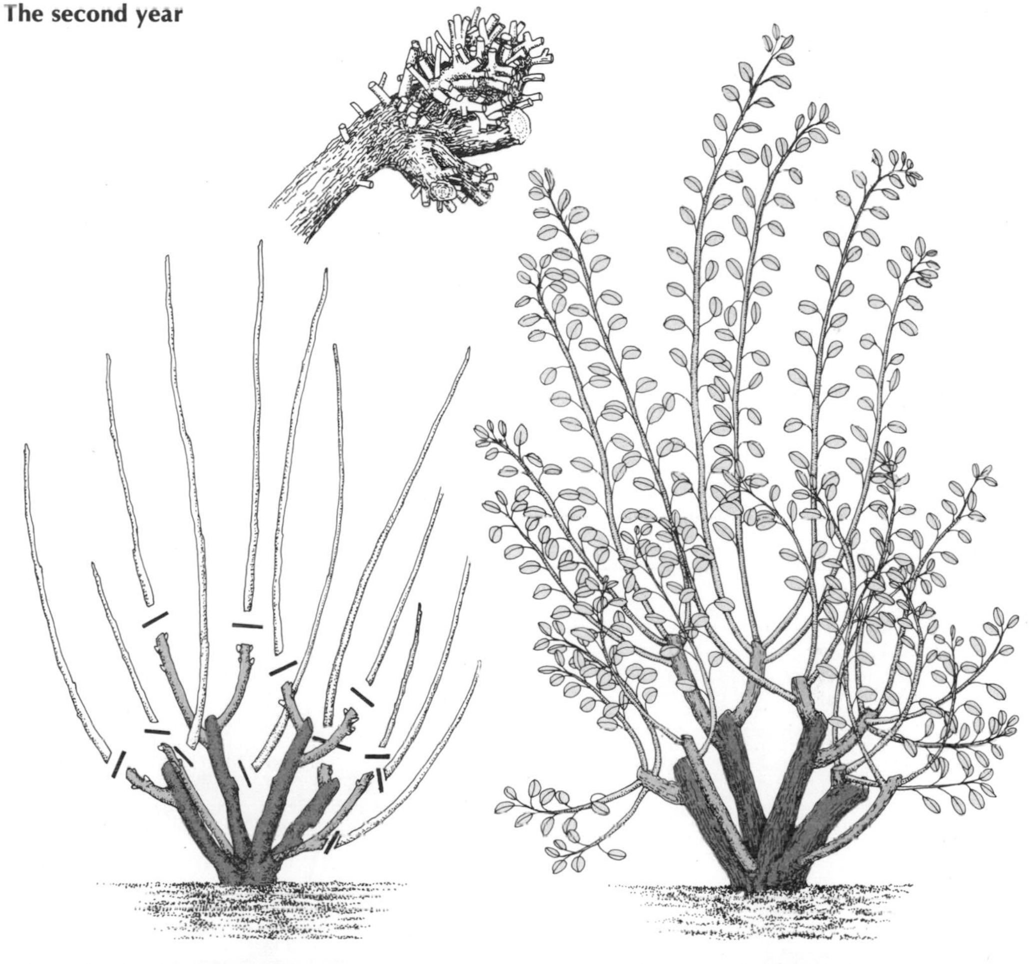

3 March. Cut back hard the previous season's growths to above a bud within 1–2 in of the framework. If a higher framework is needed cut back these growths to the appropriate height. Remove any surplus or weak growths to ensure that the framework branches are well spaced.

4 July to August. The established plant with a strong, basic, woody framework and numerous vigorous growths.

Deciduous Shrubs

Rubus cockburnianus
This method is suitable for such shrubs as *Rubus cockburnianus* and its relatives, the white-stemmed brambles. These are grown for the effect of their white, branched stems in winter. They do not form a woody framework but sucker from the base to produce annual replacement shoots, similar to their relative the raspberry.

Pruning simply consists of cutting all growths down to ground level between March and April each year. If the previous season's growths remain they will flower in summer, but they will not be particularly decorative. It is better to remove these before active growth starts. Pruning will encourage the plant's energy to go into producing vigorous new growths rather than being shared between flower and shoot production.

Where growth is poor one or two of the previous year's shoots may be left at pruning time, this provides food for the plant early in the season and helps to stimulate basal growth during the summer.

The first year

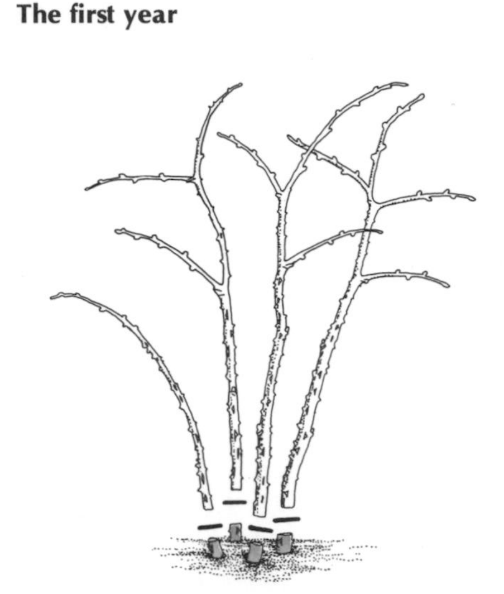

1 March to April. White-stemmed bramble at planting. Cut out all growth close to ground level. Mulch well.

2 October. Vigorous shoots branched towards the top have grown during spring and summer. In autumn the foliage falls and the stems remain attractive during winter.

Second and following years

3 March to April. Cut out all growth close to ground level.

Cornus alba
This method is applicable to *Cornus alba* and many willows grown for the colored bark of the young shoots. They usually withstand hard pruning immediately after planting.

The first year

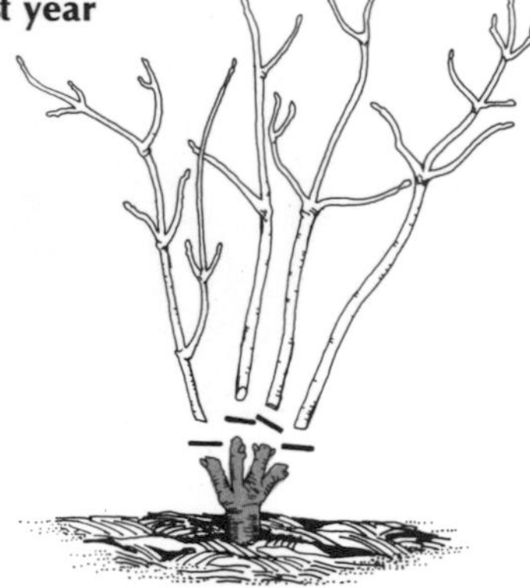

1 March to early April. *Cornus alba* at planting. Cut back hard all main shoots to within a few inches of the base. Cut out any weak basal growths. Mulch the plant well.

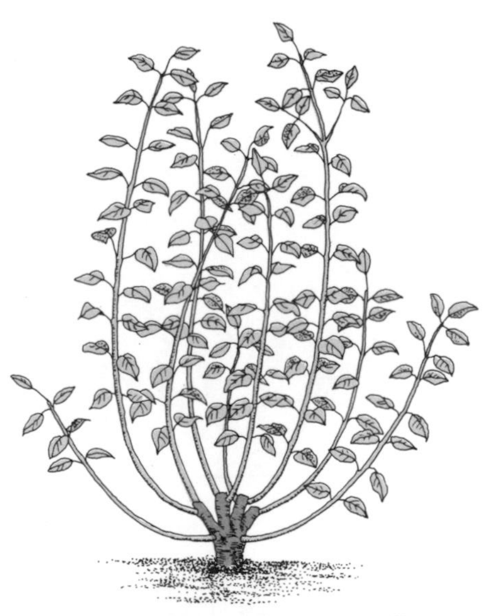

2 October. Vigorous whippy, usually unbranched shoots have grown during spring and summer. Once the leaves have fallen the colored stems form an attractive feature throughout the winter.

The second year

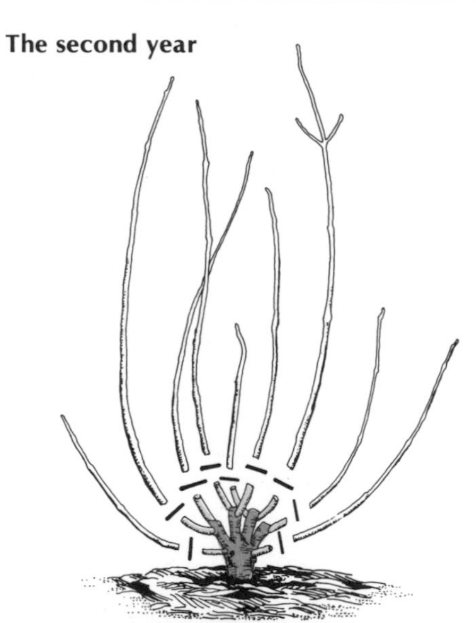

3 March to early April. Cut back hard all main shoots to within a few inches of the base. Cut out any weak basal growths. Mulch the plant well.

POLLARDING

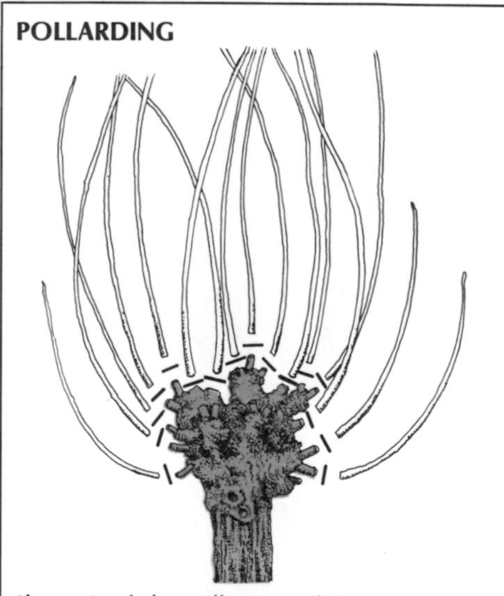

If required the willows and *Cornus* can be allowed to develop a single woody stem or stems to the required height and then pruned back in the same way. This method of pruning is usually known as pollarding.

Evergreen Shrubs

Group 5 includes the evergreen shrubs. Most evergreens are naturally bushy and reasonably compact in habit. Provided sufficient room is available they should be allowed to develop naturally with only minor pruning. This usually amounts to no more than the removal of spent flowers or wayward shoots and branches that would detract from the overall symmetry of the shrub.

Dead, diseased and mishapen shoots can be removed at any time of year. But any winter damaged growth is best cut back between April and May, just as the growth buds are beginning to swell. This gives the maximum period for new shoots to ripen before winter. Pruning earlier in the year makes the plant vulnerable to wind and frost damage, while summer and autumn pruning will produce soft growth. This will almost certainly be damaged or killed during the following winter.

A small number of evergreen shrubs or subshrubs benefit from harder pruning, it helps them to maintain a compact habit or increase their flowering potential. This may involve cutting such plants as cotton lavender (*Santolina*) almost to ground level each spring or shearing over old growths of the rose of Sharon (*Hypericum calycinum*) and *Mahonia aquifolium*.

Early training

Early training is confined to slightly shortening any lateral growths which spoil the overall symmetry. Occasionally the leader shoots of young evergreen shrubs such as camellias may be spindly, rather weak, and lack any lateral branchlets. In these circumstances the leader should be cut back a few inches at planting. This will encourage laterals to grow from lower down. The uppermost new lateral should be trained to replace the leader. Do not cut the leader back more than a few inches, hard pruning may stimulate too much lateral growth and no adequate replacement leader shoot will develop. If the weak leader shoot is left, a plant which is bushy at the base and thin at the top will develop.

The pruning and management of *Eucalyptus* differs from that of other evergreens because of its unusual growth characteristics; it is described separately.

Training

April to May. A young camellia with a well-developed leader. Cut back the uppermost vigorous lateral slightly; if left, unbalanced growth may result.

April to May. A young camellia with a weak leader and few laterals. Prune back the weak leader to a strong bud to stimulate vigorous lateral growth.

June to July. Lateral growths have formed. The uppermost lateral is trained in as the replacement leader.

DEAD-HEADING

Some evergreens, rhododendrons for example, flower and seed abundantly. Unless seed is required to increase stock the spent flower trusses should be removed as soon as possible. This will prevent the plant forming seed pods and directing its energy into producing strong new shoots and flower buds for next season's display. Dead-heading should be carried out immediately after the flowers fade and before seed pods begin to form. Carefully snap off the spent flower truss between finger and thumb. Take care not to damage the growth buds, which are present in the leaf axils directly below the flower truss.

Evergreen Shrubs

Lavender

Unpruned lavenders develop into woody, gnarled shrubs with bare lower stems sparsely topped by grey foliage. It is not worth while trying to rejuvenate mishapen or unkempt plants; they seldom produce satisfactory young growth if cut back into the old wood. It is better to replace them with young plants, which should be pruned hard in April to establish a low bushy habit.

Pruning consists of clipping over the bushes every April. Remove an inch or so of the previous season's growth to stimulate fresh young shoots that produce flowering spikes later in the season. Tidy gardeners will remove the old flower stems in early autumn to keep a neat appearance in the plant. Other gardeners may prefer to remove the stems the following April when undertaking annual pruning. In cold climates it is worth leaving these old flower stems until the April pruning because they help to protect the foliage from severe weather conditions.

Do not prune lavenders immediately after flowering as is sometimes recommended. This only stimulates late young growth that is liable to winter damage.

Heathers

Tree heathers (*Erica arborea* and its allies) do not require regular pruning. However, the removal of awkwardly placed or wayward branches is occasionally necessary. This should be carried out in April. Renewal pruning in April to May can be successful with tree heathers and some larger species and hybrids.

Most summer- and autumn-flowering heathers (*Calluna vulgaris, Erica ciliaris, E. vagans, Daboecia cantabrica* and their variants) benefit from regular trimming. If left unpruned they usually become leggy with shorter, less attractive flower heads.

Trimming should be carried out between March and early April because the russet or bronze coloring of the old flowers is attractive during the winter months. The old flower spikes of those heathers, which are grown for their brightly colored winter foliage, should be trimmed after flowering in October. They may require a further trim in March to early April.

Winter-flowering heathers are naturally either compact or spreading in habit, and when they have finished flowering in April can be gently trimmed to remove the old flower heads. No further pruning is required.

1 March to early April. Trim back the previous season's flower head to a point just below the lowest flowers on the spike. Use shears (or scissors on young plants), taking care to follow the natural growth habit of the individual plants. Avoid the flat "table-top" cut by varying the angle at which the blades of the shears are held.

2 August to September. *Calluna vulgaris* in flower; a compact plant with long flower spikes. Do not trim the old flower heads, they are attractive throughout winter.

The first year

1 April. Young lavender as received 9 in tall. At planting prune hard to remove straggly shoots and encourage new growth.

2 September. Vigorous bushy growth is produced during spring and summer. A few flower spikes develop during the first season.

Second and following years

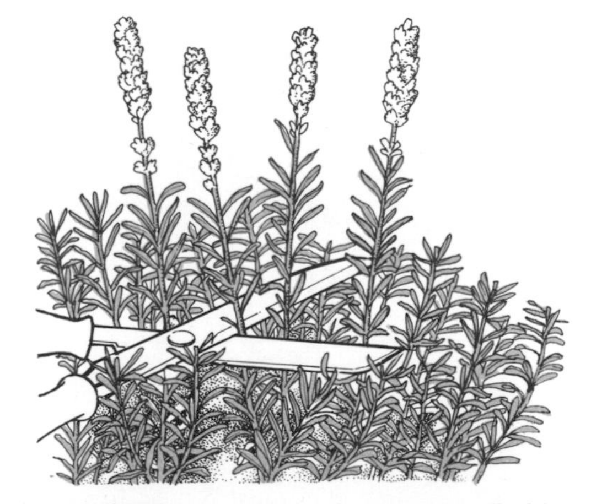

3 April. Clip over the bush removing all old flower spikes and 1 in of the previous season's growth. Follow the natural outline of the plant with the shears so that a flat "table-top" appearance is avoided.

4 September. Old plant after flowering showing the form that should be created by regular pruning.

Eucalyptus

The pruning method used for *Eucalyptus* will depend on whether the species is to be grown as a tree, as a bush, or pruned to produce a densely rounded ball-shape mass of twigs. The *Eucalyptus* produces new shoots from both the base and the stem and lends itself to several different methods of pruning and training.

The first year
It is essential to plant young specimens that are no taller than 2–4ft, and that have grown steadily and have not been allowed to become pot-bound. If the main roots have been constricted they seldom develop satisfactorily and the root system does not provide the necessary strong anchorage and support.

When planting *Eucalyptus* the top of the root ball should be placed 1–2in below ground level in a shallow depression that is filled with soil at the end of the season. This depression initially provides a basin to hold water for the young plant, and it protects the swollen base, or lignotuber, that develops on *Eucalyptus* plants. This is important as the lignotuber is capable of producing new shoots from dormant buds if damage occurs to the main stem.

Staking is important in the early stages to make sure that the root system becomes established and that wind-rock is minimized. The most satisfactory system is a triangle or square of stout stakes; each stake should be about 1ft from the trunk.

THE DEVELOPING TREE
The tree will require no further pruning unless it grows very rapidly so that the height is out of proportion to the spread. If this happens prune the leader to encourage side-branching.

Training a *Eucalyptus* as a tree with a long, straight trunk.

The first year

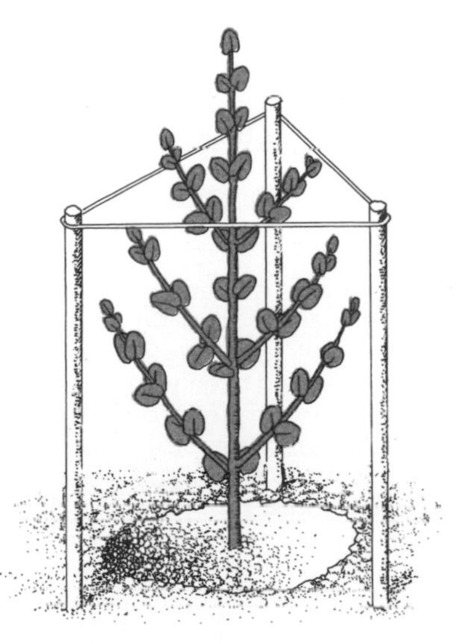

1 April to May. Plant the young tree in a shallow depression with the top of the root ball 1–2in below ground level. Stake the plant.

2 October. The plant has grown strongly throughout the summer. No pruning, except for removing dead branchlets, is required. If a double leader develops, cut out the badly placed shoot as soon as possible. Fill the planting depression with soil to protect the lignotuber.

1 Mid-March to April. Cut back the leading shoot by one-third of the previous year's growth just above a strong side-shoot that forms an acute angle with the stem.

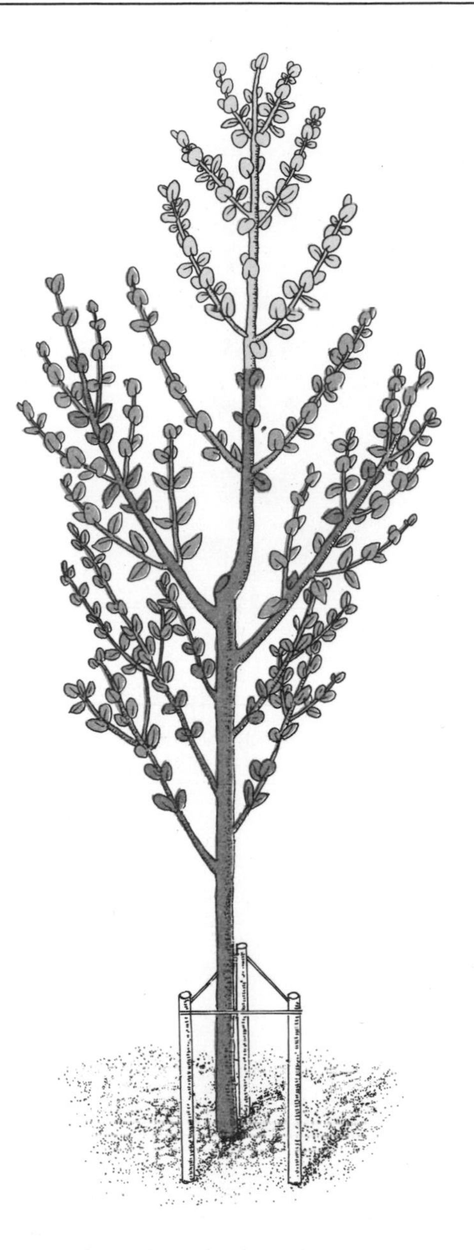

2 October. The side-shoot has straightened to form a new leader shoot. Within two or three years the trunk will appear as straight as that of an unpruned tree.

Eucalyptus

Pruning annually is a simple and effective method of growing *Eucalyptus* in small gardens. Eucalyptus will provide attractive mounds of foliage for most of the year. Some species, such as *E. gunnii*, have beautiful young foliage and are particularly suited as foliage plants.

A variation of this method is to cut back *Eucalyptus* in the same way as willows. This involves inducing the young tree to form a leg of the required height and then pruning back the shoots to the top of the leg in mid-March to early April each year. The resulting plants can be rather ungainly in habit if not carefully trained.

The first year

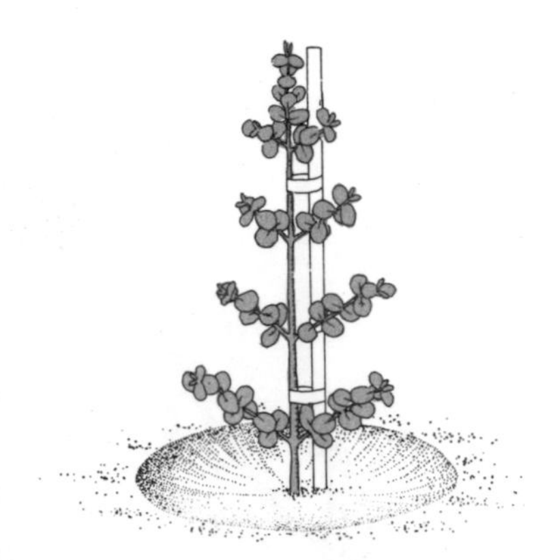

1 April to May. Young *Eucalyptus* planted in a shallow depression with the top of the root-ball 1–2in below ground level. A single stake is sufficient.

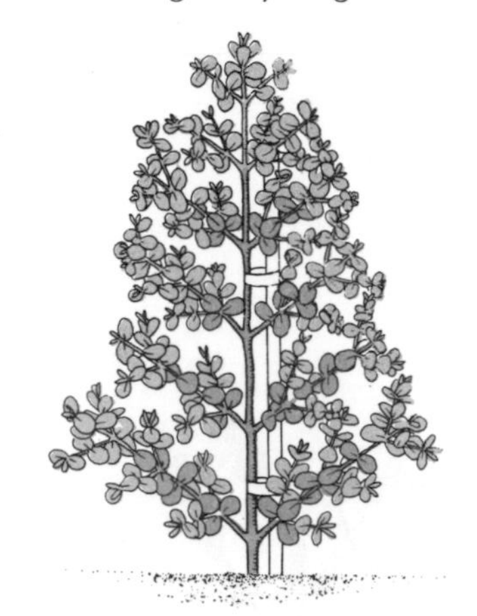

2 October. Fill the planting depression with soil. The plant will have grown strongly during the summer and have a well-established root system.

The second year

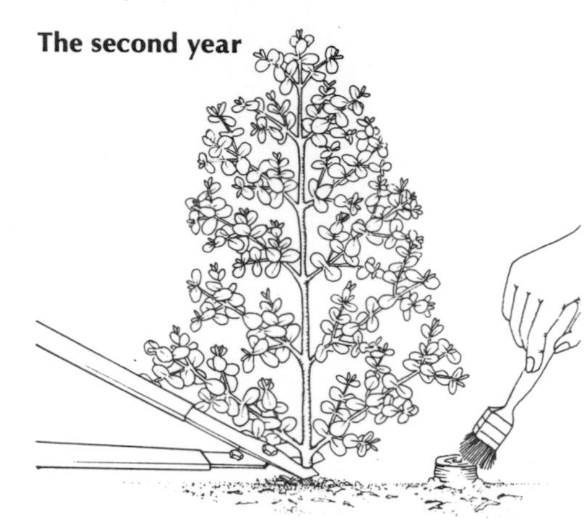

3 Mid-March to early April. Cut the stem close to ground level. Cover the cut stem with a wound paint. Apply a good basal mulch.

4 July. Strong basal shoots develop. Tip back to side shoots any vigorous upright shoots which grow more rapidly than the rest. This prevents them becoming dominant and reverting to a tree form.

Third and following years

5 Mid-March to early April. Cut back the stems close to ground level. Cover the cuts with a wound paint. Apply a basal mulch.

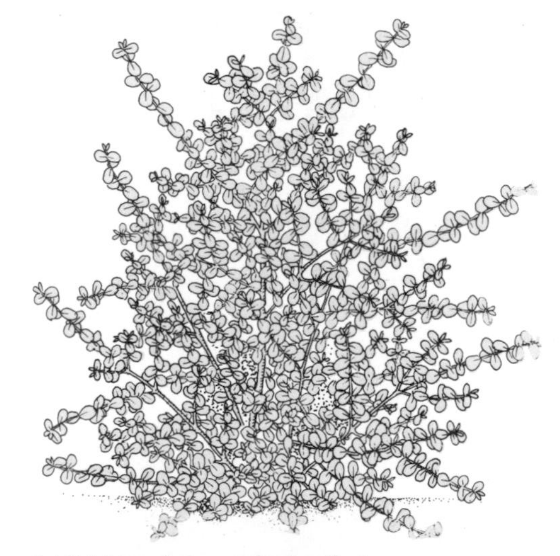

6 Mid-March to early April. A mature pruned plant. Feed with a dressing of 1oz per square yard of sulfate of ammonia and add a mulch of well-rotted compost or manure following pruning.

EUCALYPTUS GROWN IN BUSH FORM

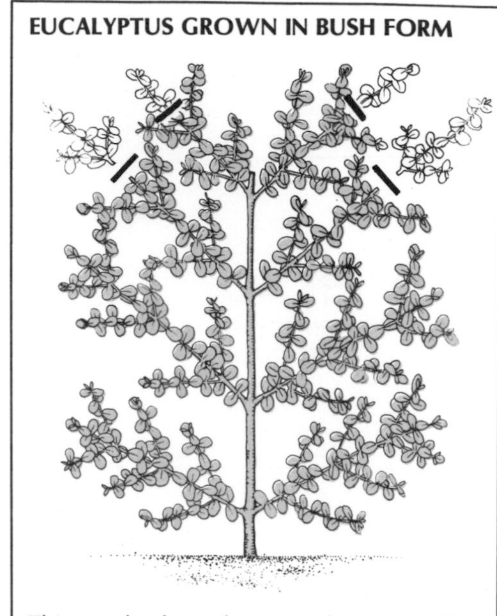

This method produces a plant considerably larger than a round-pruned *Eucalyptus*, but of similar growth habit. The first staking should be similar to that given to *Eucalyptus* grown as trees. During the first season after planting and until the following summer no pruning is required.

In June cut back the leading shoot to the group of side shoots which developed close to the end of the terminal shoot last season. In July and August trim back any side shoots that grow faster than the others to avoid them becoming dominant.

In following years prune back upright shoots that outgrow the bushy outline of the plant each March and April, repeating the process in June.

Eventually *Eucalyptus* grown as bushes may become too large for the area. They can readily be rejuvenated by cutting the plant hard back in mid-March or early April to a low rounded framework of branches. A mass of shoots will grow from these branches and from the base. These will require summer pruning to prevent any becoming dominant. Once the outline of the bush has been re-formed the normal pruning routine can be continued.

Renovation

In spite of the gardener's good intentions many vigorous shrubs, such as *Philadelphus*, lilacs and the hardy hybrid rhododendrons, either become too large for their space or become overgrown through neglect. If you move to a new house, you sometimes find the garden full of unpruned shrubs that appear beyond redemption.

One course of action is to dig them up and start again with young shrubs. This may certainly be the best method in some circumstances, but many shrubs have remarkable powers of recovery and with drastic pruning can be rejuvenated in a short period of time.

The first year

The process is simple. Cut down all the weak stems to ground level and cut back the main stems to within a foot of the base. Pare over the wounds with a sharp knife and cover them with a preservative paint as a protection against decay.

With deciduous shrubs such as lilacs this should be a winter operation done while the plants are dormant. Evergreens such as rhododendrons and laurels should be dealt with in late spring, when they will be beginning their period of growth.

Rejuvenation treatment must always be accompanied by generous feeding with manure or compost mulches the spring following the initial pruning and for several years thereafter. It is also very important to keep the plants well watered, particularly during the first year.

The second year

This drastic pruning stimulates the growth of dormant buds on most of the pruned stumps and frequently large clusters of shoots develop. During the following winter cut back most of these shoots to the point of their origin on the stumps, leave only two or three of the strongest and best-placed shoots on each stump to form the new framework of the rejuvenated shrub.

Third and following years

In the third and following years the pruning technique appropriate to the shrub concerned should be employed, following the instructions given on the previous pages.

Further growths will appear from the stumps for a year or two after rejuvenation pruning. Cut out these entirely as they appear, unless they are suitably placed to fill a gap in the framework. Any of the stumps that have not produced worthwhile growths after the first year should be cut out cleanly at ground level.

Some people may feel this process is too drastic, if you feel that the plant is in poor health and may not recover from complete amputation cut out only a proportion of the main stems. The process can then be completed by removing the remaining old growths after flowering in summer or the following winter. This two-step renovation process is suitable for deciduous shrubs such as *Philadelphus*, which naturally renew themselves from basal growths. With evergreens it is best to deal with the plant as a whole to avoid the uneven growth which occurs when renovation is carried out over two seasons.

Although not all shrubs will respond to this treatment most shrubs do recover satisfactorily and within three or four years the shrub should be healthy and flowering profusely once again.

Deciduous shrubs

1 Winter. An old lilac that has become bare at the base and bears the flowers at the top of the plant.

2 November to February. Cut back all strong stems to within 1–2ft of ground level. Cut out entirely any remaining weak growths. Cut out any stump that is badly placed and may spoil the overall balance when the young shoots develop. Cover all cut surfaces with a wound paint. Mulch the base of the plant with compost or manure.

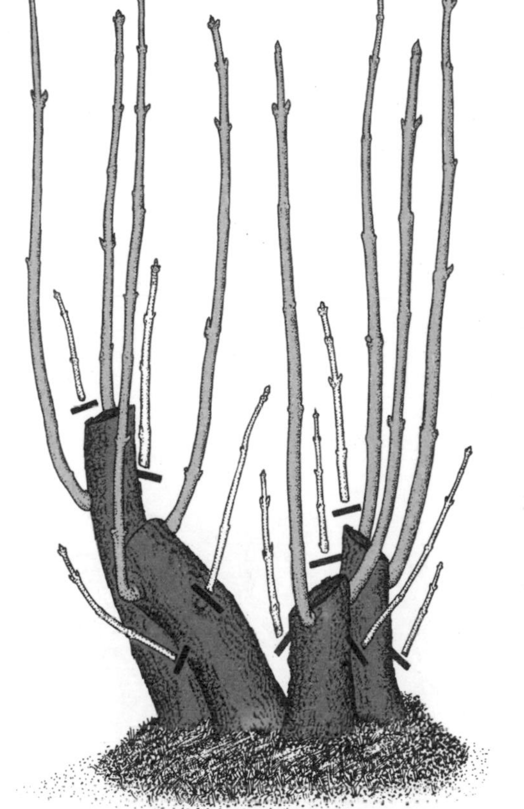

3 October. During spring and summer strong shoots have developed from dormant buds below the cut surfaces of the stumps. Cut back new shoots leaving two to three of the strongest and best placed on each stump to form the new framework.

Renovation

Shrubs can be rejuvenated over a two-year period. This method is suitable for twiggy shrubs such as *Deutzia* and *Philadelphus*.

The first year

The second year

1 November to February. An old *Deutzia* full of twiggy growth. Cut to the base all twiggy growth when the plant is dormant. Leave any new strong basal growths. Cut out one-half of the very old stems to within a few inches of ground level. Apply a wound paint to the end of the thick stumps. Add a mulch of well-rotted compost or manure.

2 June to July. Plant flowers sparsely from laterals on remaining growths. Vigorous basal and near-basal shoots develop.

3 November to February. Cut out the remaining old stems. Apply a wound paint and mulch well. Cut out any new weak growths.

4 June to July. A few flowers are produced from laterals from last year's growth. Vigorous basal shoots and strong laterals are produced.

EVERGREEN SHRUBS

The first year

The second year

1 Winter. An old laurel, which has grown straggly and too large for its position in the garden.

2 Early May. Cut back all strong stems to within 1–2ft of ground level. Cut out entirely any remaining weak growths.

3 At the same time, cut out any stump which is badly placed and may spoil the overall balance. Mulch well.

4 Early May. Strong shoots have developed. Cut out new shoots leaving two or three of the strongest and best placed on each stump.

Hedges: introduction

Many deciduous and evergreen shrubs that respond to clipping by producing dense, compact growth can be used for garden hedges. Clipping a hedge is only pruning to achieve a particular purpose and the same general principles apply (see page 37).

Formal hedges require regular restrictive clipping or trimming to keep their shape. Informal hedges, however, need only enough pruning to prevent them from becoming overgrown with straggly, stray shoots.

Normally hand or electric clippers will be used for trimming hedges. With broadleaved evergreens such as common laurel (*Prunus laurocerasus*) pruning shears should be used, as pruning with hedge clippers will mutilate many larger leaves and spoil the overall effect of the hedge until new growth has developed. Where the hedge is too long for trimming with pruning shears use hedge clippers for the main cut and follow this by using pruning shears to trim any badly damaged ugly foliage.

The feeding of hedges is often neglected. It is important to maintain healthy growth and as the individual plants in any hedge are only 1–3ft apart at most there is considerable competition between the roots. Annual mulches of well-rotted compost or manure are advisable to maintain vigor. Use plenty of mulch for your hedges—remember that you are clipping away much of the plant's food-producing unit when removing the leaves. As with specimen shrubs good treatment brings good results.

Topiary, the art of shaping shrubs and trees, particularly evergreens, into various animal and other designs is a specialist operation and is not dealt with here. The principles of clipping are the same as those applied to evergreen hedges.

Initial training

The importance of correct initial training cannot be overemphasized, as the success of the hedge depends on the treatment given to it during the first two or three years.

Gardeners are usually reluctant to prune young hedging plants at all during the first year or two, but it is essential to prune newly planted hedges to some extent to make sure that they do not grow too high too quickly.

They should be encouraged to establish strong bottom growth otherwise the base may remain relatively bare while the upper part of the hedge is dense. The severity of this initial pruning will depend on the kind of hedging plant that is used.

A deciduous hedge allowed to develop without hard initial pruning. Note the lack of basal shoots.

A deciduous hedge hard pruned at planting. Dense, even growth has resulted throughout the hedge.

Formal hedges

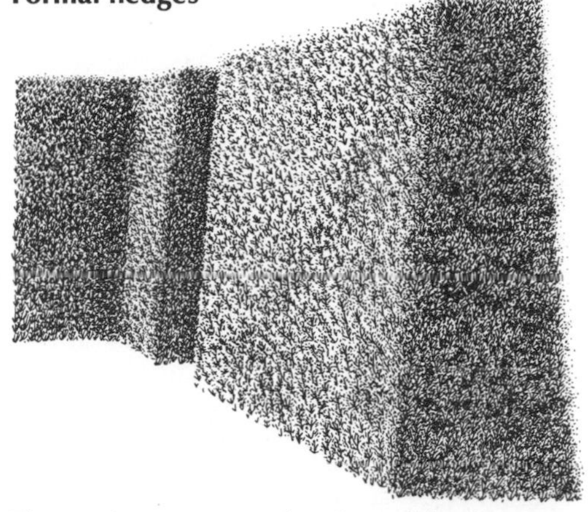

The main purpose of a formal hedge is to provide a barrier, screen or wind-break. The aim, therefore, must be to produce a hedge of the required height and width that is well-furnished with growth throughout.

There is no need for the width of even vigorous hedges to exceed 1–2ft with good initial training. Remember that the wider the hedge the more work involved and the more space in the garden used.

Formal hedges should always be slightly tapered on both sides so that the base is wider than the top. If a hedge, particularly of an evergreen shrub, is wider at the top than at the base it is liable to be damaged and the branches opened up by severe winds or snow.

When clipping a formal hedge start at the bottom to establish the basic width required and then work upwards. The blade of the clippers should be tilted in toward the hedge so that the tapered sides can be maintained.

With hedges over 6ft tall there is always a tendency to allow the top to become wider than the base after a few seasons simply because it is much easier to use shears at arm height or below than it is to wield them above the head. Avoid this by using two step ladders with a standing board in-between.

For convenience, the training and clipping of formal hedges can be divided into three groups based on the pruning required during the first two years. The timing and frequency of trimming mature hedges varies with the plant used, but with few exceptions they are covered in these groups.

INFORMAL HEDGES

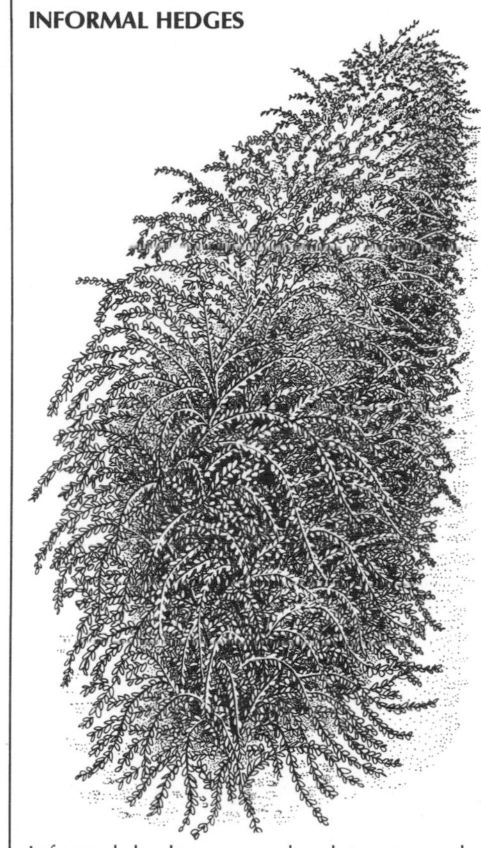

Informal hedges can also be extremely attractive and have the advantage of requiring less pruning and maintenance than formal hedges. Many flowering shrubs, such as *Berberis* × *stenophylla*, deutzia, roses, fuchsias and potentillas, make excellent informal hedges. They are pruned in the same way as when grown as specimen shrubs. Those flowering on old wood are pruned and shaped immediately after flowering, while those flowering on the current season's wood may be shaped in early spring.

With shrubs that produce berries and flower on old wood pruning or trimming should be delayed until the berries have disappeared. Pruning after flowering would mean that most of the flowers that would develop into berries would be cut away.

Hedges

Group 1 includes fairly upright plants such as hawthorn (*Crataegus*), privet, snowberry (*Symphoricarpos*), blackthorn (*Prunus spinosa*), myrobalan plum and tamarisk that require hard pruning after planting.

The first year
At planting between October and March cut back each plant to 6in from ground level. This encourages strong basal shoots to form and avoids the bare base that occurs if the plants are left unpruned.

The second year
In the second year, hard winter pruning is needed to maintain the density of growth and establish the strong basal framework of the hedge. Usually this second hard pruning will ensure that a dense hedge continues to develop, but if it is still fairly thin the same technique can be used again.

Third and following years
Thereafter trimming to shape during the growing season is all that is necessary. The period between clipping will depend on the hedging plant concerned and, to some extent, on the climate of your area. Most hedging plants in this group will need regular trimming every four to six weeks from April or May until September to keep them neat.

A number of evergreen shrubs such as *Lonicera nitida*, box and *Escallonia* are best placed in this group. They differ only in the timing and severity of the pruning during the first two years. They are best planted during March or April, when the main stems and laterals are cut back by one-third. This is repeated the following March or April, cutting back the previous season's growth by one-third. In the third and subsequent years they are treated in the same way as other hedging shrubs in Group 1.

The first year

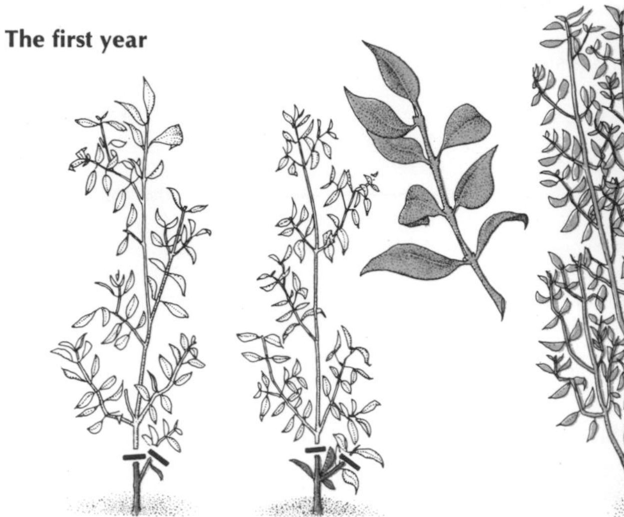

1 October to March. After planting cut back each plant to 6in from ground level.

2 June to July. Trim back laterals lightly to encourage further side-shoots.

The second year

3 February to March. Cut back the previous season's main growths by one-half. Trim remaining laterals to within a few inches of the framework stems.

4 May to September. Trim back laterals to maintain the tapered sides.

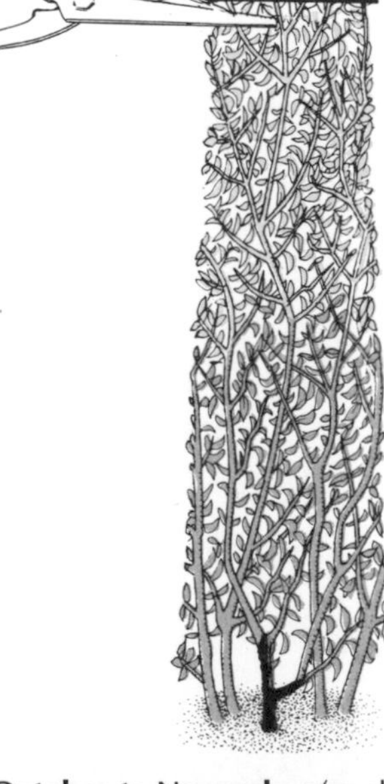

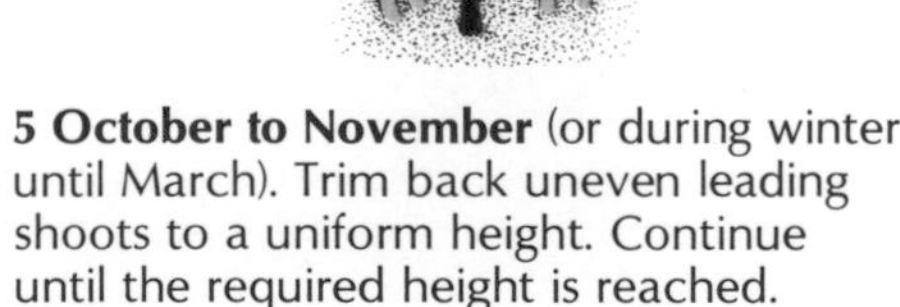

5 October to November (or during winter until March). Trim back uneven leading shoots to a uniform height. Continue until the required height is reached.

Third and following years

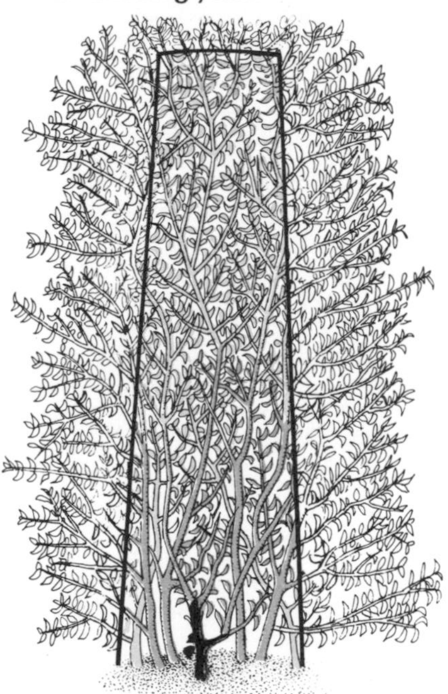

6 May to September. Every four to six weeks trim back top growth and laterals to maintain the shape required.

Hedges

Group 2 includes stocky shrubs that are naturally bushy at the base. Examples include beech, hornbeam, hazel and many deciduous flowering shrubs such as *Forsythia* and *Ribes sanguineum*.

The first and second year
Initial pruning for this group is less severe than in Group 1. Cut back the leading shoots and longer side-shoots by one-third of their length at planting. Repeat the process in the second winter to prevent straggly growth developing and to thicken up the base of the hedge or shrub.

Third and following years
In the third and subsequent years clipping to a tapered shape during the growing season is all that is required. June and late August to early September are the best times if two cuts are possible; if not cut once in late August. When the required height is reached, clip back the top growth.

With flowering shrubs such as *Forsythia* grown formally, trim immediately after flowering and lightly again in August.

Group 3 contains the conifers used for hedges and many evergreens. At planting the leader shoots are left unpruned and only untidy straggly laterals are cut back slightly to encourage further laterals to appear.

The leading shoots need not be pruned at all until they have reached the height required for the hedge before being stopped. Pruning in the second and subsequent years consists only of trimming the side growths to the required shape.

Established hedges in this group will only need trimming once or twice during the summer. A single cut in late August is usually sufficient, but with the stronger-growing species the hedge can become rather untidy by midsummer. A neat appearance can be achieved throughout the growing season by clipping in June and again in late August.

Some formal hedges in this group are also attractive in flower and in fruit, particularly cotoneaster and pyracanthas, which make their young growth after flowering. Remove the young growth as it ripens in late July or August, leaving the faded flowers to form fruit by the autumn.

The first year

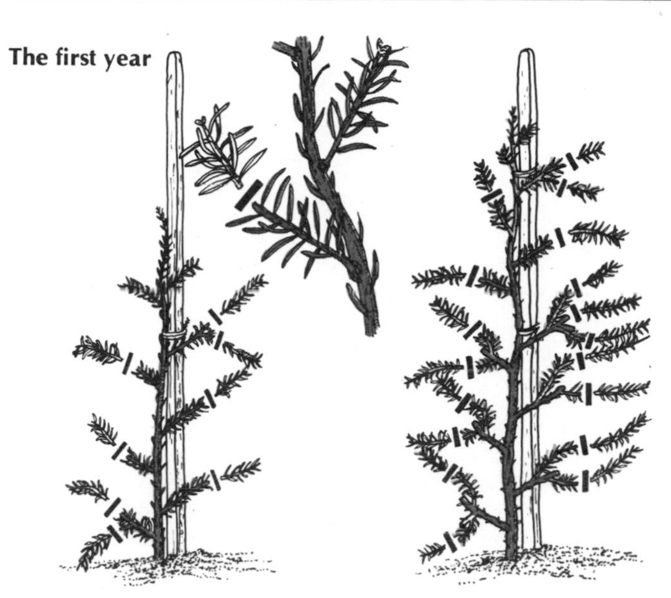

1 October to March. At planting prune straggly laterals. Stake the main leader shoots.

2 June and late August. Trim back laterals to the required shape. Tie in the leaders as they grow.

Second and following years

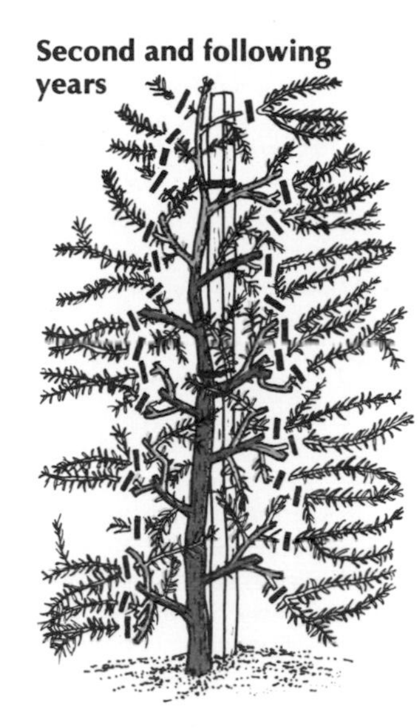

3 June and late August. Trim back laterals to the required shape. Tie in the leaders. Stop the leaders at the required height.

The first year

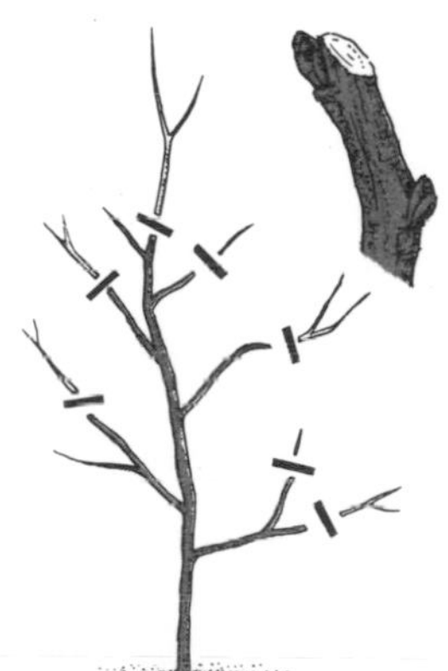

1 October to March. After planting cut back main stem and strong laterals by one-third.

The second year

2 October to March. Cut back main stems and strong laterals by one-third.

Third and following years

3 June and late August. Trim back laterals to begin shaping tapered sides.

RENOVATION

Inevitably some hedges will become too wide or overgrown through neglect. In most cases it is better to clear out the hedges and replace them with a young hedge. A few species, however, respond well to drastic pruning. The method is similar to that described for shrubs, but instead of cutting the plants to the base cut back one side of the hedge to the main stems. Repeat the process on the other side of the hedge the following year, or sometimes two years later. With evergreens this pruning should be carried out in April or early May and deciduous species should be treated in late winter, when they are dormant. Ample feeding and watering is essential to help the hedge recover from this brutal treatment.

This technique can be used very successfully with yews, hollies, cotoneasters, pyracanthas, *Rhododendron ponticum* and many deciduous hedging plants.

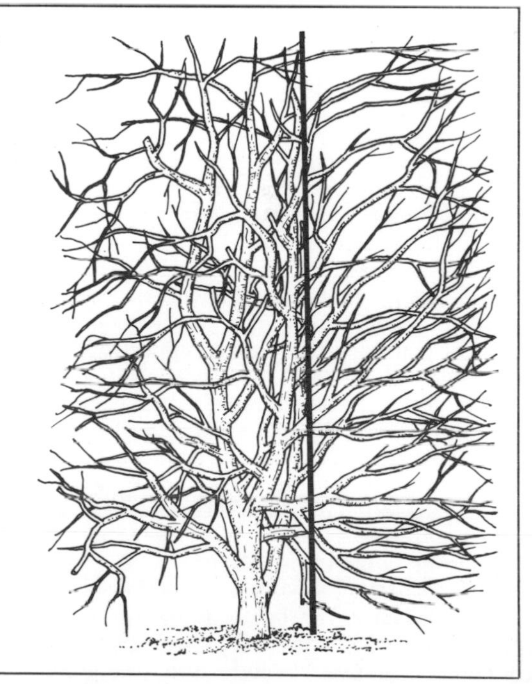

Climbing and Wall Plants: introduction

House walls and fences add an extra dimension to gardening by providing suitable locations to grow a wide range of climbing plants and trained shrubs. Many people grow a climbing rose or a clematis against the house, but wall or fence space that is readily available is seldom used effectively.

All houses walls, fences, the sides of sheds and garages—whatever their aspect—could and should be ornamented with plants. Apart from the obvious advantage of masking some of the less attractive areas of the house, planting is a method of merging house and garden, creating the single living unit that in Mediterranean countries is achieved by the vine-covered patio that links them together. Walls and fences also provide shelter for slightly tender plants that are not hardy in the open garden.

It is also possible to create additional vertical growing space by means of pergolas, arbors, pillars and other devices or to plant climbers to scramble through trees or, occasionally, hedges.

When considering the pruning of the many plants that can be used in these vertical plantings it is important to bear in mind the growth habits and the details of basic cultivation that can affect the training and subsequent pruning of climbers and wall shrubs.

The plants used can be divided into various groups based on their growth habit.

1. The natural clingers, such as ivy and Virginia creeper, which support themselves by aerial roots or sucker pads. No support system is needed.
2. The twiners, a large group, including honeysuckle, clematis and wisteria, which climb by means of curling or twining leaf tendrils, leaf stalks or stems. A support system to which they attach themselves is required.
3. The scramblers and floppers, which clamber through other plants in the wild using hooked thorns (roses) or by rapid elongation of their willowy shoots (*Solanum crispum*). A support system is needed to which the growth can be easily tied.
4. Shrubs which are slightly tender and benefit from the protection of a wall or fence. They may either be lightly pruned if space allows or trained and hard-pruned if space is limited. Examples include the evergreen *Ceanothus*, *Carpenteria californica* and *Fremontodendron*. If the plant is trained to stay close to the wall it requires support systems to which the growths can be tied.

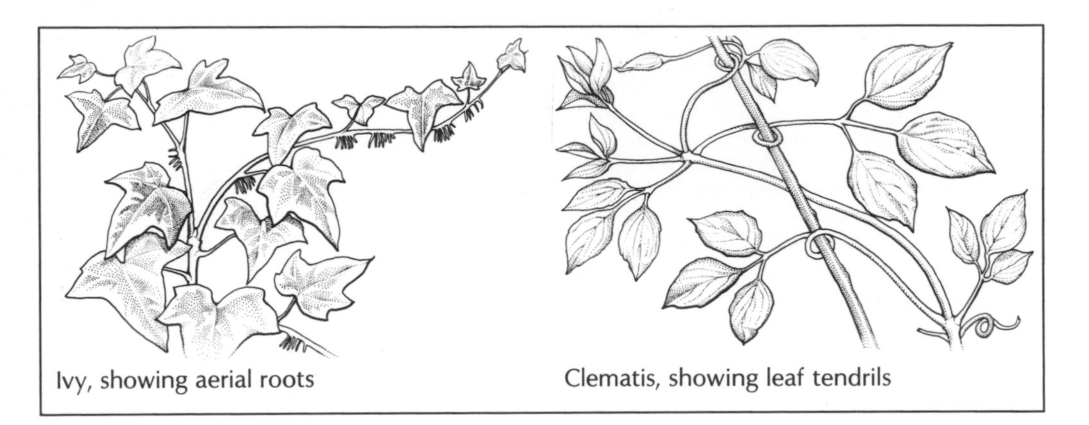

Ivy, showing aerial roots

Clematis, showing leaf tendrils

Many hardy shrubs can be trained against walls or fences in the same way and it is particularly useful to do this in small gardens, where space does not allow such large plants as *Philadelphus* and *Forsythia* to be grown in the open.

Select a plant to fill the area comfortably without the need for constant restriction to keep it within bounds. A rampant Virginia creeper on a bungalow, however attractive initially, will require constant and prompt attention to prevent its questing growths from dislodging tiles and damaging the gutters. A well-trained clematis, *Ceanothus* or pyracantha is much more satisfactory in the same position.

The dullest fence can be enlivened and the hard, straight edges lost by growing *Clematis montana* vertically to the top of the fence and then training and pruning the growth horizontally along the upper 6–12 in as far as is required. Even the difficult areas of low walls beneath windows can be clothed with trained shrubs such as *Caryopteris*, *Daphne odora* or variegated *Euonymus* if correct initial training and pruning is carried out.

Aspect is very important in deciding what plants to grow. It is no use planting sun-loving *Ceanothus* on a north-facing wall or fence. They may grow but they will seldom thrive, often becoming straggly and unkempt, whereas pyracanthas will grow, flower and fruit well.

Never plant directly against a wall or fence, always leave 9–12 in between the plant and its support system. The soil close to the wall is usually very dry. There may be difficulties with poor growth, die-back or sparse flowering.

Unless the plant climbs naturally by suckers or aerial roots some artificial system of supporting it against a wall or fence is required. Make certain the support system, which should be erected before planting, is adequate to support the plant in strong winds or heavy snowfalls. Careful training and pruning can be ruined in a very short time by failure to provide a strongly anchored support system of wire, chain-link or trellis.

Initial training and subsequent pruning

All the precepts of good pruning apply equally as much to climbers and wall plants. In particular the "3 D's," the removal of all dead, damaged and diseased wood, should be carried out regularly.

The gardener prunes to obtain the maximum coverage and the maximum effect of foliage, flower and fruit. This makes it necessary to restrict the natural habit of the plants concerned, and particularly where space is limited pruning must be aimed, in part at maintaining balanced and not excessive growth, which would require fairly drastic annual pruning of very vigorous species.

The importance of early training to establish a sound basic framework of branches cannot be overemphasized. Gardeners will often be reluctant to cut back vigorous growth on young plants, but in some situations this is essential to obtain maximum coverage of the wall or fence and to avoid the problem of excessive growth outward from the supports that is particularly prevalent with wall shrubs. The aim of the gardener must be to maintain growth as close to the wall or fence as possible.

Initially this involves considerable directing and tying in of shoots to cover the area of wall or fence concerned and cutting back outward-pointing growth (breastwood) to encourage lateral (sideways) growth.

The pruning of established plants will vary to some extent with the mode of growth. Some climbers such as ivies and Virginia creeper which cling with aerial roots or sucker pads will require no more than the removal of wayward shoots. With other shrubs regular annual pruning is needed to keep the plants neat, within bounds and free-flowering.

Generally follow the rules for pruning shrubs. Those plants which flower on the previous year's wood before midsummer, for example *Ceanothus impressus*, *Forsythia suspensa* and *Clematis macropetala*, are pruned immediately after flowering. Those which flower after midsummer on the current season's shoots are pruned either in late winter (*Clematis* × *jackmanii*) or in early spring (*Ceanothus* × *burkwoodii* and *Ceanothus* 'Autumnal Blue').

Some plants require a more complicated program if they are to flower profusely. Summer pruning—cutting back laterals and breastwood to form flowering spurs—is used. The leading shoots are trained in as required to fill space in the framework while the lateral and breastwood shoots produced during the growing season are cut back leaving only 2–5 leaves on the shoots, the severity of pruning depending on the plant concerned.

This technique is particularly applicable to the Japanese or flowering quinces (*Chaenomeles*) and *Wisteria*. They both need firm control to prevent unruly overvigorous growth, which, if left, results in a limited number of flowers. Summer pruning encourages flower bud formation on the spurred-back laterals, the food being channelled into forming flower buds on the spurs rather than into forming long growth shoots.

1: summer + fall – new wd

Clematis

The complicated instructions for pruning *Clematis* that are often found can be reduced to three categories based on the age of the growth on which the flowers are produced.

Some *Clematis* flower entirely on the current year's growth, while a number of spring-flowering species and hybrids produce all their bloom on short shoots from the previous year's wood. A third group, which includes many well-known hybrids such as 'Nelly Moser', produce flowers from last season's growth during early summer and a further display of rather smaller flowers in late summer and autumn from the current year's young shoots.

Vigorous species such as *Clematis montana* can be grown through trees and left unpruned unless they become completely out-of-hand. If this occurs it is simple to renovate them by cutting the old stems hard back to within 2–3ft of ground level in late winter or early spring. In most instances dormant buds on the old, woody stems are stimulated into growth and within a few seasons they should be flowering freely. As with all renovation techniques it is important to feed and water the plants well.

Left unpruned most *Clematis* develop into tangled masses of growth, bearing their flowers high up above the bare woody stems. The following techniques aim to provide the maximum coverage and the most lavish flowers in the space available.

Pruning at planting is important but often overlooked. Many *Clematis*, particularly the larger-flowered hybrids, will tend to grow rapidly upwards on a single stem during the first season after planting unless checked at an early stage.

At planting the stem should be cut back to the lowest pair of strong buds to encourage the plant to produce further basal growth. The two stems produced from these buds can be stopped again to increase the number of basal shoots, but this is usually unnecessary.

This initial pruning applies to all *Clematis*, whether planted dormant in January or February or in leaf during spring or early summer. Most *Clematis* species will break naturally to form bushy, well-furnished plants, but it is a practice to prune them at planting to ensure that this occurs.

Group 1 contains all the *Clematis* species and hybrids that flower in summer and autumn entirely on the new growths produced during the current season. If left unpruned they begin growth in the spring from where they flowered the previous season and rapidly become bare at the base with flowers at the top only.

Pruning is very simple and consists of cutting back all of the previous year's growth virtually to ground level in late January or February. The pruning cuts should be made immediately above the lowest pair of strong buds on each stem.

Examples of *Clematis* in this group are *C. orientalis*, *C. tangutica*, *C. texensis* hybrids such as 'Gravetye Beauty' and 'Etoile Rose,' *C. viticella* and its derivatives; and among the large-flowered hybrids *C. × jackmanii*, 'Ernest Markham,' 'Hagley Hybrid' and 'Perle d'Azur.'

The first year

1 January to February. A newly planted *Clematis*. Cut back to the lowest pair of strong buds. Mulch well.

2 May to June. Train in the strong young growths and any basal growth. Flowers may appear in late summer.

The second year

3 January to February. Cut back all growths to the lowest pair of strong buds on each stem. Mulch well.

4 May to June. Train in young growths and further basal growth as it develops.

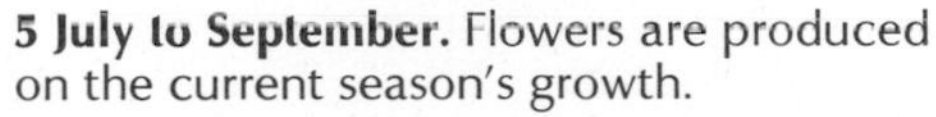

5 July to September. Flowers are produced on the current season's growth.

Third and following years

6 January to February. Cut back all growths to the lowest pair of strong buds on each stem. Mulch well.

Clematis

Group 2 consists mainly of vigorous spring-flowering species, which flower between April and June on short shoots from growth produced the previous summer.

Examples of species in this group are *Clematis montana* and its forms, *C. chrysocoma, C. alpina* and *C. macropetala*.

The first two species are very hardy and attempting to restrict them to limited areas on a wall or fence usually results in a good deal of work. They thrive best given ample space on a house wall or in a tree and left unpruned or merely sheared over after flowering to keep them tidy. If left unpruned they may require rejuvenation after a few years. This involves cutting them to near ground level in winter.

The first and second years
Initial pruning at planting will encourage vigorous growth that can be gently guided to cover the area available and to form the basic framework over a two-year period.

Third and following years
Once this has been achieved the pruning of mature plants consists of cutting away all the flowered wood to within a few inches of the main framework immediately after flowering.

This stimulates vigorous long growths that can be trained or guided in as required, or allowed to cascade naturally. This growth will provide next season's flowering display and must not be winter-pruned.

The first year

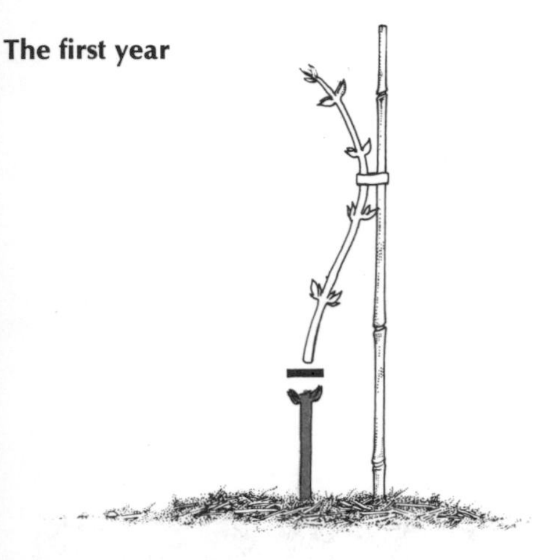

1 January to February. A newly planted *Clematis* with a single main stem. Cut back the stem above the lowest pair of strong buds. Mulch well.

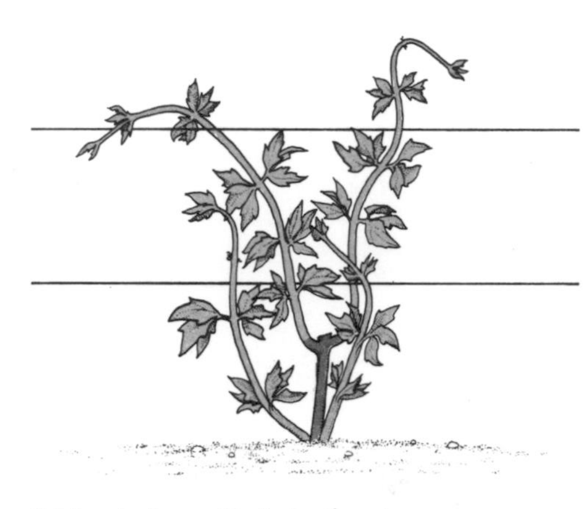

2 May to June. Train in the strong young growths and any further basal growths that may have developed.

The second year

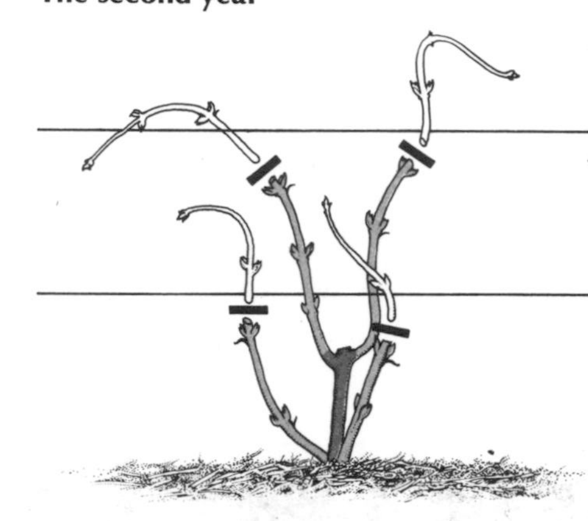

3 January to February. Cut back all the main growths trained in the previous summer by one-half their length to a pair of strong buds. Mulch well.

4 April to June. Train or guide the new shoots as required. Prune back any laterals that have flowered low down on the plant to one or two pairs of buds from the base.

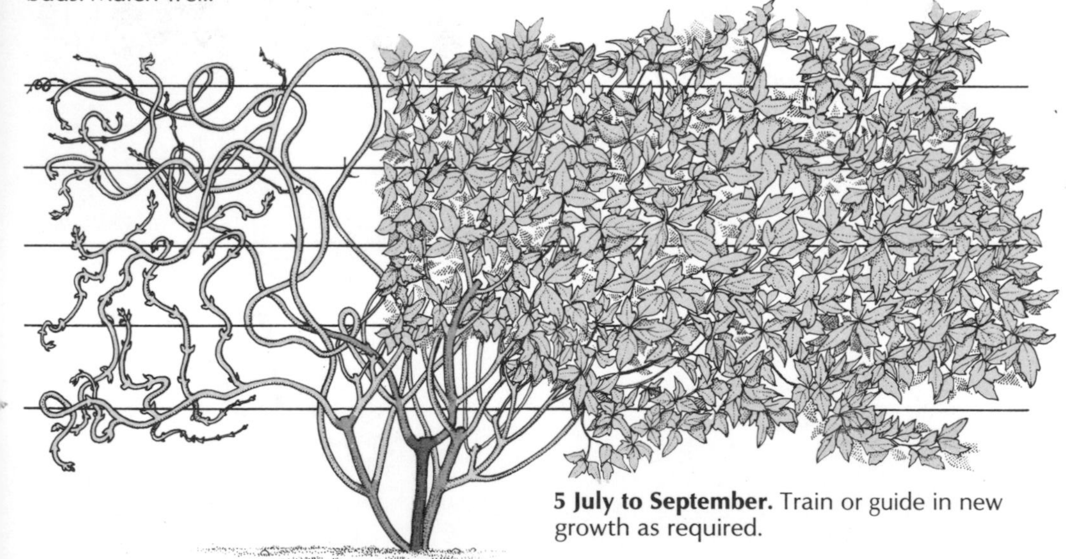

5 July to September. Train or guide in new growth as required.

Third and following years

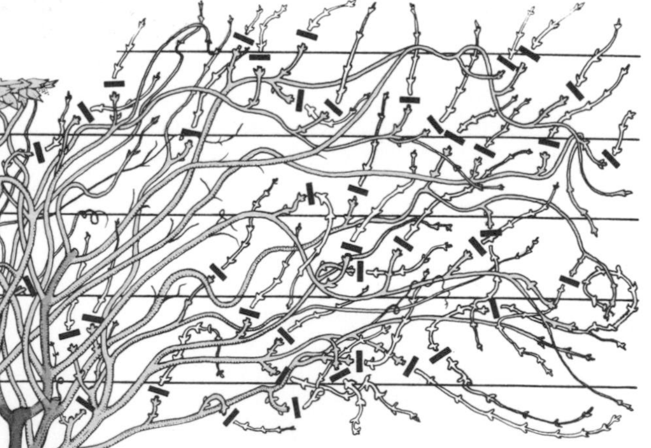

6 June. Prune back all growths that have flowered to one or two buds from the framework branches.

Clematis

Group 3 contains all the hybrids that provide large, sumptuous flowers from May to July on the previous year's wood. While the flowers are being produced on side-shoots from the old wood new growth is being formed. This produces further crops of medium-sized blooms during late summer and early autumn.

Popular varieties in this group include 'Lasurterr,' 'Nelly Moser,' 'The President,' 'Henry,' 'Mme le Coultre,' 'William Kennett' and the double-flowered 'Duchess of Edinburgh' and 'Vyvyan Pennel,' which may produce single blooms late in the season.

The growth habit of Group 3 *Clematis* makes them difficult to prune satisfactorily without a good deal of work, and they may be left entirely unpruned or only lightly pruned until they become straggly and out of control. Then the rejuvenation process described in the introduction can be applied. Alternatively they may be treated as Group 1 and pruned back hard to base each January to February, but then they will only flower in late summer.

Neither of these treatments allows the full flowering potential of these *Clematis* to be exploited, but a simple renewal system can be instituted with mature plants to provide the maximum flower during summer and autumn. It involves the same basic training as Group 1, but mature plants are renewal-pruned with one-quarter to one-third of the old shoots being cut to within a foot or so of the base. This is done between May and July, depending on the variety, immediately after the first flush of bloom has been produced on the previous season's growth. Alternatively the renewal pruning can be carried out annually in January or February, but this means a smaller display of flowers in early summer.

Strong shoots arise from the pruned-back stems and will grow vigorously during summer and possibly provide a few autumn blooms. Ample feeding to maintain vigor is required, but using this method the gawky "bird's-nest" effect so commonly seen is avoided.

This renewal system works more easily with wall- or fence-grown plants, where the shoots can be spaced out evenly. On pergolas or grown among shrubs *Clematis* in this group are best left unpruned or trimmed after the initial flowering as it is difficult to disentangle the cut-back stems.

The first year

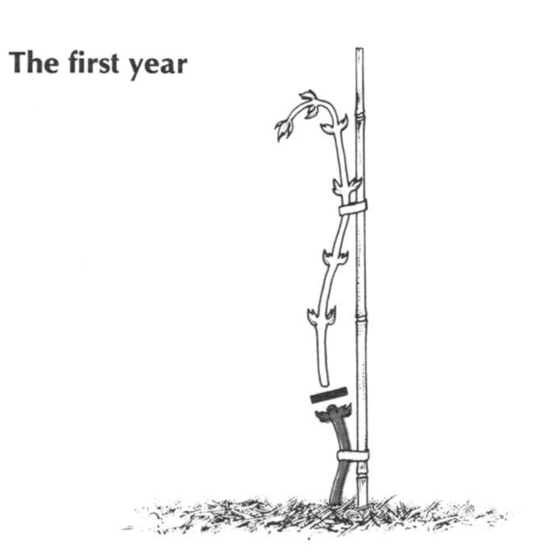

1 January to February. A newly planted *Clematis* with a single main stem. Cut back the stem to above the lowest pair of strong buds. Mulch well.

2 May to June. Train in strong young growths and any basal growths which develop. A few flowers may be produced in late summer.

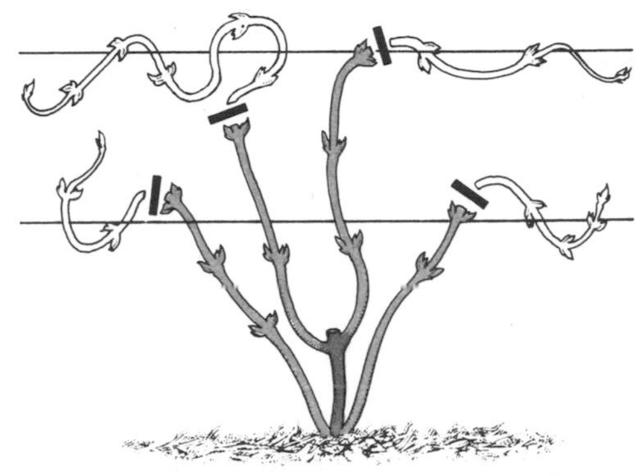

3 January to February. Cut back all the main growths trained in the previous summer by one-half to a strong pair of buds. Mulch well.

4 June to September. Train or guide in new growths as required. The basic framework has been established. Some flower will be produced in summer and autumn on the new growth.

Third and following years

5 June to July. Plant will flower on old wood. Immediately after flowering cut one-quarter to one-third of the mature shoots to within a foot or so of the base. Water and feed well.

6 August to September. Plant flowers on young shoots. Guide into place basal shoots that develop from the cut-back stems.

Wisteria

The pruning of *Wisteria* baffles most gardeners as the tremendous vigor of their whiplike summer shoots seems almost impossible to control. It is however, quite possible to keep them restrained and trained into a reasonably confined space—although they are capable of clambering a hundred feet or more up a tree or along a wall. Successful control demands a good deal of attention from the gardener as pruning needs to be carried out twice during a season to ensure adequate flowers and to confine the plant's naturally robust growth.

The first year
A young *Wisteria* planted in winter or early spring will normally produce one or two vigorous basal growths that increase rapidly in length. Few or no lateral shoots develop naturally at this stage. If the plant is to be grown in espalier form to cover a wall or fence the main shoot must be cut or tipped back to $2\frac{1}{2}$–3ft from ground level at planting.

This stimulates two or three lateral buds to develop and these new shoots should be trained into the positions required. Tie in the upper shoot vertically and the other growths at an angle of approximately 45 degrees. If the laterals are trained in a horizontal position initially their growth may be checked. At this stage the branches are flexible and easily positioned on the support system.

The second and following years
The following winter cut back the leading shoot leaving $2\frac{1}{2}$–3ft of wood above the uppermost lateral. Bring down the laterals to a more or less horizontal position. At the same time cut back the horizontal leaders of those laterals by about one-third of their length. This stimulates further lateral growth and a similar training process is carried out during the following years to form a new vertical leader and further well-spaced horizontal laterals to form the arms of the espalier.

Train in a new horizontal leader for each pruned-back lateral and cut back surplus laterals or sublaterals in early August to within 6–9in (4–5 leaves) of the main framework branches to form flowering spurs.

This process is continued annually until the desired number of well-spaced lateral branches is obtained. The aim should be to produce an espaliered plant with horizontal branches not less than 15–18in apart. This allows the long pendulous inflorescences to hang down gracefully from the spurs without crowding those on the branches below.

Further basal growth that develops should be cut out completely as soon as it is seen.

The first year

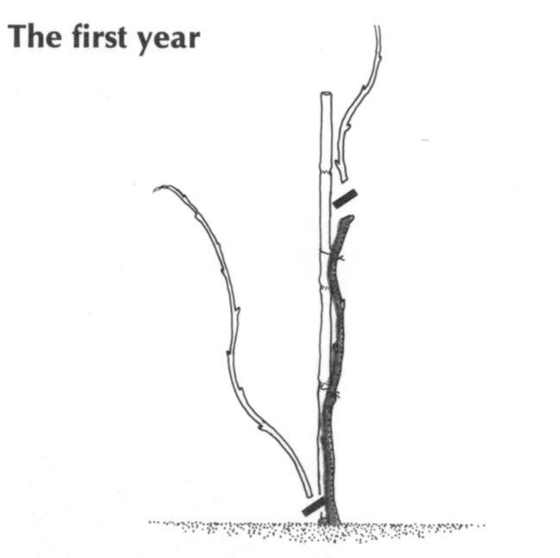

1 Winter to early spring. Young *Wisteria* at planting. Prune or tip back the strongest growth to $2\frac{1}{2}$–3ft from ground level. Stake this main shoot. Remove to base any surplus shoots that are present.

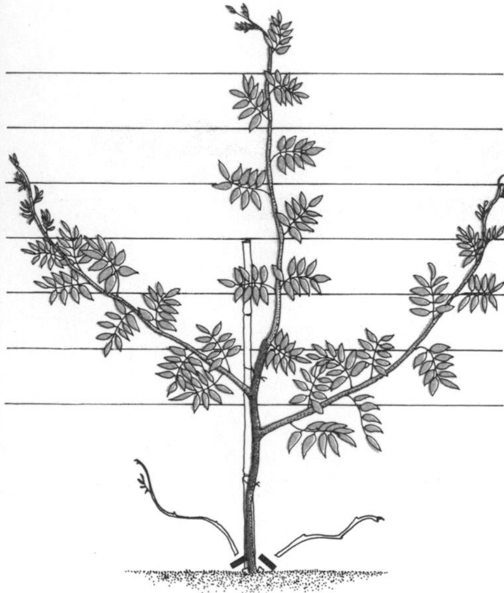

2 June to early August. Two or three vigorous shoots develop from lateral buds. Train in the uppermost vertically. Tie in other laterals on the support framework at approximately 45 degrees. Remove any new basal growths. Tie in further extension growth. If sublaterals are produced, cut them back in early August to 6–9in.

The second year

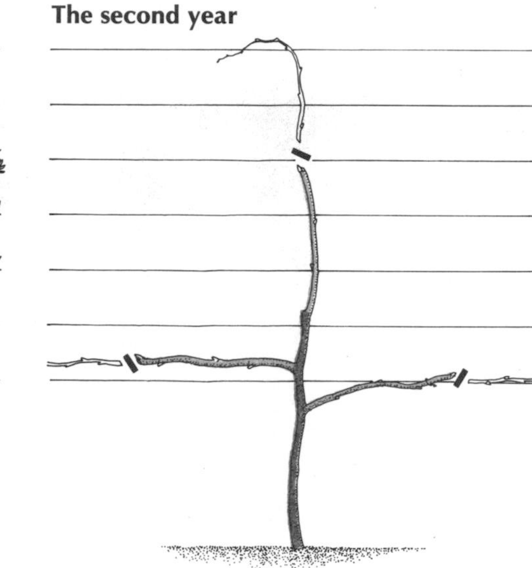

3 December to January. Cut back the vertical leader to within $2\frac{1}{2}$–3ft of the uppermost lateral. Bring down the laterals trained at 45 degrees to a horizontal position and cut back their leaders by one-third.

4 June to early August. Vigorous shoots develop from lateral buds on the vertical leader. Train in the uppermost vertically as the new leader. Tie in other laterals on the support framework at an angle of about 45 degrees. Remove any further basal growth. In early August cut back any surplus laterals and sublaterals to 6–9in.

The third year

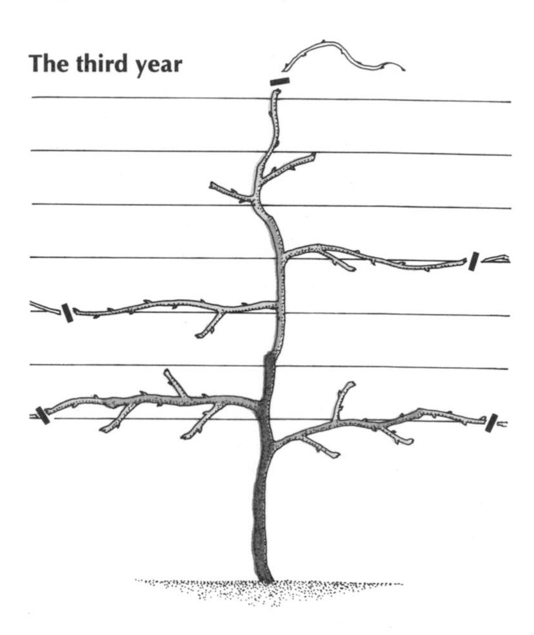

5 December to January. Cut back the vertical leader to within $2\frac{1}{2}$–3ft of the uppermost lateral. Bring down the laterals trained at 45 degrees to a horizontal position and cut back their leaders by one-third. Cut back last season's growth of leaders on horizontally trained branches by one-third.

Wisteria

The mature plant
Once the basic framework of branches has been trained to fill the area available any further extension growths, which may reach 10–12ft in a season, and lateral growths are pruned back in early August to within 6in (4–6 leaves) of the main branches to form flowering spurs. This summer pruning is followed by a further shortening of these spurs in winter (December and January) to 3–4in leaving only 2–3 buds on each spur shoot. The following season's flowers are borne on these spurs. In winter the plump flower buds are easily distinguished from the flattened growth buds so the flowering potentiai is easy to predict.

A difficult procedure that will provide more flower buds involves pruning back the extension growths to 6in at two-week intervals during the summer. This stimulates further laterals to form and constant pinching back produces more congested spurs.

Wisteria can be grown in a number of ways and trained as espaliers, fans, and as low-standard shrubs or semi informally to be used against walls or fences. The same pruning technique is used for mature plants, but the initial training will differ slightly with the method used. Wherever possible it is best to train the main branches more or less horizontally as the maximum display is obtained from plants trained this way.

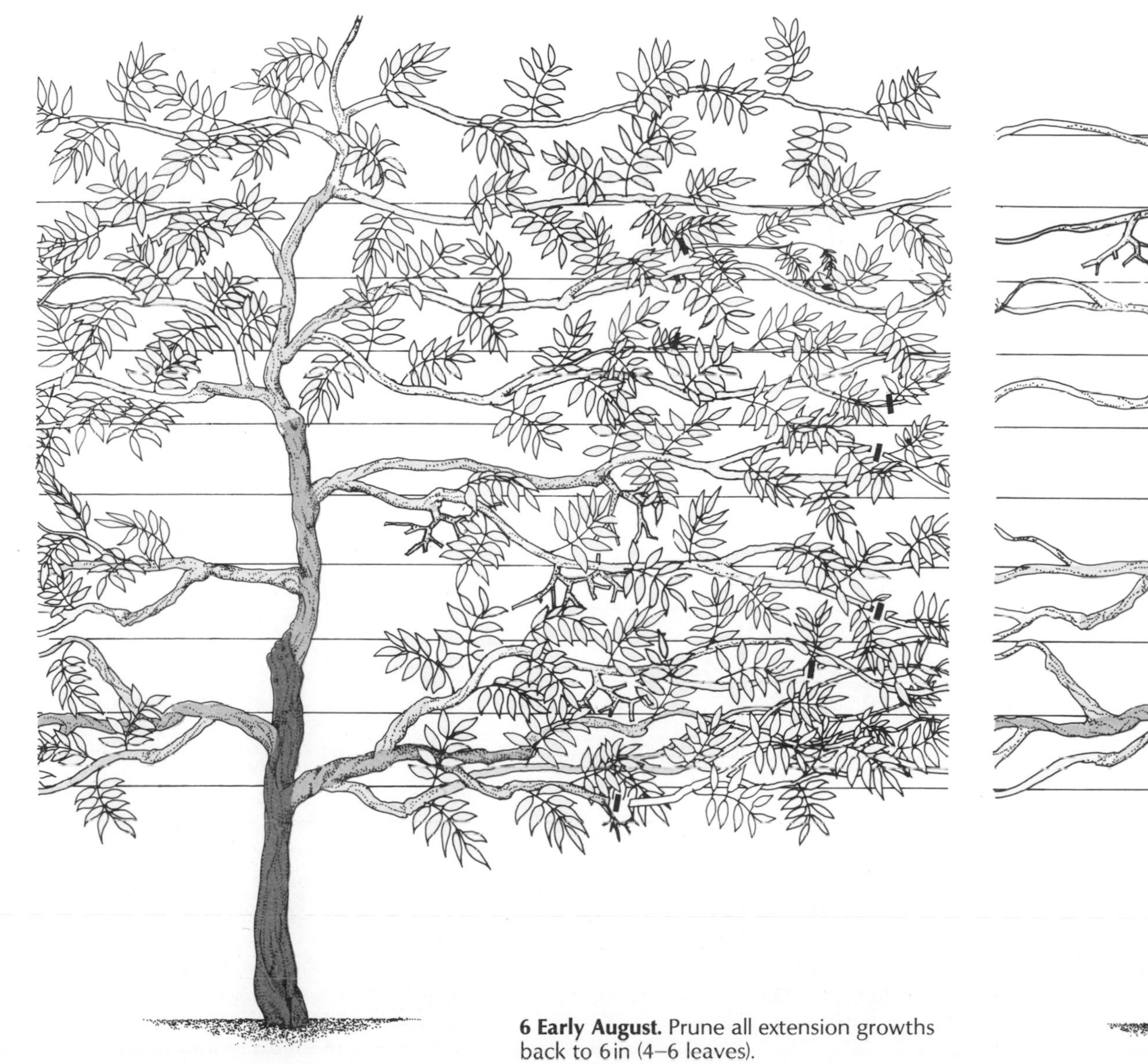

6 Early August. Prune all extension growths back to 6in (4–6 leaves).

7 December to January. Prune the same growths back to 3–4in (2–3 buds).

Ceanothus and Honeysuckle

The shrubby evergreen *Ceanothus* species and hybrids are suitable for training as wall plants, where their abundant blue, powder-puff flower heads show to the best advantage. Most *Ceanothus* flower in May on growth produced the previous summer, but a few, such as 'Autumnal Blue' and 'Burkwoodii,' flower on both last season's and the current year's growth and require slightly different pruning treatment.

The first year

Ceanothus should always be planted in spring as pot-grown plants. Training consists of tying in the main shoot vertically as it grows and fanning out the laterals to fill the available space as evenly as possible. Growth is rapid and it is important to tie in the young shoots regularly during spring and summer to ensure that they are guided in the direction required. If left they will tend to grow away from the support structure and become difficult to manage as the growth ripens. Breastwood is produced abundantly and, if not suitable for training into the framework, should be clipped over once in June to encourage dense, tight growth and to maintain the plant close to the wall or fence.

Second and following years

Continue training and tying in extension growth until the space provided has been filled. Immediately after flowering clip over the previous season's growths, which will normally have flowered during May, to within 3–4 in of the framework. The dense growth produced during the summer provides flowers the following spring.

It is important to prune a wall-trained evergreen *Ceanothus* regularly each season so that a compact mat of growth is maintained against the support structure. If it is left unpruned it will quickly grow away from the wall or fence and is liable to be damaged by strong winds or snow. *Ceanothus* resent hard pruning into old wood and it is difficult to maintain the neatly tailored look which is so attractive with well-grown specimens if regular training is not carried out.

Pruning of the few evergreen *Ceanothus*, which flower mainly on the current season's growth, is carried out in April. The initial training and method of pruning is the same. Pruning in early spring means the loss of any early bloom, but ensures that the plant maintains a tight habit and flowers generously in summer and autumn.

HONEYSUCKLE

The climbing honeysuckles can be divided into two groups for pruning purposes, based on their flowering habit.

The first group, typified by *Lonicera japonica*, the rampant Japanese honeysuckle, produces flowers in pairs in the axils of leaves on the current season's growth. The only pruning necessary is to restrict the exuberant growth. This involves clipping away any unwanted growth in March or April each season. This stimulates fresh young growth which quickly covers the sheared surface and will flower later in the season.

The second group includes the much more popular Dutch honeysuckle *L. periclymenum* 'Belgica' and a number of related species and hybrids such as *L.× americana, L.× brownii, L. sempervirens, L.× tellmanniana* and *L. tragophylla*. These bear flowers on laterals produced from the previous season's growth.

If space allows they may be permitted to climb through old trees or on walls and left completely unpruned so that the growth wanders and cascades in a natural manner. They tend to form "birds'-nests" on bare stems (like some *Clematis*) and if they are to be grown in positions where tangled growth and bare stems will be unsightly, mild pruning is required immediately after flowering each season. This simply involves cutting back some of the old weak growths and some of the shoots which have flowered to a point where vigorous young growth is developing. The young growth can be tied in to the framework as it develops, but is more effective if left to cascade down so that an informal curtain of flowers is produced.

The first year

1 April to May. Tie in the leader vertically. Spread out and tie in lateral growths. Cut out badly placed shoots and trim back breastwood to 2–3 in.

2 June to July. Rapid extension growth has occurred. Tie in leader and lateral shoots. Trim breastwood to 3–4 in from the supports.

The second year

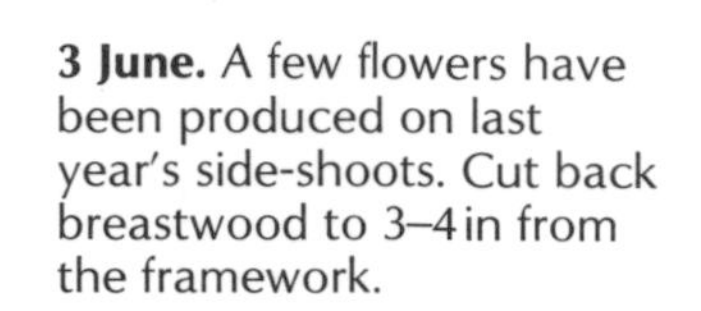

3 June. A few flowers have been produced on last year's side-shoots. Cut back breastwood to 3–4 in from the framework.

Third and following years

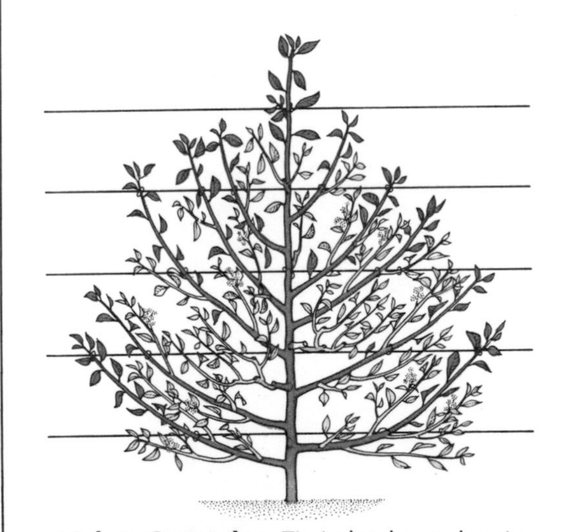

4 July to September. Tie in leader and main lateral shoots as they develop.

5 June. Cut back all breastwood that has flowered to within 4–6 in of the framework. Tie in extension shoots as they develop.

Chaenomeles and Pyracantha

Most varieties of the common "Japonica" or "Flowering Quince" are excellent plants for training against walls or fences. They flower well even on northern and eastern aspects, where they are particularly useful for early spring color.

The first year

Although *Chaenomeles* can be trained formally as espaliers or fans a less exact arrangement than that described for *Wisteria* better suits their growth habit.

The basic framework is built up by training in a leader and spacing out more or less horizontally any laterals against the wall or fence. If several basal shoots are present on the young plant these can be spaced out evenly against the support structure as it is not essential for a main leader to be established unless a formal espaliered plant is required.

Most *Chaenomeles* produce laterals and sublaterals freely without the need to stop the main shoots. These are trained in as required to complete the basic framework. Very little flower is produced during the first year or two after planting.

Cut back any outward-pointing shoots (breastwood) or sublaterals not required to form part of the framework to 4–6 leaves from the base after they have made their initial summer growth.

Further sublaterals usually develop on these cut-back shoots and these should be pruned to 2–3 leaves in late summer so that a stubby spur system is formed.

Second and following years

After flowering in spring vigorous extension growth is produced. Unless any shoots are required to train in to fill gaps in the framework summer-prune all new growths to 4–6 leaves from the base in June to July. Cut back any secondary shoots produced from this summer-pruned growth in early autumn, again to 2–3 leaves. This summer pruning builds up flowering spurs that are covered in bloom the following spring. In time these spurs may become congested and some will require to be thinned out each winter to maintain a balanced plant. This winter thinning may be done annually on established plants, pruning back all the summer growth originally cut to 4–6 leaves to two buds in winter if required. It produces a neater plant, but specimens which are only summer-pruned with an occasional winter-thinning of spurs flower equally well.

PYRACANTHA

Pyracantha is ideal for covering walls and can easily be trained to form almost any pattern of growth and grow around the windows and doors of houses. It also lends itself to formal training as an espalier, cordon or fan and is particularly valuable for northern and eastern aspects.

The first year

If a formally trained plant is required, the training is similar to that used for espalier apples. Usually it is more convenient to use the less formal system described for *Chaenomeles*, making sure that the basic framework branches are well spaced and that excess lateral growths and breastwood are cut back in July or early August to form spur shoots and to maintain growth close to the wall or fence.

Mature plant

The bunches of white flowers, which are followed by red or yellow berries, are formed in the leaf axils of short spur growths on the previous year's shoots. After flowering growth shoots appear during late June and July, hiding the young berries. On mature plants these need to be summer-pruned so that the fruit can be seen to full effect. Cut back the young growth as soon as the berries begin to ripen in mid- or late July or August to within 3–4in of the main framework. Secondary growth often occurs and a second trimming in early September can be given if needed. This pruning not only exposes the fruits so that they ripen well and can be seen but also produces the next season's flowering spurs.

The first year

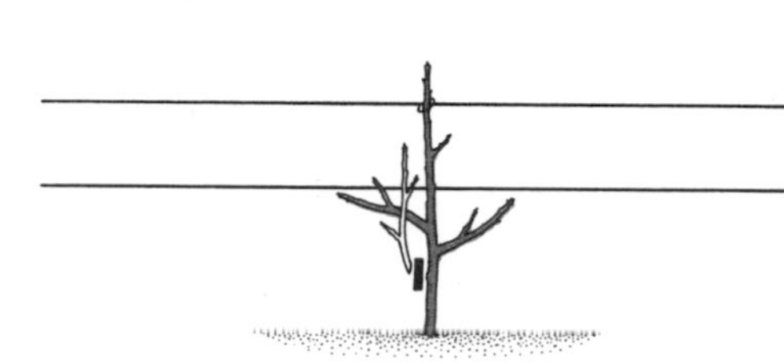

1 October to March. Train in the leader vertically. Space out laterals more or less horizontally. Cut out any awkwardly placed shoots that cannot be trained.

2 Late June to July. Train in the leader, lateral extension growths and new basal shoots to form main framework. Cut back breastwood or crossing shoots to 4–6 leaves.

Second and following years

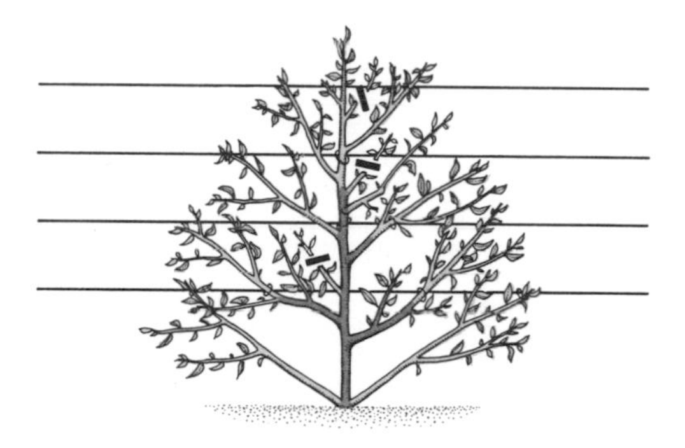

3 August to September. Train in late growth. Cut back any breastwood or surplus laterals to 2–3 leaves.

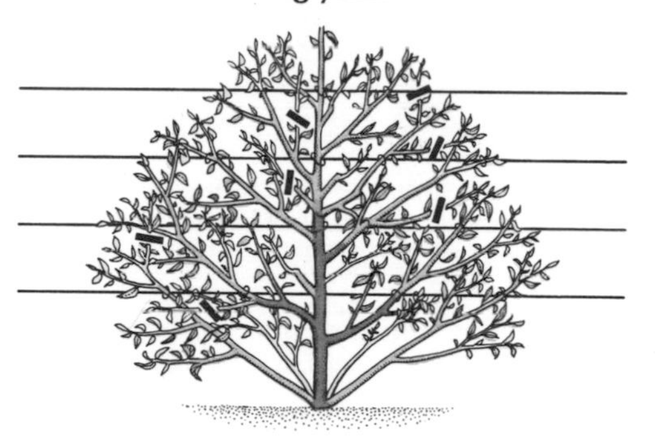

4 June to July. Train in the leader, lateral extension growths and new basal shoots to form main framework. Cut back breastwood or crossing shoots to 4–6 leaves.

Mature plant

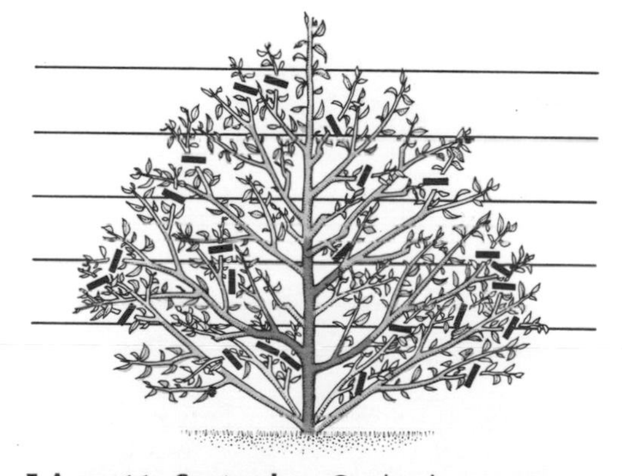

5 August to September. Cut back summer growth (sublaterals) to 2–3 leaves from base.

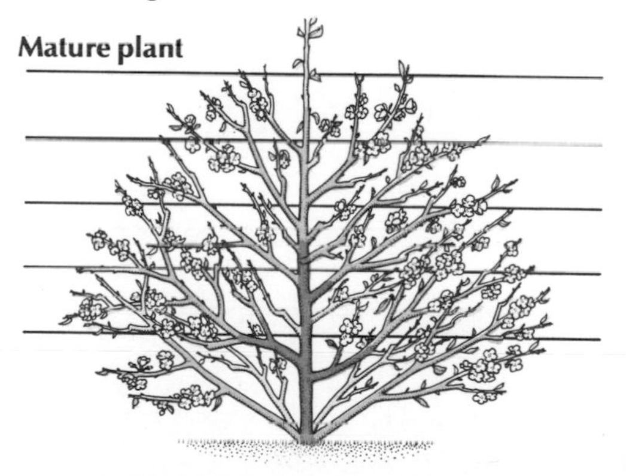

6 March to April. When the allotted space is filled stop the leader and main laterals.

Vines: introduction

It will be evident to those who have travelled in wine-growing districts that grapes are produced from vines grown in a wide variety of forms, ranging from closely pruned stumps to free-growing ramblers. A further contrast is available when you think of the vines grown in traditional fashion under glass. But whichever way the vine is trained it can clearly be seen that the grapes are produced on laterals formed in the current year.

It is important that this should be appreciated, because it is very easy to allow the vine, whether grown outside or under glass, to produce too many laterals and therefore too many bunches of small and perhaps useless grapes. Equally, the way in which the grapes are produced means that the vine has to grow quickly and freely if the berries are to ripen before the beginning of winter.

Pruning is of great importance, because it is the method by which the gardener—or viticulturist, if you seek promotion—can reduce the number of competing growths and thereby concentrate the energies of the vine in the desired directions.

Pruning is a constant but rewarding task—constant in that it takes place not only in the dormant season but also during the period of active growth, rewarding in the sense that the results can be so readily observed.

Most gardeners think of pruning as the wholesale removal of large shoots, but vine pruning is more subtle. It is often necessary to pinch out growing points, or remove unwanted shoots when they are still tiny, or to take away surplus bunches in the embryo stage, or to thin out the bunches by removing individual berries to ensure that dessert grapes are large and luscious.

All these tasks are aspects of pruning, the disciplined technique by which the grower exercises control over his vigorous plants.

The following pages set out in detail the pruning of vines under glass and outdoors. There are, however, some general points that should be kept in mind.

THE FRUIT

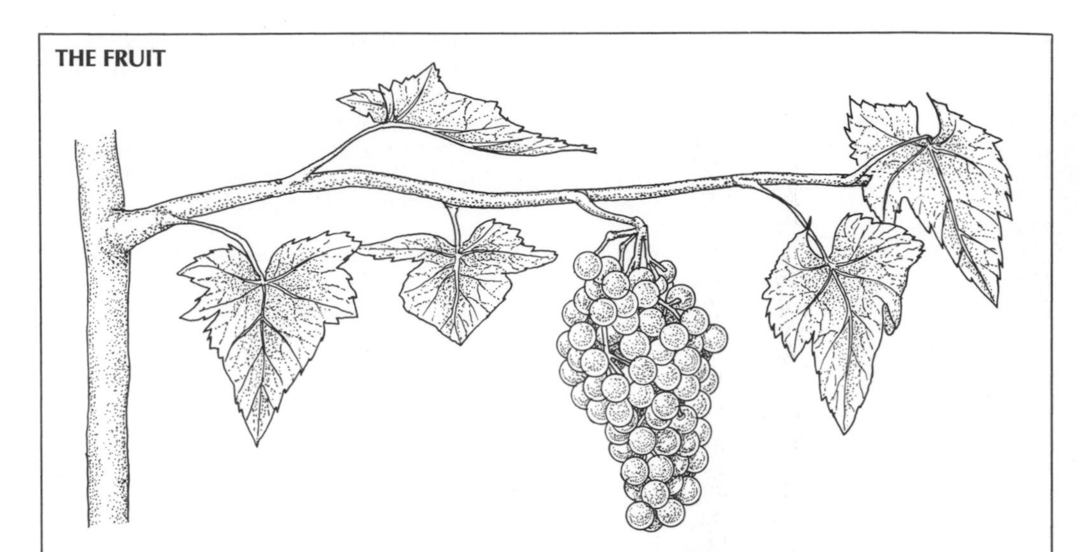

Grapes are produced on new laterals. The aim of the pruner is to reduce the number of laterals and bunches, to avoid overcropping. One bunch per lateral is usually enough.

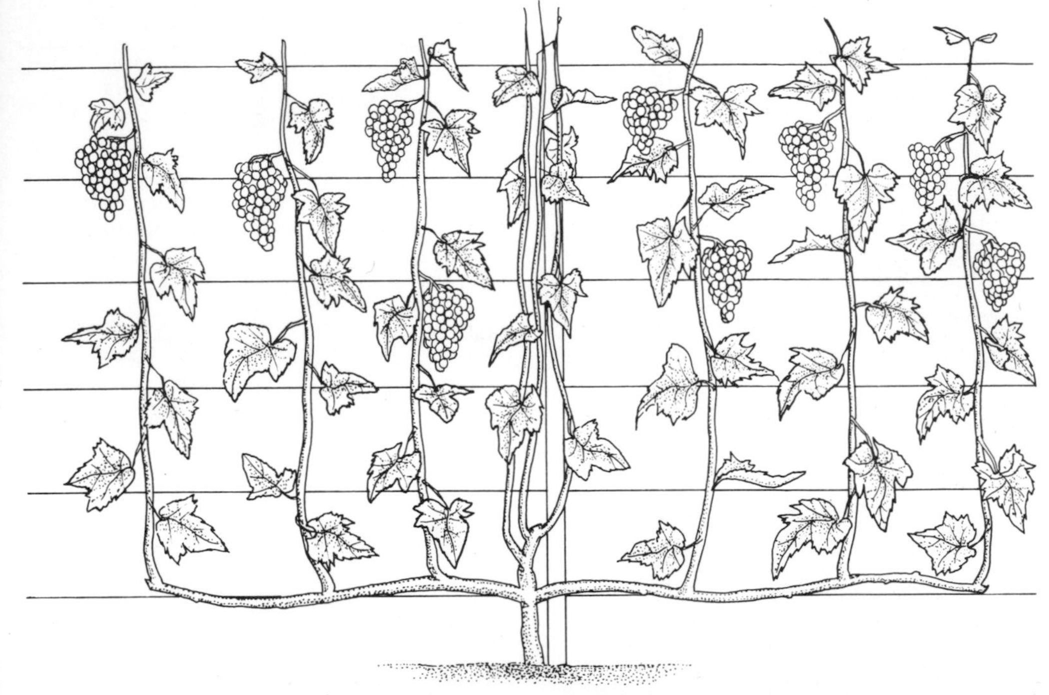

Vines grown under glass are usually produced as single vertical rods carrying horizontally trained laterals. Each lateral carries one good bunch of grapes.

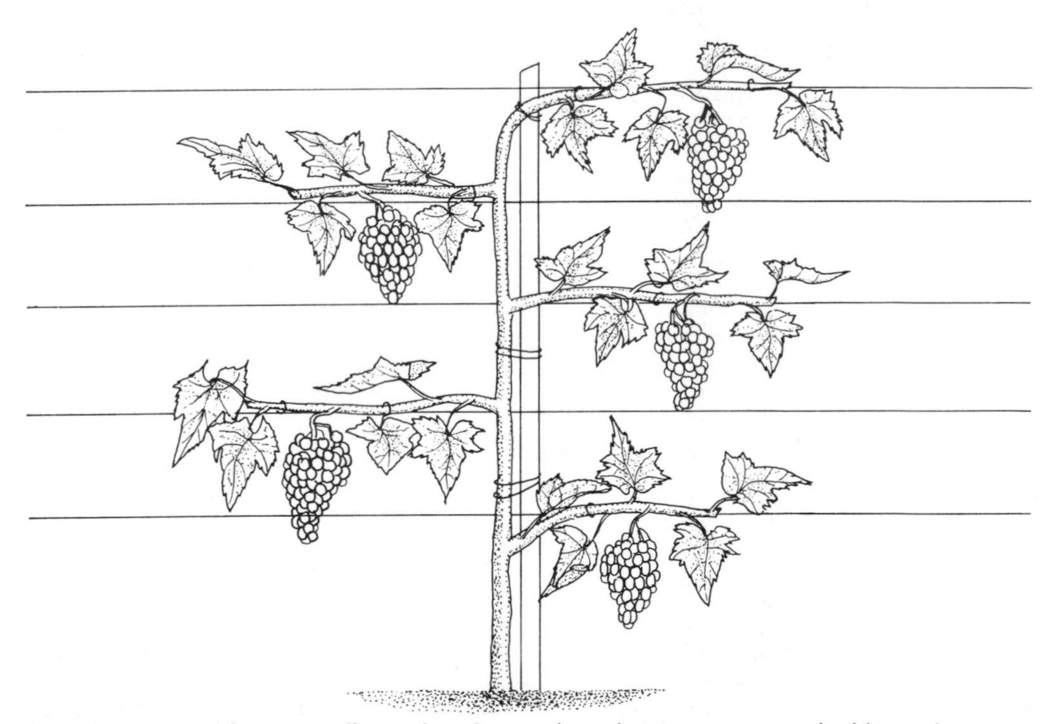

Vines grown outside are usually produced as horizontal rods carrying vertically trained laterals. It is necessary to build in replacement rods each year.

Indoor Vines

It is difficult to separate the pruning of vines grown under glass from the other factors that are involved in successful cultivation. These include the preparation of the border in which the vine is to be grown, the choice and number of varieties, planting distance, and the important question of heat. But these are beyond the scope of this book, which deals only with training and pruning.

It is unusual to find a greenhouse devoted entirely to vines, and it is assumed that only one vine is being grown in a mixed plant house provided with enough heat to keep out frost, thus permitting a growing season long enough to ensure the ripening of varieties such as 'Black Hamburgh,' but not suitable for the choice Muscats.

The first year

The young vine should be planted from a container during the dormant season, which lasts from November to February. It can be planted as a one-year-old vine or a two-year-old plant that the nurseryman will have pruned hard after the first year's growth and transferred to a larger container.

The rod should be severely pruned back to two buds from ground level on planting. The most common mistake is to allow the vine to crop too early, on a weak stem. The hard pruning is designed to prevent this.

As a result of the initial pruning two or more growths will be produced. Only one—the strongest—should be allowed to develop. Stop the other growths when they are about 4in long by pinching out each growing point and stopping any subsequent sublaterals at one leaf as they appear. The retention of the leaves of the stopped laterals will encourage the strengthening of the stem without undue competition with the selected main growth.

At the end of the first growing season the vine enters into a necessary period of dormancy. The leaves fall and the plant rests, or appears to be at rest. In reality important chemical and biological changes are taking place internally. Because of these, pruning should be carried out early, in December, as soon as the leaves have fallen.

The amount to be removed will depend on the length and thickness of the rod—the longer and thicker the less severe the pruning.

As a generalization, the young vine at the end of its second year of growth should be cut back by two-thirds.

The second year

The following spring and summer the topmost bud will form the new extension leader, while the remaining buds will break to produce laterals. These laterals should be thinned out, if necessary, by removing unwanted shoots when they are about 1in long. The aim should be to space the laterals at intervals of about 6in as they appear, taking care that those retained are alternate rather than sub-opposite.

About two of the retained laterals can be allowed to fruit, providing the vine is growing strongly. The fruiting lateral should be stopped, by pinching, at two leaves beyond the embryo bunch. Unfruited laterals should also be stopped when they reach a length of about 2ft. The leader is allowed to grow on unchecked during the summer.

The following December shorten the leader by one-half, and cut back each lateral to about 1in, aiming to leave two buds.

The first year

1 November to February. A one-year-old rod at planting. Cut back to two buds from ground level.

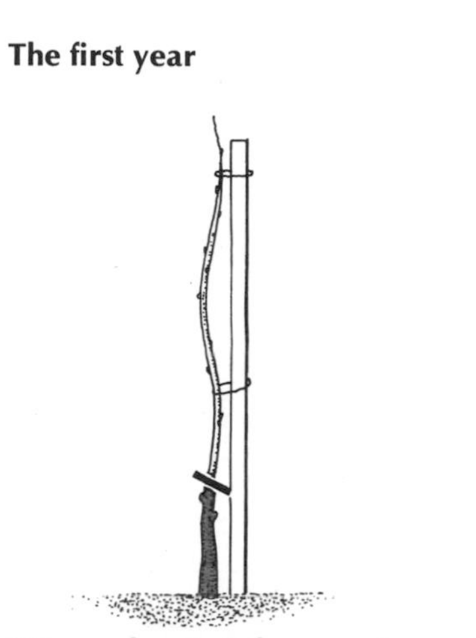

2 April to September. Two or three new growths develop. Leave the strongest untouched. Pinch out the growing points on the others when about 4in long. Pinch out subsequent sublaterals to one leaf.

3 December. As soon as the leaves have fallen cut back the vine by two-thirds.

The second year

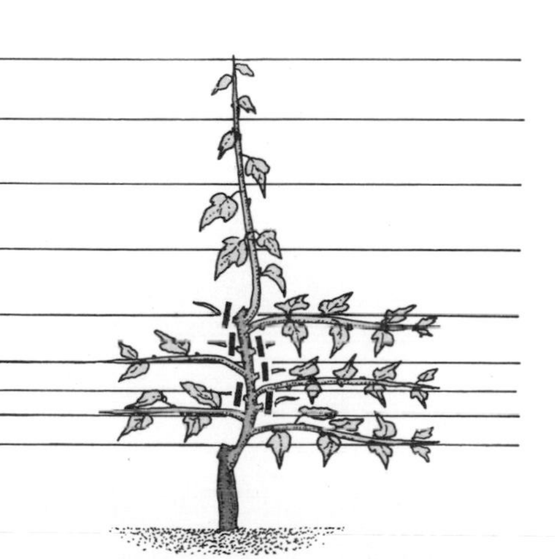

4 March to April. The topmost bud forms the new extension leader. Thin laterals if necessary by pinching out when they are 1in long. The aim is to produce laterals alternately on opposite sides of the stem.

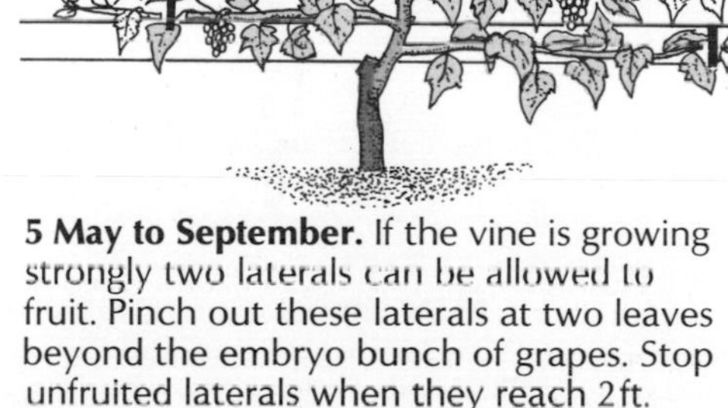

5 May to September. If the vine is growing strongly two laterals can be allowed to fruit. Pinch out these laterals at two leaves beyond the embryo bunch of grapes. Stop unfruited laterals when they reach 2ft.

6 December. Shorten the leader by about one-half. Cut back each lateral to about 1in, leaving two buds.

Indoor Vines

Third and following years

Pruning is now straightforward. The single rod is allowed to grow in stages until it reaches the limit set by the height of the greenhouse, when it is stopped in the summer and pruned back to 1in each winter.

Stop the laterals at two leaves beyond the bunch of grapes and pinch out any sub-laterals to one leaf. After picking the fruit it makes a neater looking plant if you cut back the laterals by about one-half, but this is merely a preliminary to the winter pruning, when each lateral is cut back to 1in, leaving a neat but slightly outraged-looking vine consisting of a straight, single rod clothed in tight spurs, brimming with potential fruitfulness.

Each spring and summer carefully regulate and space the new laterals so that only one develops from each spur. It is best to secure each fruiting lateral to a wire and to bring it gradually to the horizontal.

Care must be taken not to overcrop. As a general rule not more than twelve well-spaced bunches should be allowed. Another rough measurement is to allow one bunch for each foot of bearing length.

Third and following years

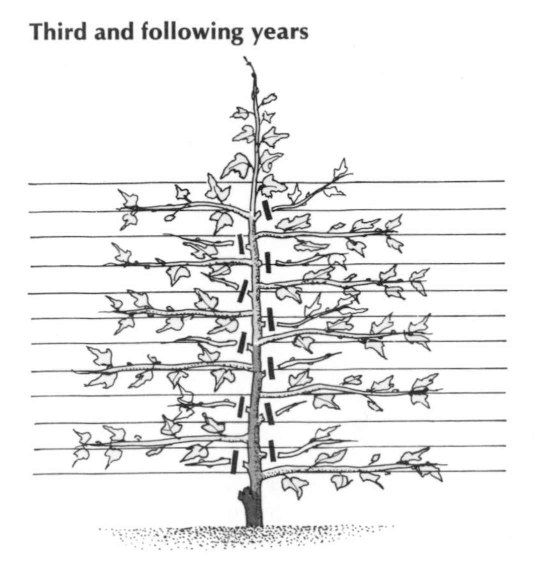

7 April to July. Throughout spring and summer thin and space the laterals to 6in so that only one develops from each spur. Secure each fruiting lateral to a wire, gradually bringing it to the horizontal.

8 August. Stop each fruiting lateral at two leaves beyond the bunches of grapes. Pinch back any sublaterals to one leaf.

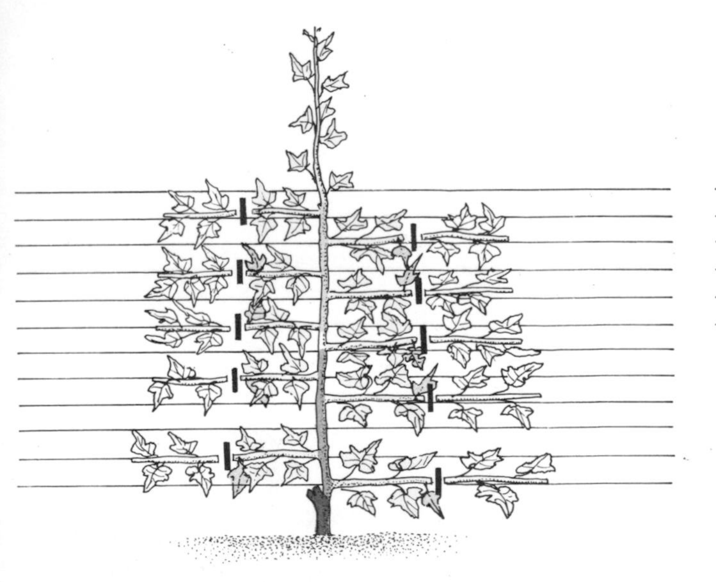

9 September. After picking the fruit cut back the laterals by about one-half.

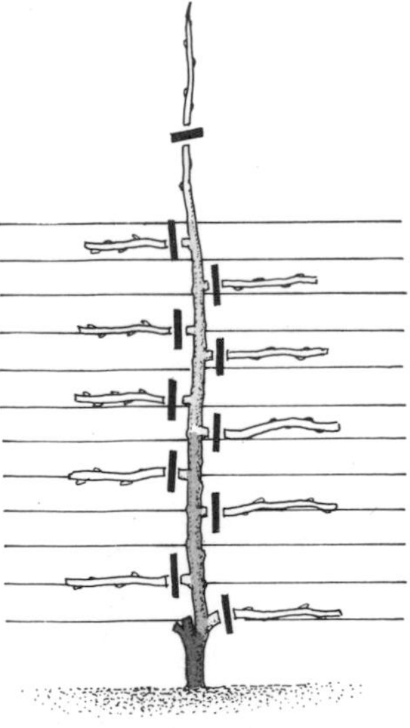

10 December. Cut back the leader by one-half and the laterals to 1in or two buds.

The mature vine

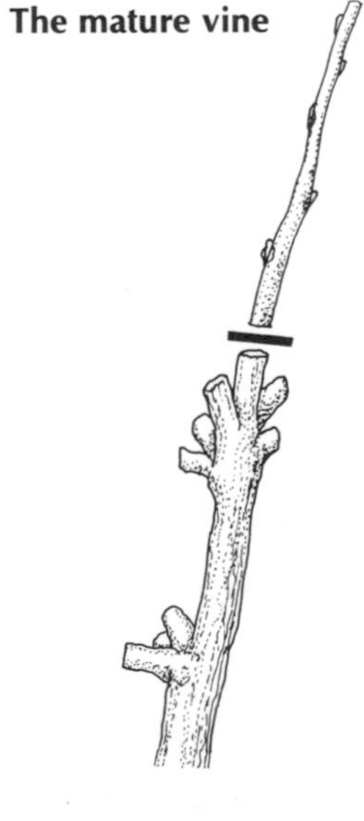

11 Stop the leader in summer and cut it back to 1in in winter.

THINNING THE FRUIT

When the grapes begin to swell, thin with a pair of long-bladed scissors. Leave plenty of grapes at the shoulders of the bunch but remove most of the interior berries, always aiming for well-balanced shape. This process may need to be repeated. Try not to touch the berries or the bloom may be spoilt. Move the bunch gently with a twig.

Outdoor Vines

Occasionally dessert varieties of vines are grown outdoors. They can be grown against walls and trained as single or multiple vertical rods in the manner described for vines grown under glass. But for the most part outdoor vines are intended for wine production, with dessert quality as an occasional bonus. In recent years there has been a considerable revival in viticulture, linked with the domestic art of wine-making.

Visions of vast wine-vats should, however, be put firmly aside. It is important to realize that only after very warm summers is a bumper crop likely to ripen. In some years the crop will be virtually useless but nevertheless excellent wines have been produced from grapes grown in sheltered, but often sunny sites.

Since the growing season is comparatively short it is essential that the varieties are quick-maturing. To assist this process the pruning should be severe—designed to control the number of fruit-bearing laterals and to ensure that these are fully exposed to sunlight.

A number of systems of training and pruning have been tried with these desirable aims in view, but the most popular is that known as the Guyot system. There are two variants. One, relying on a single bearing rod, is used for the weaker varieties, the other, known as the Double Guyot system, is used more generally. It is very easy to switch from one system to the other, according to the way in which the vines respond to a particular combination of soil, site and pruning.

The Double Guyot System

A system of posts and wires, or similar supports, is necessary to ensure that the horizontal bearing rods and vertical laterals are properly trained. The aim is to produce two strong new main growths each year, which are trained the following winter—one is trained to the left and one is trained to the right—along a wire 18in above the ground.

During the following spring and summer strong vertical laterals that carry the fruits grow from these horizontal arms. As the laterals appear secure them to three additional wires arranged at spacings of about 1ft above the bottom wire. Sometimes double wires are used so that the growths can be tucked in quickly rather than tied individually.

In addition to the fruiting laterals three other strong growths should be taken up from the center. These are the all-important annual replacement shoots, next year's bearing rods, two of them destined to be trained horizontally at the end of the first growing season, when their predecessors should be cut out entirely.

Only two are needed as bearing rods, those most readily placed for horizontal training. The third, most central shoot, is pruned back severely to generate new replacement rods.

Clearly, if the single Guyot system is used only one horizontal replacement is secured to the support each year.

The first year

Between November and February plant a well-rooted, strongly growing one-year-old vine from a container, and prune back to about 6in from ground level, taking care to leave two good buds.

During summer allow only one shoot to develop and train this to a vertical 6ft tall stake. Pinch back any laterals that develop to 1in as they appear.

A year after planting you should be the proud owner of a strong single rod, perhaps 6ft in length. Cut it back to within 2ft of ground level, this ensures three good buds are left at the top, the lower two ideally being sub-opposite and in the line of the supports. If, however, growth during the first summer has been weak, typified by a thin shoot of say 4ft in length, it is best to start the whole process over again, cutting back to 6in and deferring cropping for a year.

The second year

The topmost three buds will grow vigorously upwards throughout summer and should be trained vertically. Pinch back any other laterals to 1in as they appear.

In November cut back severely the shoot from the topmost bud to leave three good buds. Gently persuade the remaining two towards the horizontal, by tying them to the bottom wire, one shoot to the right and one to the left. Prune the tip of each to leave about 3ft of strong shoot, giving a total of 6ft of bearing rod.

The first year

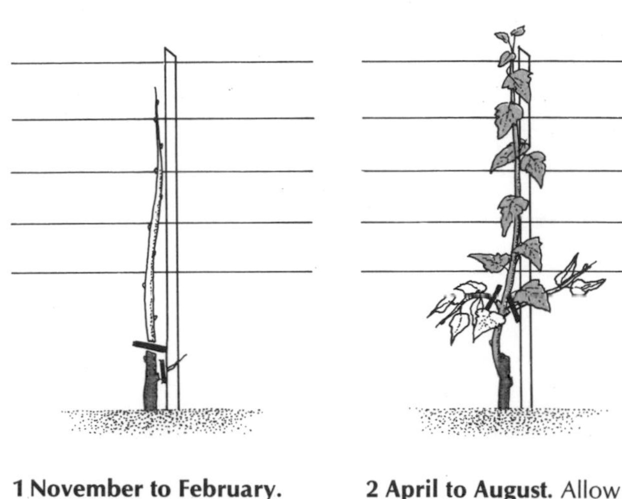

1 November to February. Plant a one-year-old vine. Cut back to about 6in from ground level, leaving two good buds.

2 April to August. Allow only one shoot to develop and train it to a vertical 6ft stake. Pinch back to 1in any other shoots as they appear.

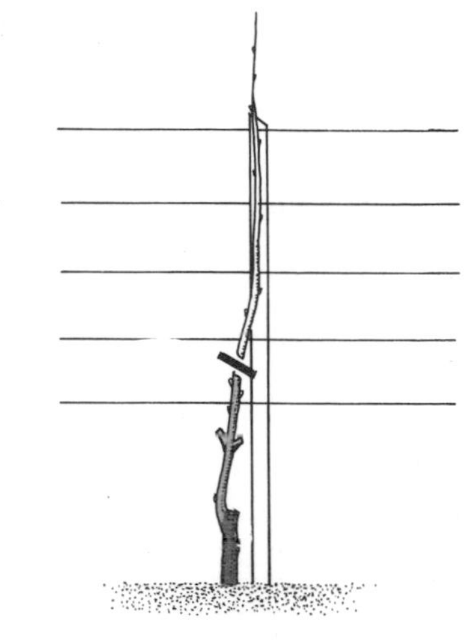

3 November. Cut back the central rod to within 2ft of ground level, leaving three good buds. The lower two should be sub-opposite and in line with the supports.

The second year

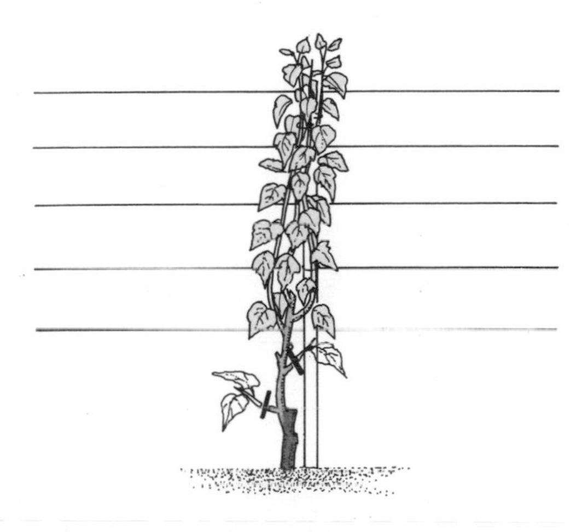

4 April to August. Train the three shoots vertically. Pinch back any laterals that are produced to 1in as they develop.

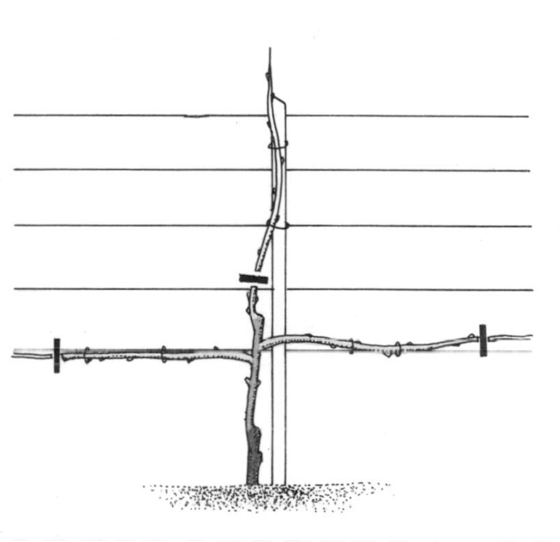

5 November. Cut back the shoot from the topmost bud to leave three good buds. Lower the remaining two shoots and tie them to the wire. Prune back each one to leave about 3ft of strong shoot.

Outdoor Vines

Third and subsequent years
During summer, fruiting laterals appear from the horizontal rods. If too many are produced they should be thinned out at an early stage so as to space the remainder at intervals of approximately 6–8in. Those carrying the strongest embryo bunches of grapes are the lucky survivors. Stop each fruiting lateral as it grows above the top wire, leaving at least two leaves beyond the bunch.

In November cut out to base the two bearing rods and all their attendant laterals. The three central shoots are treated as before; the upper shoot cut to three good buds, the other two trained horizontally and cut to about 3ft.

Do not worry unduly if it proves impossible to produce neat horizontal arms. Nature sometimes resists our tidy concepts, but avoid marked curves if possible, otherwise laterals of uneven strength are produced.

Third and subsequent years

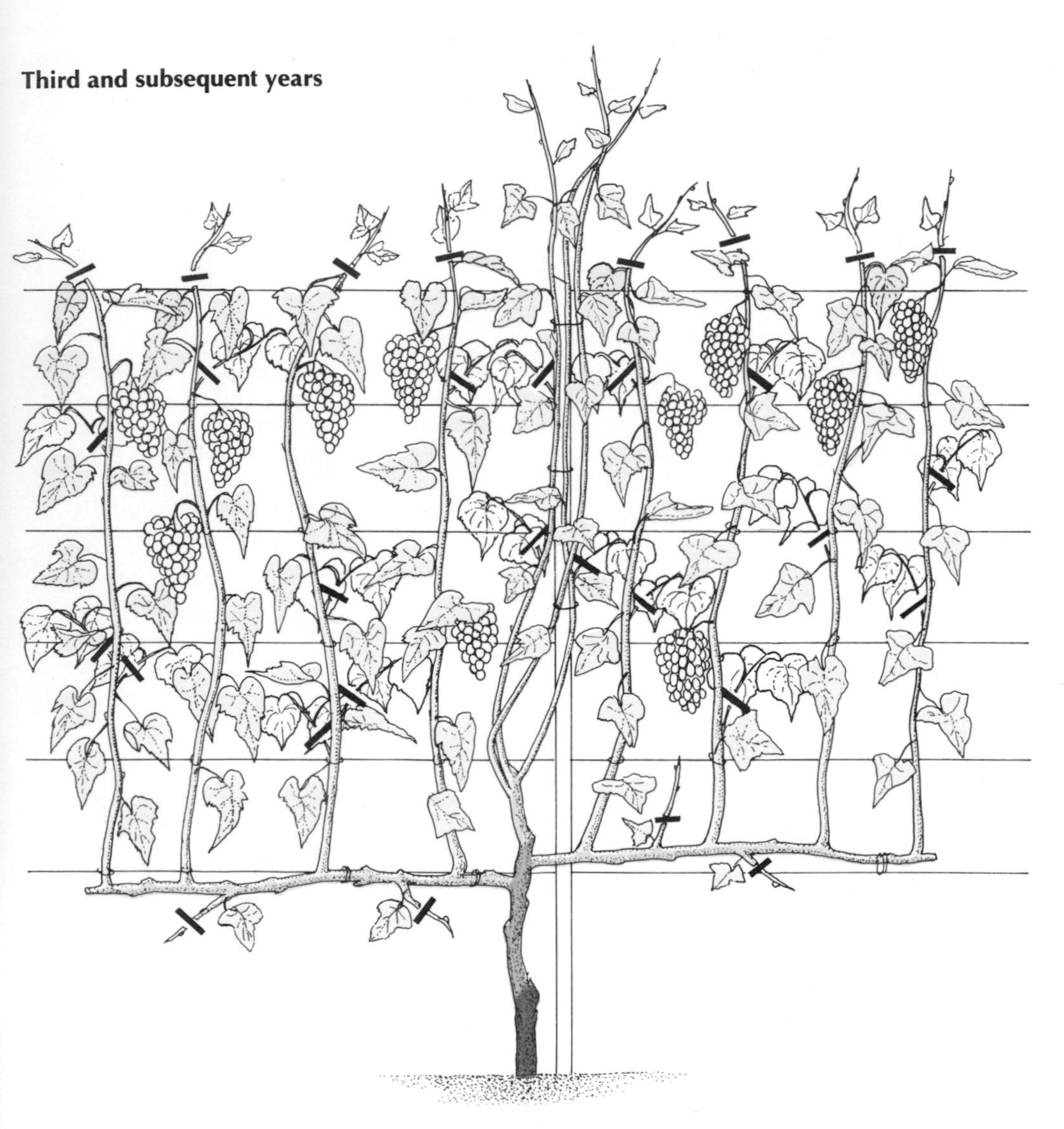

6 April to August. Train three shoots vertically from the centre. Pinch back any laterals that are produced on them to 1in as they develop. Fruiting laterals grow upwards from the horizontal rods. If necessary thin them to 6–8in apart. Stop each fruiting lateral above the top wire leaving at least two leaves.

7 November. Cut out to base the two bearing rods. Cut back the shoot from the topmost bud to leave three good buds. Lower the remaining two shoots to the horizontal and tie them to the wire, one to the left and one to the right. Prune back each to leave about 3ft of strong shoot or less if growth is weak.

Fruit Trees: introduction

There is a great deal of unnecessary mystery attached to the pruning of fruit plants. This has partly arisen because fruit growing is an ancient craft and has gathered its proper share of folklore.

The pruning of fruit trees is very often overdone. If there is any uncertainty the tree is best left untouched. Every pruning cut must have a purpose.

The forms in which trees can be grown are dealt with on page 54. The special training of such forms as cordons and espaliers are covered on the following pages. Technical terms are unavoidable, so definitions of the frequently used terms in the pruning of fruit trees are of use to any fruit gardener.

Maiden is a term used to describe a one-year-old, used in a "maiden tree," "maiden wood" or "maiden shoot."

Scion is the desired variety of fruit that is grafted on to the rootstock or root system of another tree. Where the two join is known as the *union*.

A branch is essentially a limb that grows from the trunk. Primary branches are the first formed and secondary branches grow from the primary branches. A *leader* is a shoot that has been selected to extend a branch. A *lateral* is a side-shoot.

Spurs are very short laterals (side-shoots) that terminate in flower buds. They may occur naturally or they can be induced by the pruning of laterals.

Flower buds, or blossom buds, are unopened flowers. These are often referred to as *fruit buds*, but that may be optimistic. Buds that open to give rise to a shoot, as distinct from a flower, are called *wood buds*.

Suckers are shoots which grow from below ground or below the union.

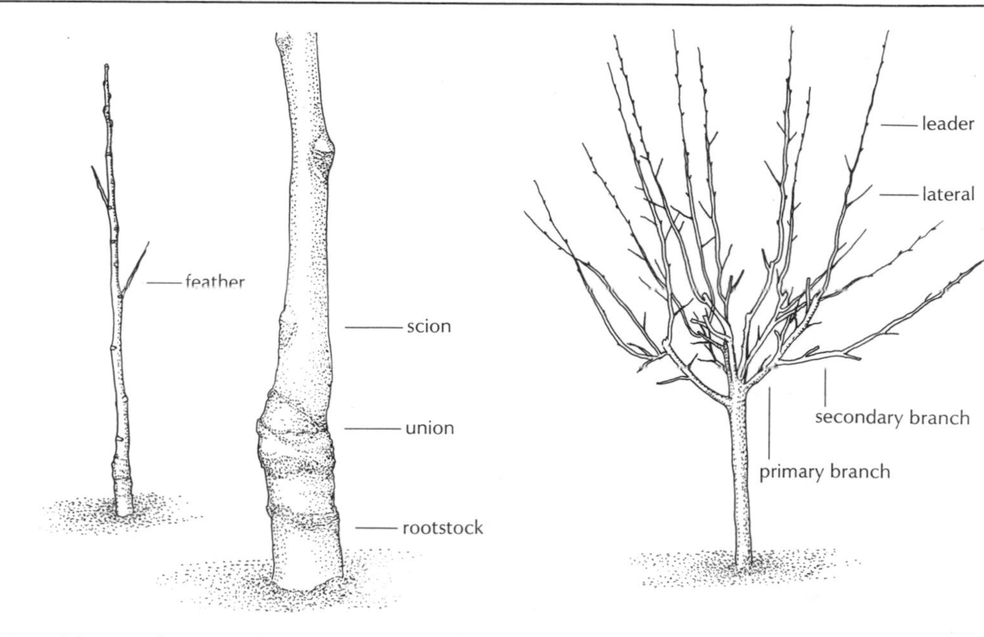

A maiden apple tree. Above the union is the scion and below the union is the rootstock. Laterals on a maiden stem are called *feathers*.

A three-year-old, open-center bush apple tree, showing a primary branch, a secondary branch, a leader and a lateral.

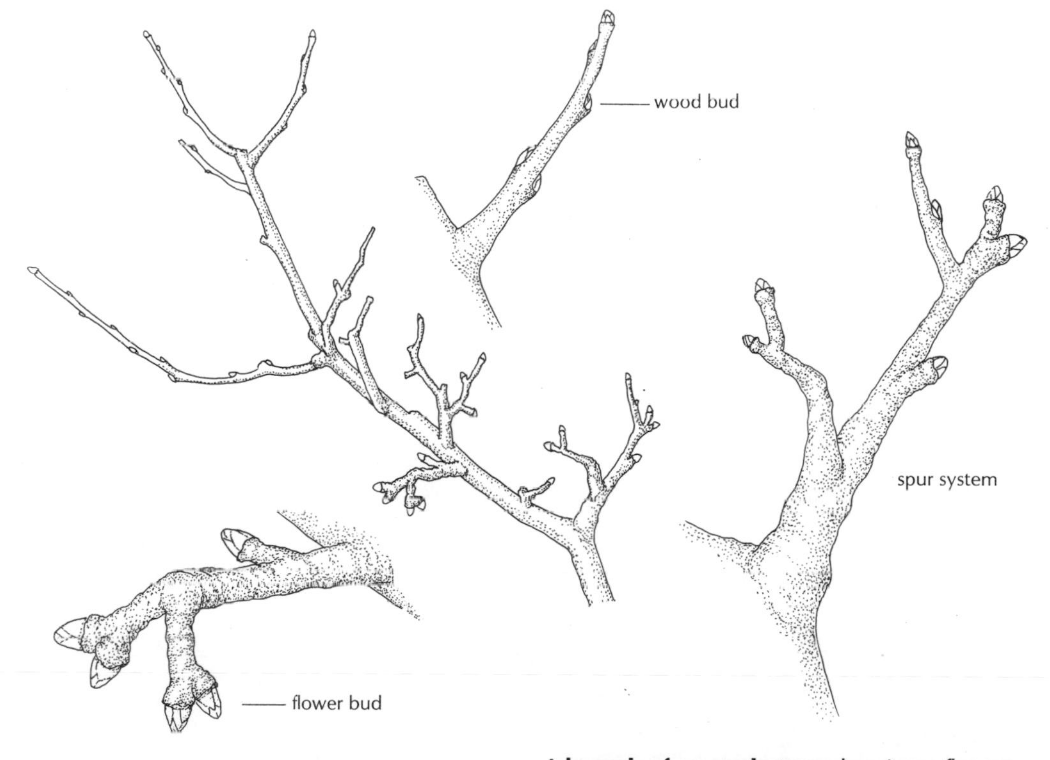

A branch of an apple tree, showing a flower bud, a spur, a spur system and wood buds.

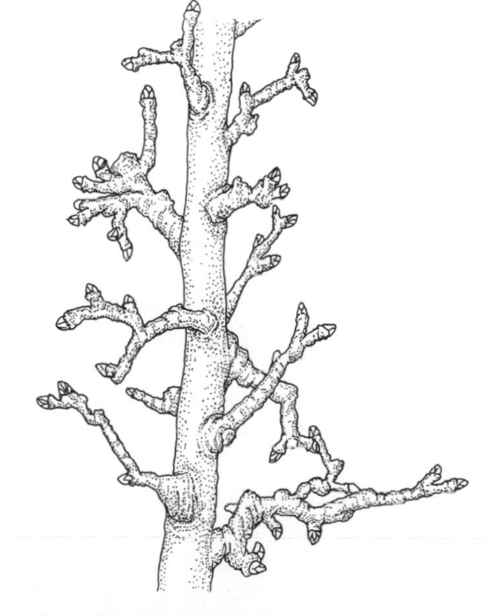

Complicated spur system on a three- or four-year-old branch.

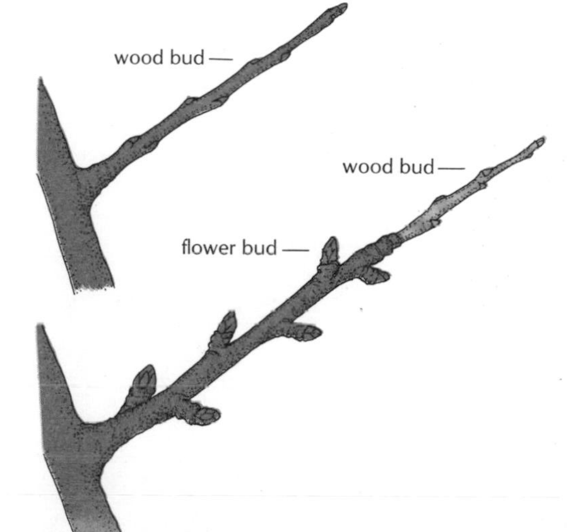

A maiden lateral, showing wood buds and a two-year-old shoot showing wood buds and flower buds on the two-year-old wood.

Forms of Tree

Both apple and pear trees can be fitted into almost any garden. The vigor of the tree depends not only on the nature of the soil and climate but on the extent of pruning, the amount of fertilizing and on the rootstock that is chosen.

The rootstock is of particular importance. The East Malling rootstocks have been selected to provide a wide range of tree vigor and performance. There are many different apple rootstocks in the Malling series. The most suitable for home gardeners are, in order of vigor: M9, M26, MM106 and MM111. A rootstock that produces an even smaller tree than M9 will soon be available as M27. As far as pears are concerned the choice of rootstock is between Quince A or Quince C.

Although not directly concerned with pruning, making the correct choice of rootstock is very important. Avoiding the very vigorous rootstocks will ensure a relatively small tree in the garden. Having made the choice great care must be taken not to undo all the good work by burying the union—the junction of stock and scion—when planting. If the scion is in the ground, it may take root and a large, but unfruitful tree may result.

Forms of tree

Apples and pears in gardens where space is limited can be grown as a dwarf bush, a larger bush, a central-leader bush, a cordon, a dwarf pyramid or an espalier. The dwarf bush apple trees are usually grown on M9 or M26 rootstocks. The larger bush is readily produced on such rootstocks as MM106 for apples and Quince A is best for pears. These two bush forms are exactly the same in structure, the difference lies only in the size.

Commercial growers now increasingly favor a central-leader bush tree, in which the main axis is continued upwards and branches are built in at regular intervals.

Cordon means a single line or stem, but fruit tree cordons can be single or multiple. The lines or stems can be trained vertically or at an angle. The essential features are spur pruning and no branching. Because of this compact linear habit, cordons can be planted closely together.

The espalier can be thought of as a series of horizontal cordons carried on one tree.

The dwarf pyramid is best described as a free-growing vertical cordon. It is easier to produce than the tightly pruned cordon.

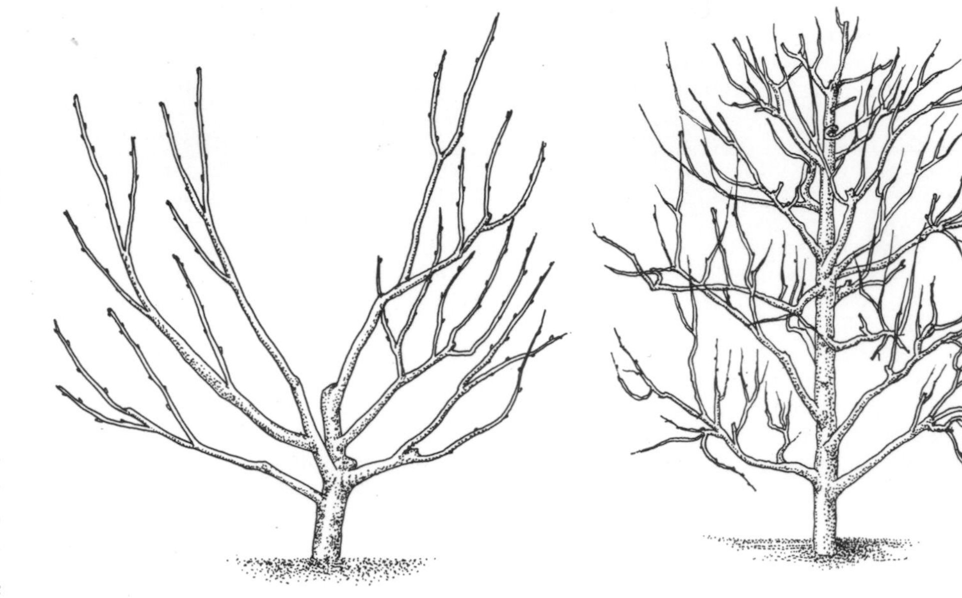

An open-center bush, showing the 2ft main stem and the radiating main branches. The form is sometimes compared to an inverted open umbrella.

A central-leader bush tree. The main stem is continued vertically so that branches arise over a greater length.

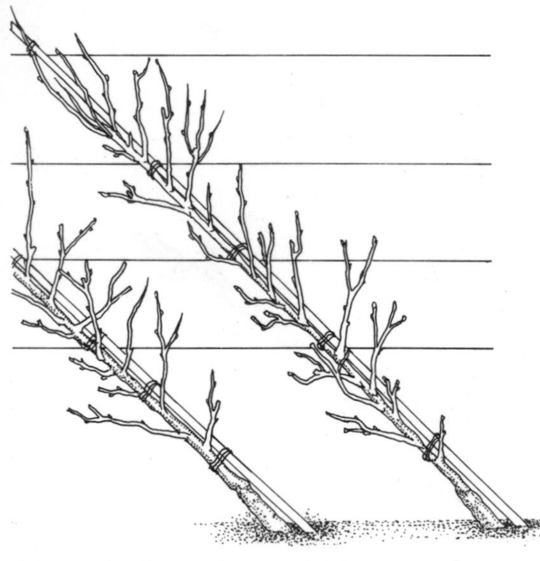

Oblique single cordons trained at an angle of approximately 45 degrees by securing to canes fixed to wires.

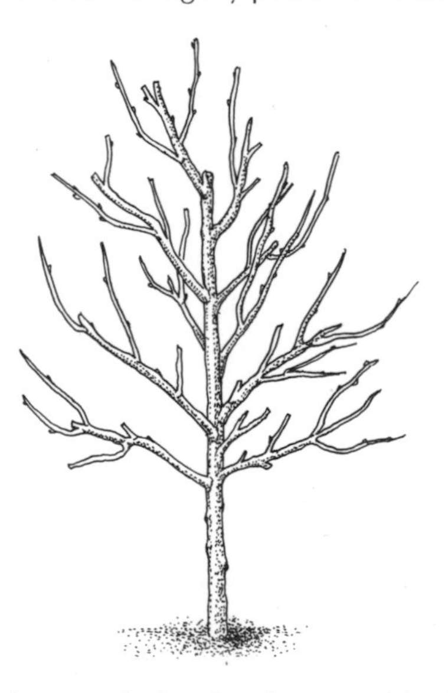

Dwarf pyramid, showing the central leader, and free-growing side branches.

Espalier, showing four tiers of horizontal fruiting arms.

Pruning for Fruit

Spur pruning
By the fifth year after planting apple and pear trees are still increasing in size but growth should slow down because of the strain imposed by fruit bearing.

The following pages discuss the formation of the permanent framework of branches. Developing this framework involves some severe pruning of the leaders to ensure strong, well-placed branches capable of carrying the heavy fruit crops. When the framework has been formed the gardener is usually interested only in the furnishing of the branches with spurs and flower-bearing laterals.

Spurs will form naturally in many cases, or they can be encouraged by pruning between November and February, or in summer. A lateral pruned back in winter to about four buds will produce one or two shoots from the uppermost buds, but usually the lower wood buds will be transformed during the summer to flower buds. (The flower buds are round and plump in appearance compared with wood buds.) Once flower buds have clearly formed cut back the whole unit to the uppermost flower bud. The foundation has been laid for a spur system close to the branch.

Each flower bud will, all being well, produce at least one apple or pear from the four or five blossoms contained within the bud. Behind this fruit a new flower bud will form, assuming the tree is properly fertilized. The spur systems are self-renewing.

After some years a spur system may get too crowded and complicated. At this point spur thinning is undertaken by the pruning away of the weaker spurs and those on the underside of the branches.

Sometimes varieties of apples and pears are divided into short-spur and long-spur and tip-bearing groups. This is an unnecessary complication. All varieties found in gardens will respond to the pruning methods suggested here.

The first year

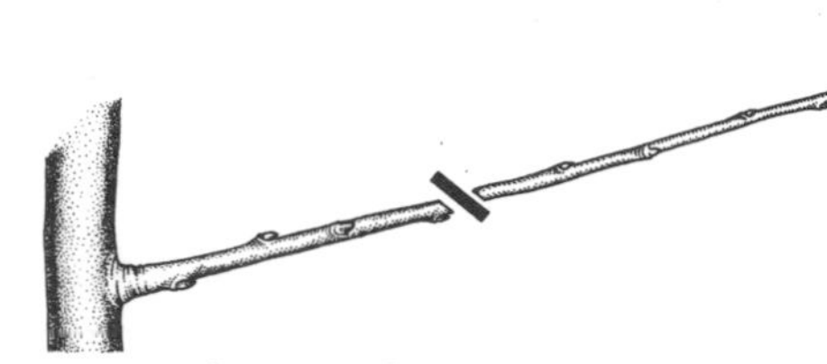

1 November to February. Cut back a maiden lateral to four buds.

The second year

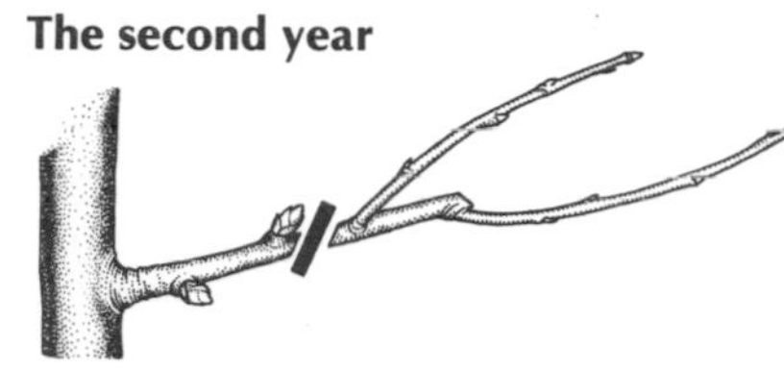

2 November to February. Cut back the lateral to a flower bud.

The third year

3 July to September. Fruit is carried on the pruned-back lateral.

The fourth year

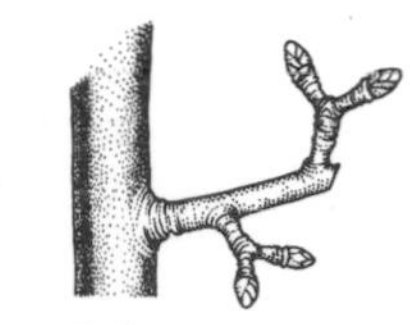

4 November to February. A spur system beginning to form.

SPUR THINNING

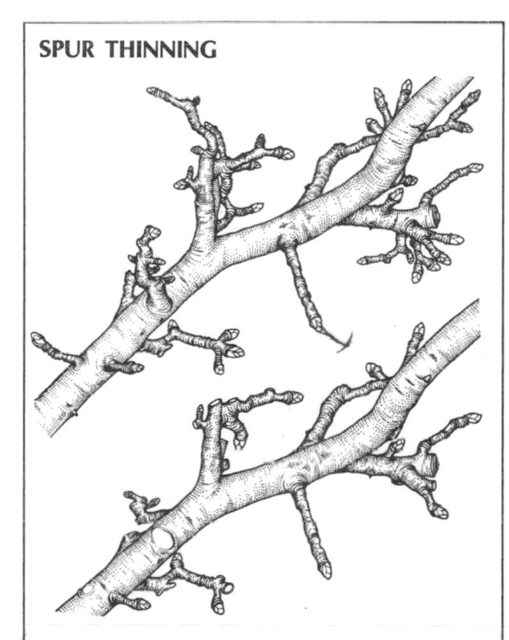

As the tree matures the spur systems will become crowded and should be thinned. Remove spurs on the underside of the branch as well.

Renewal pruning
Most commercial growers, who make a living from their fruit growing and therefore depend on heavy crops, use a system which is a combination of the older method of spur pruning and a newer system, which is called renewal pruning. It is based on the known tendency of both apple and pear varieties to produce flower buds on unpruned two-year-old laterals.

Leave strong laterals on the outer parts of the tree unpruned. During the following growing season the terminal bud on each unpruned lateral extends to produce a further maiden shoot, while most of the buds on the unpruned portion become flower buds. In winter cut back the laterals to the top-most flower bud, and the following summer the cut-back lateral produces fruits. The fruited lateral can either be retained as an elongated spur system or cut back to within 1in of its base.

This severe shortening stimulates the formation of a new lateral shoot—from this, the term "renewal"—and the whole productive cycle starts again. The best approach to pruning apples and pears is to combine spur pruning with renewal pruning.

The first year

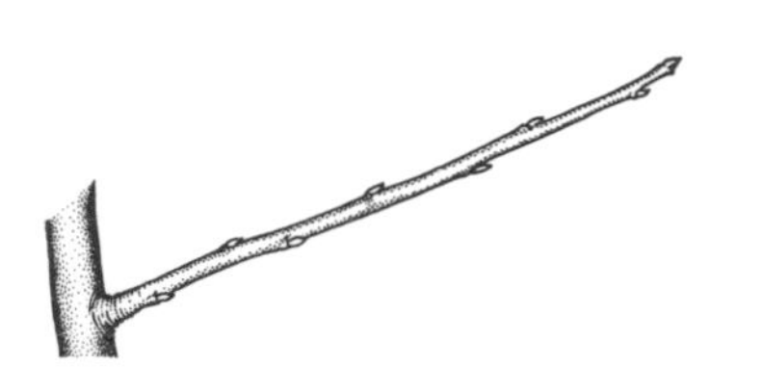

1 November to February. Select a strong, well-placed lateral and leave it unpruned.

The second year

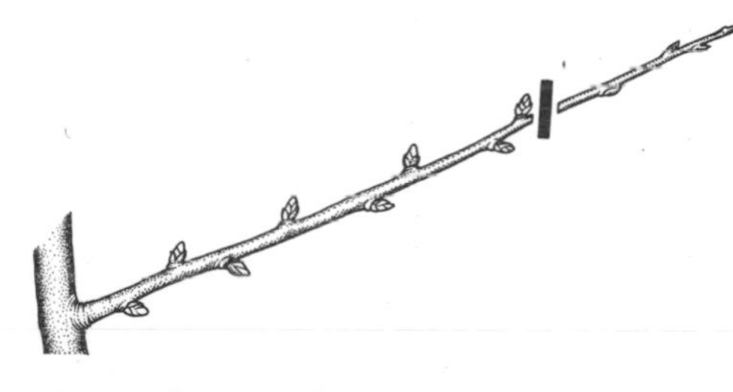

2 November to February. Extension growth has occurred. Flower buds have formed on last year's wood. Cut back to the junction between the old and new wood.

3 August to October. Fruit is carried on the pruned-back lateral.

The third year

4 November to February. Cut back the fruited lateral to leave a 1in stub.

5 October. At the end of the growing season a strong new lateral has been produced from the 1in stub. This is left unpruned, to start the renewal cycle again.

sh Tree

The bush form of tree is used for the growing of apples, pears, plums, peaches and acid cherries. There are slight variations, but the principles are the same. Training may take up to five years. Fruit buds are quite frequently set in the third or fourth year but it is usually a further season before a reasonable crop is obtained.

The first year
The work of forming the head begins with the maiden tree. This should be planted in the dormant season, from November to February. Take care not to bury the union. At planting shorten the maiden tree to about 27 in, cutting it back to just above a bud. This cut stimulates the formation of primary branches.

At the end of the growing season select four strong leaders to form primary branches, taking care to select only the branches that have formed wide angles with the main stem. The wide angles ensure strength—narrow angles may mean branch breakages later on. Cut back the stronger leaders by one-half and the less vigorous ones by two-thirds. Each cut should be to an outward-pointing bud, so that next year's extension, from the top bud, is in the correct direction.

The second year
During the second summer the branch growth following the hard pruning should be strong, the tree becomes larger, and secondary branches can be built in to fill in the space inside of the branch growth.

At the end of the second full growing season select about four more widely spaced branches. (The framework now consists of about eight branches.) Shorten these four by one-half or two-thirds, depending on the vigor of each branch. Cut back to an outward-pointing bud. Prune back laterals not required for secondary branches to about four buds to induce spurs. If the tree is growing vigorously some laterals on the outer part of the tree can be left unpruned to form flower buds.

The first year

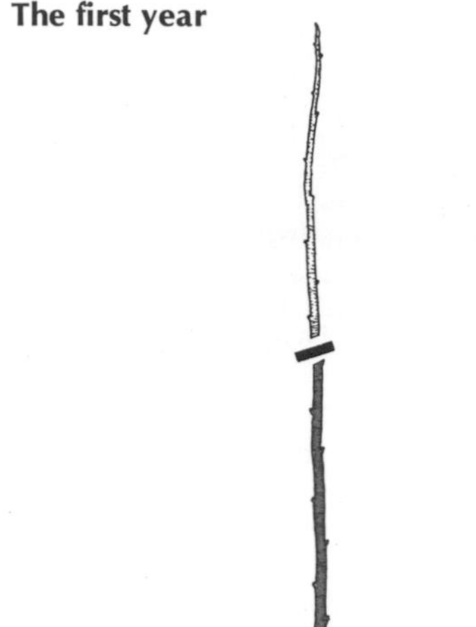

1 November to February. Maiden tree at planting. Cut back to 27 in, just above a bud.

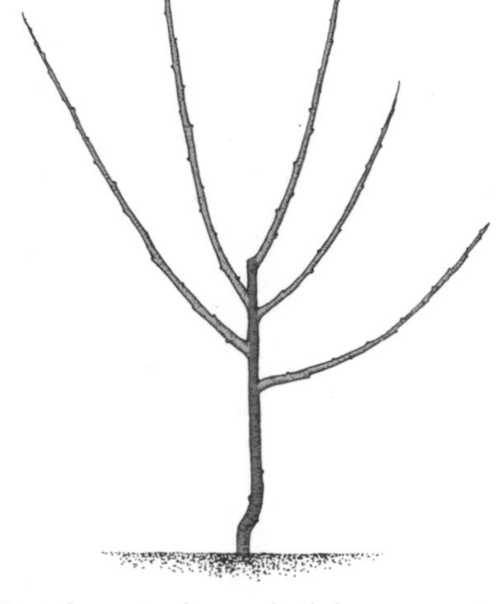

2 October. At the end of the season's growth the tree has responded to pruning and formed strong primary branches.

The second year

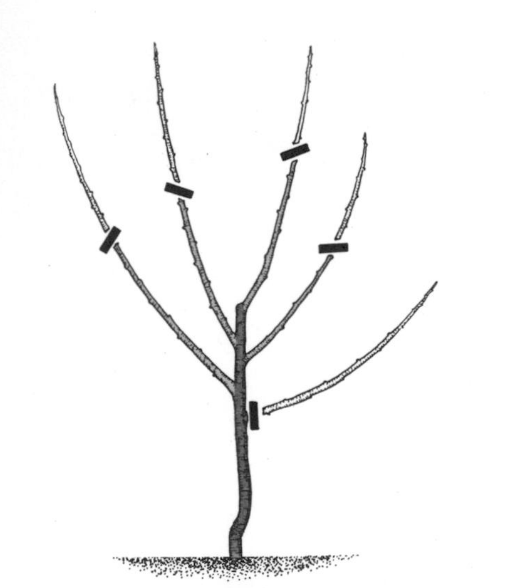

3 November to February. Select four of the primary branches that have formed wide angles to the stem. Cut back vigorous ones by one-half and less vigorous ones by two-thirds. Prune to outward-pointing buds. Remove unwanted branches.

4 October. At the end of the season's growth strong secondary branches will have formed.

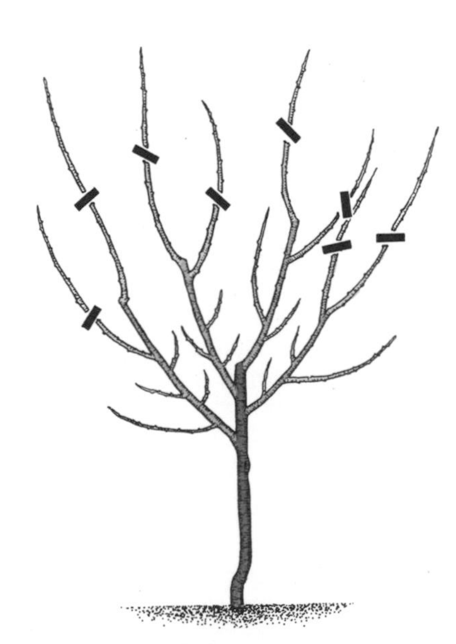

5 November to February. Select a further four well-placed new growths to form permanent branches. Cut back all leaders, shortening vigorous ones by one-half and less vigorous ones by two-thirds. Prune to outward-pointing buds.

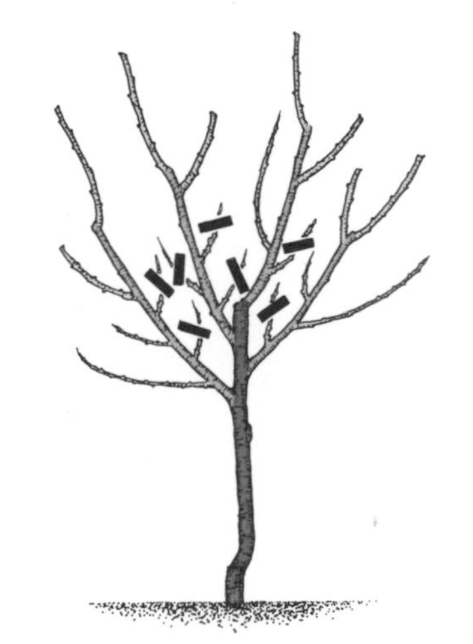

6 At the same time, prune back any laterals on the inner parts not required for secondary branches to four buds to induce spurs. Leave some laterals on the outside of the bush unpruned. Remove unwanted branches.

Bush Tree

The third year
Well-spaced leaders have been built in to form the framework of branches. Between November and February cut the stronger leaders back by one-half of the maiden extension. Weaker leaders should be pruned back by two-thirds, cutting to outward-pointing buds. The tree should now be carrying flower buds on the spurs and the unpruned laterals. Budded laterals should be cut back to prominent flower buds. Leave maiden laterals unpruned if they are on the outside of the bush. From now on the tree will be doing two jobs—increasing in size and entering the fruit-bearing stage.

Fourth and following years
The real problem lies in the pruning of the leaders after the fourth year of growth. Leader pruning is a destructive process and should be discontinued if . . .
1 the branch is strong enough
2 the leader is growing outward.
3 the branch is free from disease or breakage.
4 a sufficient number of laterals are being produced.

The essential framework of the tree has now been formed and the fruiting stage will begin. To this end prune back laterals on the inner parts to four buds to induce spurs. Leave laterals on the outside unpruned.

The third year

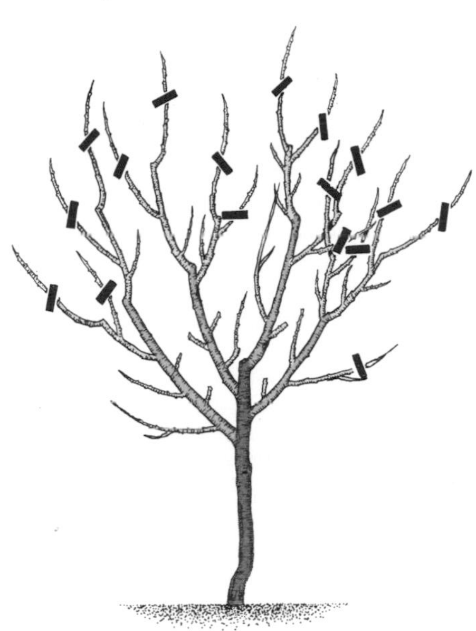

7 November to February. Cut back the vigorous leaders by one-half and the less vigorous ones by two-thirds. Cut to outward-pointing buds.

8 At the same time, prune back laterals on the inside to four buds. Leave laterals on the outside of the bush unpruned.

Fourth and following years

9 November to February. The branch framework has now been formed and leader pruning can cease, unless growth is weak. Leave laterals on the outer parts of the tree unpruned. Cut back laterals on the inside to 4in.

STANDARDS

Gardeners are sometimes puzzled by the use of the terms half-standard and standard. These terms only indicate bushes that have longer legs and larger spreads. A typical open-center bush tree has a clear 20in stem from ground level to the first permanent branch, a half-standard has a leg of approximately 4ft, and a full standard one of 6ft. Half-standards are traditionally used for plums, full standards for sweet cherries.

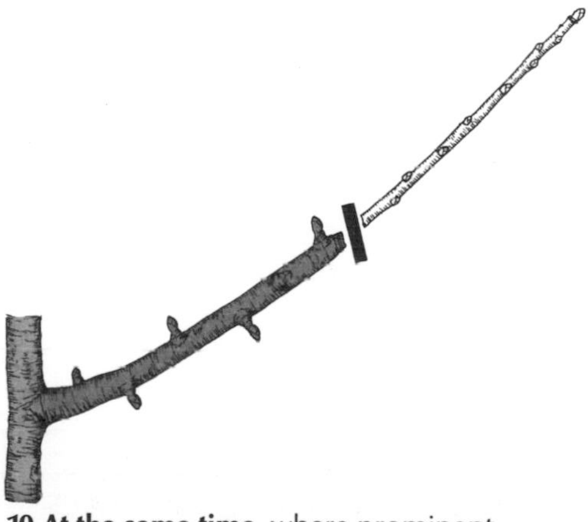

10 At the same time, where prominent flower buds have already formed on well-placed unpruned laterals, cut back the unit to the topmost flower bud.

Cordon

The great beauty of the cordon form is that the trees can be planted closely together and can be kept compact and close enough to the ground to facilitate easy management. This offers the gardener the opportunity to grow a wide choice of varieties. But cordon growing is not always successful and the fault often lies in the lack of understanding concerning training and pruning. Any attempt to work against nature involves a constant challenge, and the closely confined cordon is one of the most unnatural forms that has been devised.

It is necessary to control vigor and keep the trees within arms' reach so cordons are usually planted at an angle of 45 degrees. There is no rule that all cordons must be planted at an angle, nor to confine them to a single stem. They can be grown vertically or as double or triple cordons. However, apples and pears are usually grown as oblique single cordons.

To support the inclined cordon it is necessary to provide a post and wire fence. Bamboo or similar canes are secured to the wires at the required angle and the trees are tied to the canes not the wire. Begin with planting an unpruned maiden tree of apple or pear. It is not wise to plant older trees, and on no account permit the nurseryman to prune the maiden for you in advance. The presence of side-shoots (feathers) is a definite advantage, providing that the tree is a genuine one-year-old specimen.

The first year

In winter, preferably November, plant the unpruned maiden tree against the wire support, and tie it to the cane. Keep the union on the upper surface to reduce the risk of breakage. Do not prune the leader, but prune back any laterals to four buds.

Pruning the leader stimulates the production of vigorous laterals immediately behind the cut, and excessive and uneven vigor in cordons is to be avoided. That apart, the desired direction of the central stem of the cordon may also be lost by pruning, and there is a tendency for a length of bare, unfurnished stem to occur as a result of the vigor of the new extension leader, which grows from the uppermost bud.

Throughout the first summer no pruning is undertaken. At the end of the year the result of doing nothing often transforms the wood buds on the maiden to flower buds. Some buds may produce laterals; much depends on the choice of rootstock. Malling 9, for example, tends to form flower buds, while the more vigorous rootstocks tend to produce laterals. Do not prune the leader but shorten any laterals to four buds and sublaterals to 1in or one to two buds.

Second and following years

It is not unusual to pick a few apples from cordon trees in the second year. But do not be greedy at the expense of the long-term welfare of the trees. If the trees are not growing well, early fruiting should not be allowed. Premature flowers are best cut off as they appear, taking care to leave the rosette of leaves intact. After the second year do not remove flowers otherwise you will not obtain any fruit. The tree must be secured to the cane as it extends to maintain the required angle of 45 degrees.

Summer pruning

Begin the summer pruning of laterals. The advantages obtained from summer pruning include the stimulation of flower bud formation close to the main stem and the checking of excessive vigor. Larger fruits that are better colored and are more durable are an added bonus.

The technique is simple. From mid-July onward any laterals not required for further extensions are shortened to three good leaves from the base, ignoring the basal cluster. Sublaterals growing from existing side-shoots, should be treated more severely and cut back to 1in.

The first year

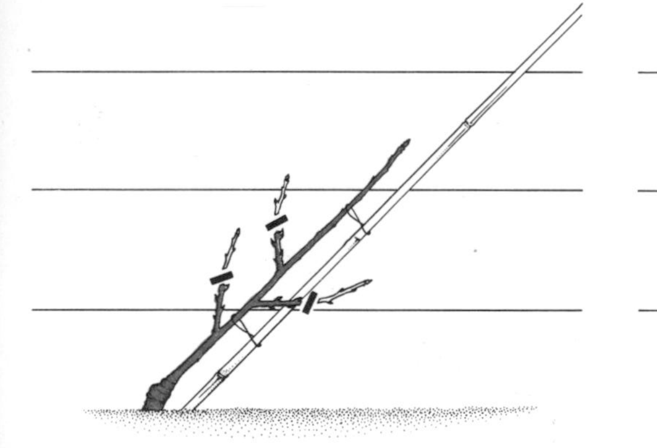

1 November to February. Plant the maiden tree, with the union uppermost, against a cane secured to wire supports at about 45 degrees. Do not prune the leader. Cut back any feathers to four buds.

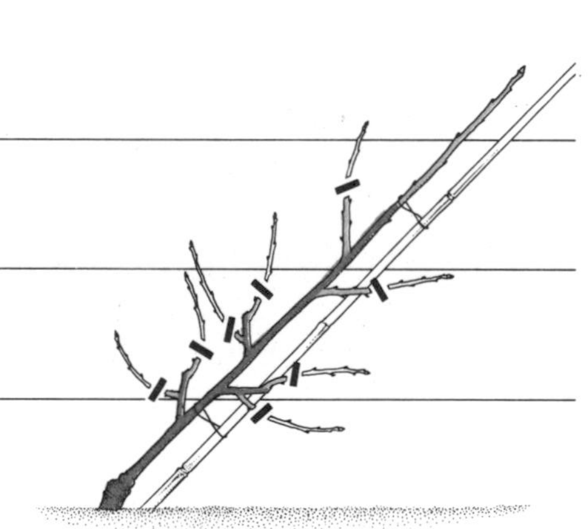

2 November. At the end of the first growing season do not prune the leader. Cut back any laterals to four buds, and sublaterals to 1in or one to two buds.

Second and following years

3 Spring. In the second year remove premature flowers as they appear, leaving the basal rosette of leaves intact.

4 Mid-July to September. Cut back laterals to three good leaves from the base, ignoring the basal cluster. Cut back sublaterals to 1in or 1–2 buds.

Cordon

At the end of the year flower buds should be apparent and fruiting can be allowed, assuming the tree is growing well. No leader pruning is undertaken, but laterals that have not been pruned in summer should be cut back to four buds. Laterals that were pruned in a previous year should now have produced obvious flower buds at the base. If so, cut back the whole unit to the uppermost flower bud. This encourages the formation of fruiting spurs (see page 55).

If a good flower bud does not form in the year following the pruning of a lateral to four buds, you should cut back the subsequent sublaterals to 1in. It is another year before prominent flower buds show. From now on this pruning program should be continued each year.

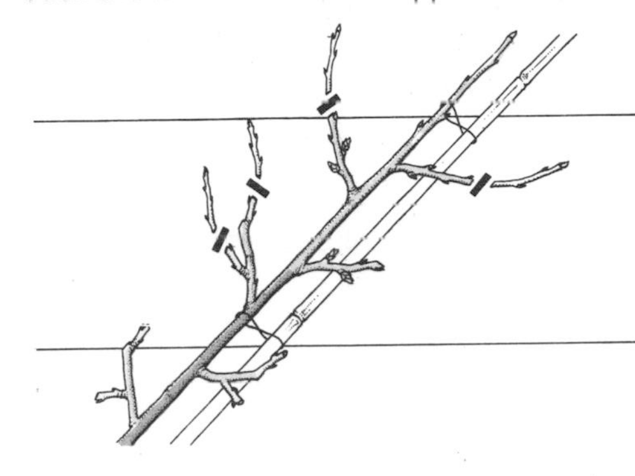

5 November to February. Do not prune the leader. No lateral pruning is required if the strong shoots were pruned in the summer as suggested. If summer pruning has not been done cut the laterals now to four buds and the sublaterals to 1in.

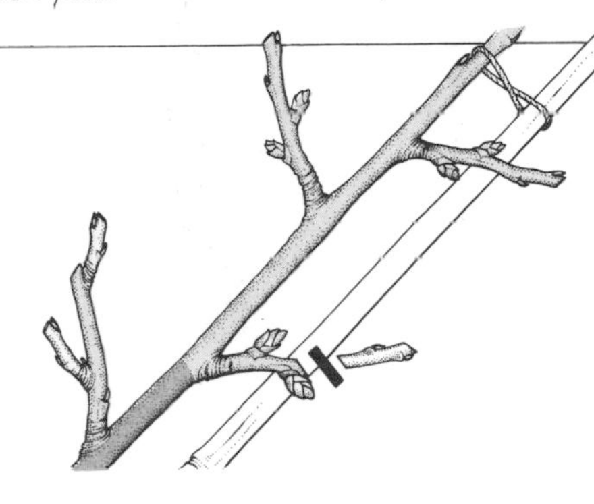

6 At the same time, to encourage the formation of fruiting spurs, cut back any summer-pruned laterals and sublaterals to the uppermost flower bud. If no flower buds have been produced cut back sublaterals to within 1in of the stem.

The fruiting cordon

1 May. When the leader has passed the top wire—about 7ft—cut back the maiden extension wood to its origin.

2 Mid-July. Cut back strong laterals to three good leaves from the base (ignoring the basal cluster). Cut back sublaterals to 1in. Cut back the leader to 1in if it was pruned the previous May.

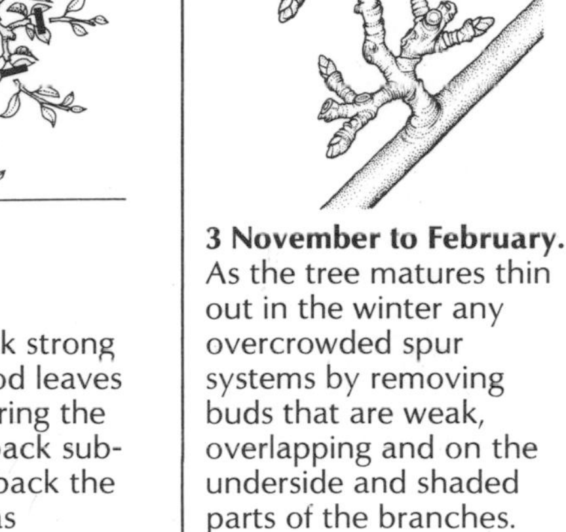

3 November to February. As the tree matures thin out in the winter any overcrowded spur systems by removing buds that are weak, overlapping and on the underside and shaded parts of the branches.

MULTIPLE CORDONS

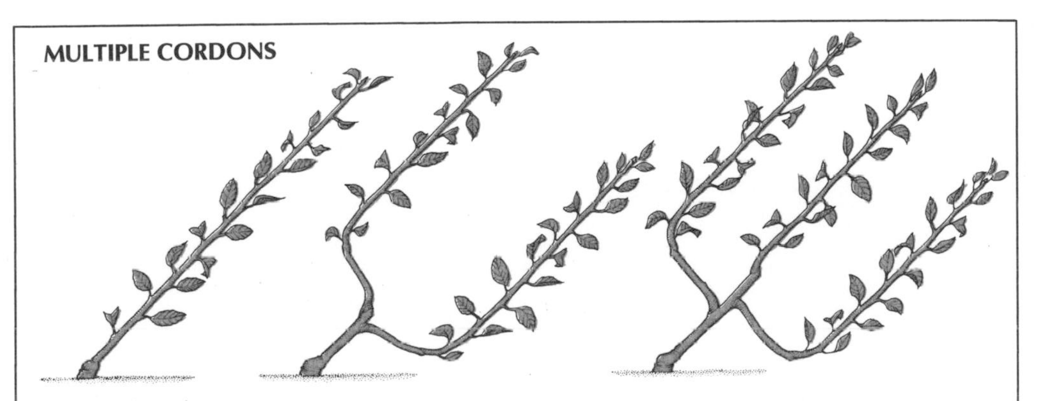

Cordons may also be formed with two, three or more arms, trained either vertically or at an angle. The training of a multiple cordon is initially similar to the formation of the first horizontal arms of an espalier. Thereafter each stem of the multiple cordon is treated as a single cordon. Vertically trained cordons are generally more vigorous and often less fruitful than those trained obliquely at an angle of about 45 degrees. The angle can be reduced further (see overvigorous cordons).

THE OVERVIGOROUS CORDON

If the mature cordon continues to grow vigorously, then the solution may be to reduce the angle of stem inclination further. This will bring the bearing parts nearer to the ground. Untying and retying is a time-consuming job but is rewarding. A new cane should be tied to the wires at an angle of about 30 to 35 degrees from the ground. The whole cordon should then be untied and secured to the new cane, taking care to retain a straight line. Lower the cordon very carefully to avoid damaging or breaking the stem. Lowering the angle will slow down the movement of sap and limit extension growth while encouraging fruit bud production. Finally, if the mature tree is still excessively vigorous, do not hesitate to bark-ring (see page 65).

don't cut out extra side br - head to 3 buds -> spurs
init. tie @ 45° - up for > vigor, down if too vig

Espalier

Strickly speaking, an espalier is a tree trained on a latticework or fence. But in common usage it has come to mean a tree form that consists essentially of a central stem from which horizontal fruiting arms are taken at about 15 in intervals, the tree being trained in one plane.

Espalier trees are often planted to form boundaries between such parts of the garden as the vegetable plot and the fruit garden, or against paths or to cover walls or fences. The shelter provided by a wall is highly beneficial to the growing of the choice varieties of pear.

The early training of an espalier calls for skill and for the enthusiast there is much pleasure to be had from building up an espalier from the beginning.

The first year

Plant an unfeathered maiden tree in the dormant season between November and February. Cut back the stem to within 15 in of ground level, making sure that room for a short leg is left, together with three good topmost buds. The two lower ones should point in opposite directions.

In spring, carefully direct the shoot from the top bud vertically and the others to the right and the left. It is difficult to obtain horizontal shoots in the first year without a check to growth and it is best to train the two branch shoots initially at angles of about 45 degrees to the main stem. This can be achieved by tying them to canes secured to the wires.

During summer the angle can be varied so that any weaker shoot is encouraged to catch up by raising it a little to the vertical.

In November, at the end of the first growing season, lower the two side branches to the horizontal and tie them to the wire and cane supports. Prune back the central leader to within 18 in of the junction with the lower arms. The intention is to further promote the three growths—one to continue the central axis and the other two to form a second tier of side branches. Shorten surplus laterals from the main stem to three buds. Prune the two horizontal leaders to downward-pointing buds, removing about one-third of each shoot. If growth has been particularly satisfactory, perhaps because of a good growing season, the leaders can be left unpruned.

The first year

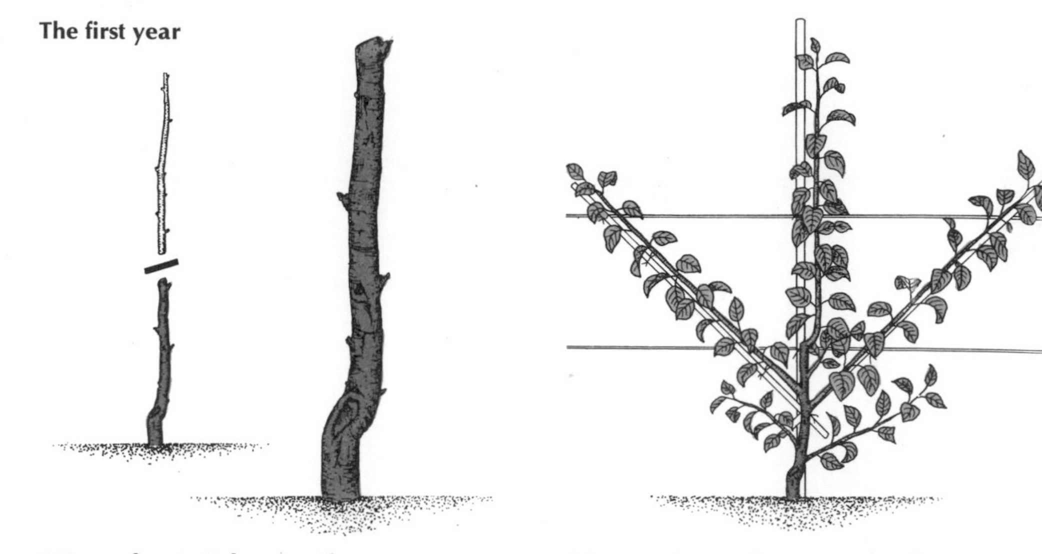

1 November to February. Plant an unfeathered maiden tree. Cut back the stem to within 15 in of ground level. Leave room for a short leg and select three good upper buds, the lower two buds pointing in opposite directions.

2 June to September. Train the shoot from the top bud vertically. Train the shoots from the two lower buds at an angle of 45 degrees to the main stem. Tie them to canes fixed on the wire support.

3 November. At the end of the growing season lower the two side branches to the horizontal and tie them carefully to the wire supports.

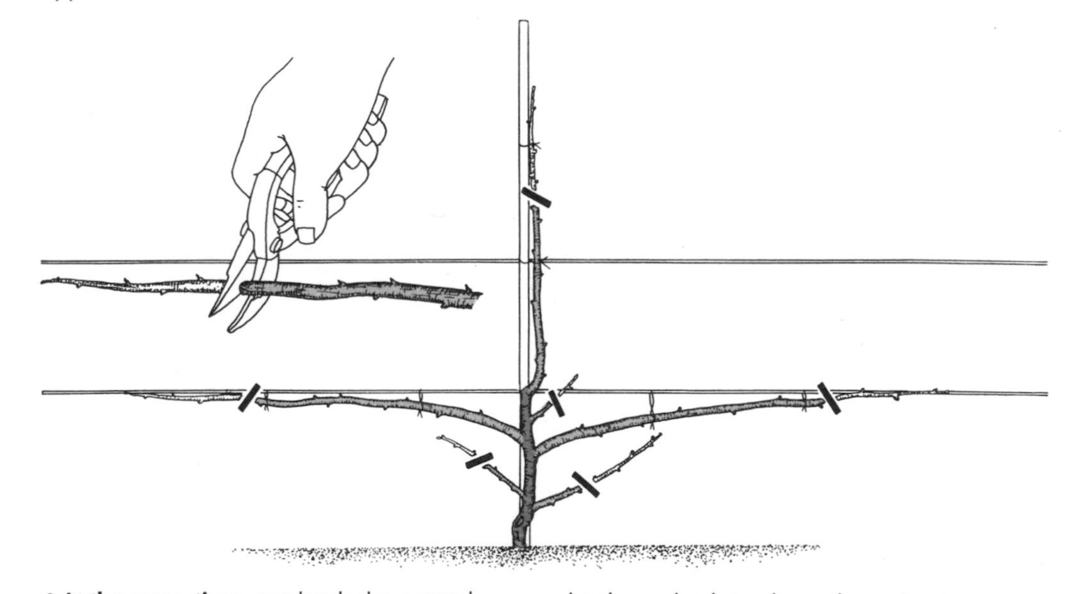

4 At the same time, cut back the central leader to within 18 in of the lower arm, leaving three good buds to form the central leader and two new horizontal arms. Cut back surplus laterals on the main stem to three buds. Prune back the horizontal leaders by one-third, cutting to downward-pointing buds.

Espalier

Second and subsequent years
The next years are a repetition of the first year. As the espalier grows tiers of branches are trained in. In November lower the side branches to the horizontal and secure them to the wire supports. Cut back the central leader to within 18 in of the last tier of arms. Cut back unwanted laterals from the main stem to three buds. The horizontal leaders should be cut back by one-third, cutting to downward-pointing buds.

Cut back competing growths from the main stem to three leaves during the summer. There is a tendency for vertical shoots to grow from the horizontal arms. These laterals are pruned in summer, cutting each back to three leaves above the basal cluster. In November train and prune both the horizontal and vertical leaders in the same way as before. This program of winter and summer pruning should continue until the desired number of tiers has been built in.

The number of tiers finally achieved depends on soil, site and inherent vigor, but four or five is usual. Eventually both the central axis and the horizontal arms fill the allotted space. After this is achieved, cut back the new terminal shoots to their origin each May and in summer prune the subsequent growth.

The fruiting stage
The fruits are carried on spur systems on the horizontal arms. The spurs are formed by the summer pruning of laterals and the cutting back of units to prominent flower buds as they appear (see page 55). Any excessively vigorous shoots are best removed completely. Left alone they are unfruitful, dominant, and competitive, reducing the fruiting potential of the tree.

After a few years of fruiting the spur systems may become overcomplicated and should be simplified by removing clusters of weak buds and those in shaded areas or those on the underside of the main branches.

Second and subsequent years

5 July to September. Train the second tier of branches in the same way as in the previous years (see caption 2). Cut back competing growths from the main stem to three leaves. Cut back laterals from the horizontal arms to three leaves above the basal cluster.

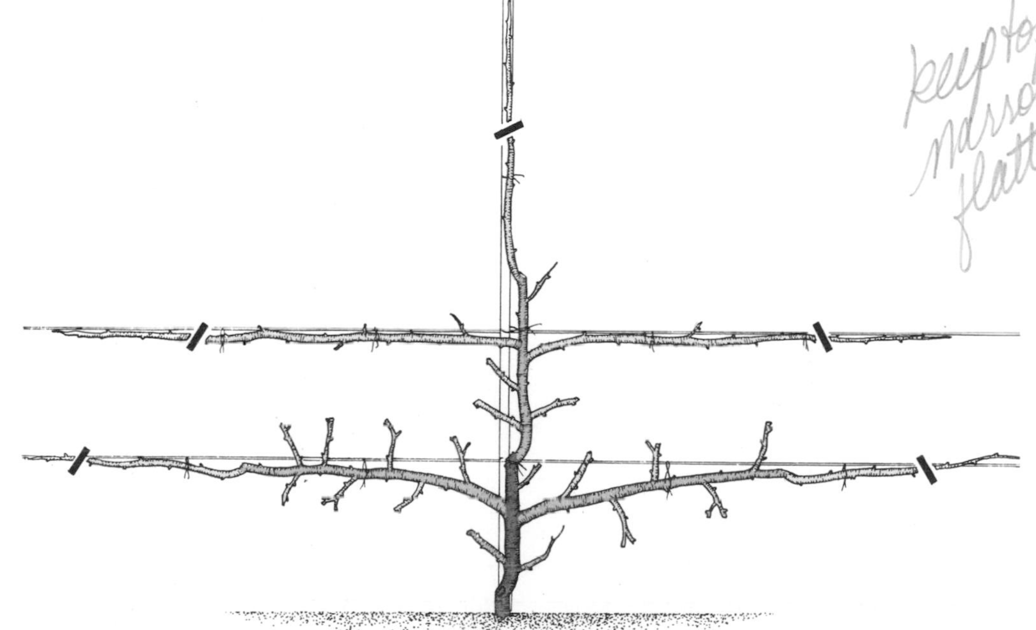

6 November. Cut back the central leader to within 18 in of the lower arm, leaving three good buds to form the new central leader and two new horizontal arms. Cut back surplus laterals on the main stem to three buds. Prune back all of the horizontal leaders by one-third, cutting back to downward-pointing buds as before.

Mature tree

7 May. When the final number of tiers is produced and the tree has filled its allotted space, cut back the new terminal growths of the vertical and horizontal arms to their origins. From now on prune them each summer as if they were laterals.

Dwarf Pyramid

The dwarf pyramid was evolved by commercial fruit growers as an easy method of producing apples and pears in a small area. The pear, in particular, when grown on Quince rootstock, responds well to this method of training, and in recent years the technique has been extended to plums (see page 68). With apples and pears the aim is to produce a central-leader tree some 7ft high with a total branch spread of about 3ft through the tree, tapering to the top.

It is essential to keep such a closely planted and compact tree under control. This control is exerted by a combination of summer pruning, early cropping, the complete removal of any vigorous upright shoots, and the choice of a rootstock capable of sustaining the balance between steady cropping and the renewal of bearing wood that is required. M9 and M26 rootstocks are suitable for apples in most gardens and either Quince A, or the re-cloned Quince C, when it becomes generally available, can be used for pears. A related form, the spindle-bush, has been developed in Europe, but has not as yet superseded the dwarf pyramid as a tree for the home gardener.

The first year

A start is made with a maiden tree, which is cut back to about 20in on planting during the dormant season from November to February. Prune to a bud on the opposite side to the graft. The result of this initial pruning is the production of four or five strong shoots. The uppermost shoot grows vertically. No pruning is necessary during the first summer.

At the end of the first season prune the central leader to leave about 9in of new growth, taking care to cut to a bud that points in the opposite direction to the last pruning. This is aimed at keeping the successive stages of the central stem as straight as possible, in a series of zig-zags. It would be easier not to prune the leader at all since the stem is straighter if it is left untouched, but the pruning is necessary to stimulate the annual production of side branches during the formative stages. These side branches, perhaps four in number and evenly spaced around the tree, are pruned back to within 8in of the maiden extension, cutting each to a downward- or outward-pointing bud to maintain the horizontal direction of the branches.

The first year

1 November to February. At planting cut back the maiden to a bud within 20in of ground level.

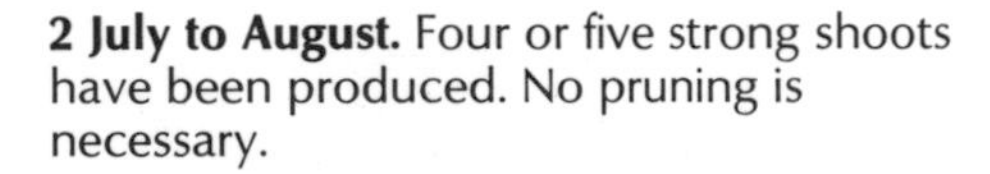

2 July to August. Four or five strong shoots have been produced. No pruning is necessary.

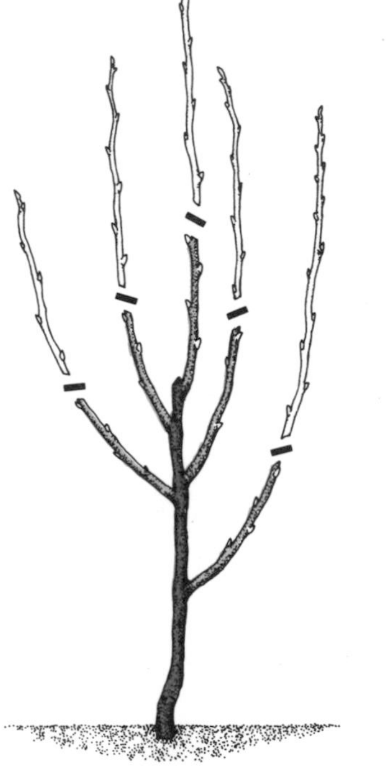

3 November to February. Cut back the central leader to leave 9in of new growth. Cut to a bud that points in the opposite direction to the last pruning. Cut back side branches to downward-pointing buds to leave 8in of the maiden extension.

The second year

4 July to August. Cut back laterals not required for the framework to three leaves or 3–4in and sublaterals to one leaf beyond the basal cluster. Leave leaders unpruned.

Dwarf Pyramid

The second year

During the second year of growth begin summer pruning. Cut back each lateral that is not required for the framework to three leaves and the sublaterals to one leaf beyond the basal cluster. This work can begin in early July for pears and about two weeks later for apples, and it should be continued throughout the summer when the shoots reach a length of 9in. Prune the central leader in winter, to leave about 9in of new growth.

Third and following years

In the third and following years pruning follows the same pattern. To stimulate new growth, shorten the central leader each winter. Take care to keep each growth vertical, by cutting to a bud on the opposite side to the previous pruning. When the tree reaches the desired height cut back the leader to its origin each May. Branch leaders should be summer pruned as laterals once they attain a total length of 18in.

Prune the laterals and sublaterals throughout the summer. Remove vigorous upright shoots completely. It occasionally means shortening branches to a downward-pointing shoot in an attempt to maintain the horizontal position of the fruiting arms. This is best undertaken in the winter. Any necessary spur thinning can be done at the same time. Take care to prevent the top portions from dominating the tree—the pyramid shape must be maintained.

Third and following years

5 November to February. Prune the central leader to leave about 9in of new growth, cutting to a bud on the opposite side to the previous pruning, so that a straight central stem is maintained. Cut back new side branches to 8in.

6 July to August. Throughout summer cut back laterals to three leaves or 3–4in and sublaterals to one leaf beyond the basal cluster. Leave the leader unpruned.

7 November to February. Prune the central leader to leave 9in of new growth. Remove overvigorous shoots entirely. Shorten branches to downward-pointing buds as necessary to maintain the horizontal position of the fruiting arms.

THE MATURE TREE

When the tree has reached the desired height of about 7ft, further extension growth should be stopped by cutting back the leader to its origin each May. Thin fruiting spurs as necessary (see page 55). Maintain the central stem throughout and retain the pyramid shape by close pruning and the removal of any upright or overvigorous shoots.

Renovation

Sometimes the gardener is confronted with trees that have become barren through neglect, but frequently the problem is one of old age. Apple and pear trees can survive to great ages, but not necessarily in a healthy state. As a general rule, to which of course there are exceptions, trees over 30 years of age are best taken out completely.

Often the problem centers on disease, in both young and old trees. Some diseases, such as scab and mildew, can be cured, and aphids, caterpillars, mites and other similar pests can be dealt with by modern pesticides. But diseases such as silver leaf, severe canker and collar-rot are often incurable and trees affected are best removed and burned. Usually the trouble is a twofold one—lack of pruning and the absence of fertilizing.

Trees left unpruned may produce a profusion of flowers but the fruit, if any, is likely to be small and affected by pests and diseases. The points just made must be stressed even in a pruning manual, because no amount of skilled pruning will restore a starved and pest-ridden tree, that has been neglected for too long, to health and fruitfulness.

The first thing to put right is the level of nutrition. This is accomplished by the removal of competing weeds and other vegetation, and the lavish application of moisture-retaining manures and appropriate nutrient-providing fertilizers.

The rootstock must also be considered. Sometimes soil has been heaped around the base of the tree and the union buried, resulting in scion rooting. This is particularly serious with pears on Quince rootstock. If inspection indicates no sign of the union above ground level, and the tree is in a barren condition, bark-ringing will be necessary (see page 65).

More frequently the opposite state occurs: the trees are stunted and lacking in vigor. In addition to manuring and the removal of weeds, it will probably be necessary to stake and tie each tree to prevent constant root damage during high winds.

The overvigorous tree

Pruning is a major contribution to renovation. It is important to consider the state of excess vigor, apart from the possibility of scion rooting, because a tree may be neglected by being subjected to oversevere pruning. Such a butchered tree is out of balance and over-vegetative. The remedy is to thin out crossing, broken, diseased and overcrowded branches, but to leave untouched the branches that are healthy and well placed. The unpruned branches may well settle down to form flower buds and resume a fruitful career in two or three years. Branches should be removed cleanly, without snags, and large wounds painted over to prevent the entry of disease and to promote natural healing. Renovation of the kind indicated is best spread over more than one year to avoid further unbalancing shocks.

Winter pruning stimulates growth, but summer pruning checks it and, assuming that the height of the tree makes the procedure sensible, the shortening of unwanted laterals from July through the summer is a great help.

Another way to remedy the overvigorous tree is to take advantage of the fact that shoots growing horizontally are fruitful and shoots growing vertically tend to be unfruitful. Horizontally inclined branches and shoots should therefore be encouraged. Tie down young upright shoots or loop one over another to form arches. This system is much better than wholesale cutting back, which merely perpetuates the problem.

The stunted tree

The other extreme—the stunted tree—is obviously best remedied in the first place by the measures involving staking and the removal of competition for water and nutrients mentioned earlier. There is usually very little new wood to prune, but the thinning of spurs and the severe shortening of any maiden wood, coupled with the necessary soil husbandry, will stimulate growth.

It is often desirable to reduce the quantity of fruit to small proportions, or to remove it all together, as it sets, for a year or two to relieve the tree of the strain of reproduction. Fruit from a really starved and neglected tree is not worth having anyway.

Once a balance has been restored between growth and flower bud formation it should be maintained by sensible pruning, in combination with correct management of the soil and adequate control of pests and diseases.

A case for the bonfire. Old age, neglect and indifferent pruning have left only unfruitful vertical growths.

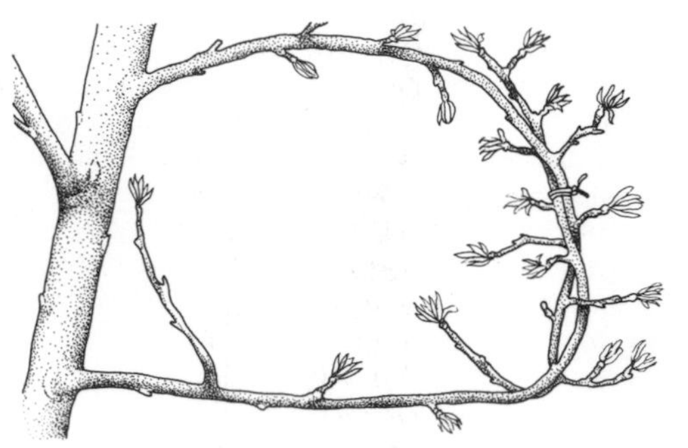

Vigorous pear laterals in flower in the second year after they have been tied down and arched.

The overvigorous tree

Left unattended, this tree has become overcrowded and unproductive.

Over two winters the crossing branches must be removed and fruitful horizontal growth encouraged.

The stunted tree

Poor growth caused by malnutrition and competition from weeds.

The weeds have been cleared, avoiding deep digging. The tree is staked and tied and a thick mulch is applied. Fertilizers and water are used to stimulate growth.

Root-pruning and Bark-ringing

Root-pruning

It seems odd to talk about the pruning of roots as well as shoots, but very occasionally gardeners resort to this ancient technique to check excessive growth of branches, particularly with plums and wall-trained figs.

If the overvigorous tree is young—say up to five years old—the best plan is to transplant it, merely digging it up and putting it back in the sam or a more suitable site will disrupt the root system. The deep and wide-ranging roots are naturally cut during the transplanting. With older trees, take out a trench around the tree some 5ft from the trunk. Prune the thick roots as they are exposed, and preserve the thin fibrous ones. Refill the trench without undue delay.

Bark-ringing

The same result, however, can be achieved with apples and pears in a much simpler manner, by an exercise in plant physiology known as bark-ringing.

If a ring of bark, $\frac{1}{4}$in wide, is removed from the trunk in May then the downward passage of sugars and similar foodstuffs to the roots is temporarily interrupted. The roots are checked and growth slows down. Bark-ringing should be used only on very vigorous trees, but can be repeated as often as necessary.

Remove the soft outer tissues down to the wood, using a sharp knife. The wound must be protected immediately by wrapping round a double layer of car masking tape, adhesive tape or similar material. The tape excludes air, pests and disease and allows the necessary healing process to take place. For ease of mind it is best to leave 1in of bark untouched, so that the ring is not quite complete.

It really is much easier to choose the correct rootstock in the first place, but the overvigorous, unfruitful tree can often be brought into bearing by bark-ringing, reduced manuring and minimum pruning.

Bark-ringing should not be used for plums, cherries and other stone fruits and is best confined to apples and pears.

Both root-pruning and bark-ringing are admissions of failure to choose the correct rootstock, or to manure or prune in the right way, and in a well-tended garden should be regarded as last resorts.

Root-pruning

1 Spring. Mark out and dig a trench around the tree some 5ft from the trunk.

2 Fold back the fibrous roots to expose the thicker woody roots. Cut back the thicker roots with a pruning saw.

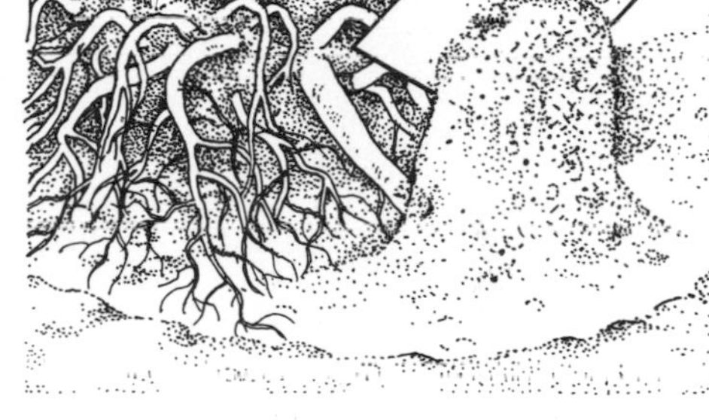

3 Retain the thinner, fibrous roots and spread them back into the trench. Cover with soil and firm the ground.

Bark-ringing

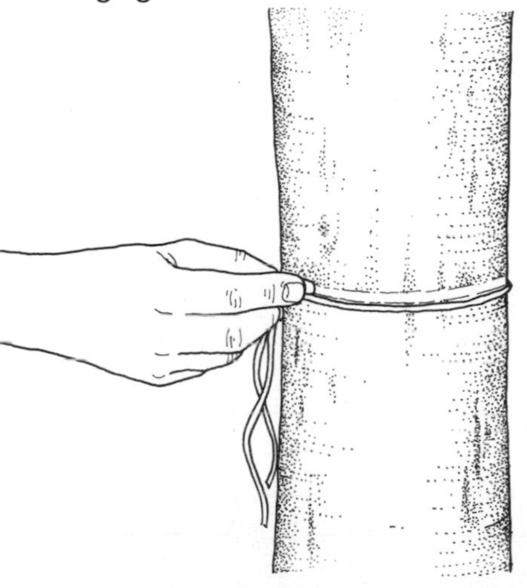

1 May. Mark out a ring $\frac{1}{4}$in wide on the main trunk of the tree.

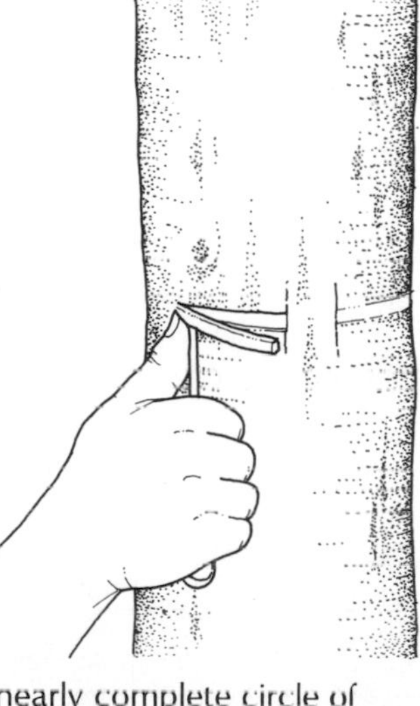

2 Remove a nearly complete circle of bark using a sharp knife. Leave 1in of the ring untouched.

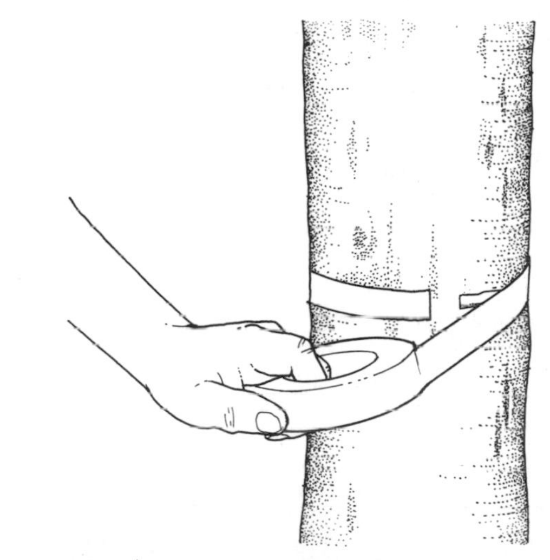

3 Cover the wound immediately with two overlapping circles of adhesive tape. Apply a smear of Vaseline to the edges of the tape to exclude air.

Sweet Cherries leaders to ½ out lat.
March

Bush Tree

The pruning of damsons can be quickly dismissed by saying that they are treated as plums, but less severely. Damsons thrive under a regime of gentle neglect not suitable for the more refined plums and gages. Gages are merely dessert plums and should receive the same pruning as other plums.

Plums are not more successful in gardens because they flower early and they are liable to spring frost damage, there is, at present, a lack of suitable rootstocks, and because they are susceptible to bird damage and silver leaf. The last three problems are directly linked to training and pruning, as is the first problem because if a suitable rootstock was available it would be possible to produce smaller trees which might not be quite so vulnerable to the worst hazards of spring frost.

Plum trees tend to be large trees difficult to manage. Recent research has resulted in the selection of a form of rootstock on which plums can be grown and kept reasonably compact. This rootstock is called St Julien A. Another dwarfing rootstock of particular promise has been issued under the name of Pixy, and this may be what gardeners have been looking for. If you can acquire trees on either St Julien A or Pixy for your new plantings, then use these in preference to the commonly employed Brompton and Myrobalan B rootstocks, which produce trees too large for most home gardens. The following notes, however, assume that most plums are still grown on older rootstocks.

Many varieties of plum possess slender branches which tend to weep. To keep the branches off the ground it is necessary to start the head on a long half-standard leg of about 4 ft.

It is a great pity, but many species of birds feed voraciously most winters on the fruit buds of plum trees, reducing the crop considerably and causing lengths of bare wood to puzzle the pruner. It is not within the scope of this book to discuss the prevention of damage, but it is important that gardeners should realize why there is so much bare wood and so little blossom on their plum trees when spring arrives.

Silver leaf is a killing disease caused by a fungus which lives inside the tree. The fungus gains entry to the tree through wounds, but entry is much less likely in the summer months. Two important points are clear. Try to avoid wounds and prune plum trees in summer.

Build up the young tree so that branch breakages and removals are minimal. Avoid large wounds if possible but treat any unavoidable large cuts with a sealing and antiseptic paint. Reduce pruning to a minimum once the young tree has formed and attempt to confine the pruning of fruiting trees to June, July and August.

The first year

Plant a maiden in the dormant season, from November to February. Stake and tie, using a double stake and cross-bar. Cut back the maiden to about 5 ft from ground level to just above a bud. Plums can be planted successfully as two- or three-year-old trees on which the head has already been formed, but such trees are more expensive and the risk of growth being checked on planting is greater.

Some four or five strong primary branches should appear during the summer following planting. It is very important that these branches should form wide angles with the main stem, be evenly spaced, and grow in the desired directions. It is essential to build-in these strong, well-placed, permanent branches, to avoid breakages and the necessity for branch pruning as the tree gets older.

The second year

Pruning can take place during winter but it is best to wait until March, when the healing of the wounds is that much quicker. Select four permanent branches, if possible, and prune back each by one-half to two-thirds of the maiden growth. Cut to an outward-pointing bud. During the growing season shoots may spring from the stem below the lowest permanent branch. These laterals should be pruned back to about 3 in. They are only temporary and are left solely to assist in the thickening of the main trunk. After the second growing season they may be removed completely. Growths from below ground—suckers—come from the rootstock and should be removed as soon as they appear by cutting at their origin rather than at ground level.

The first year

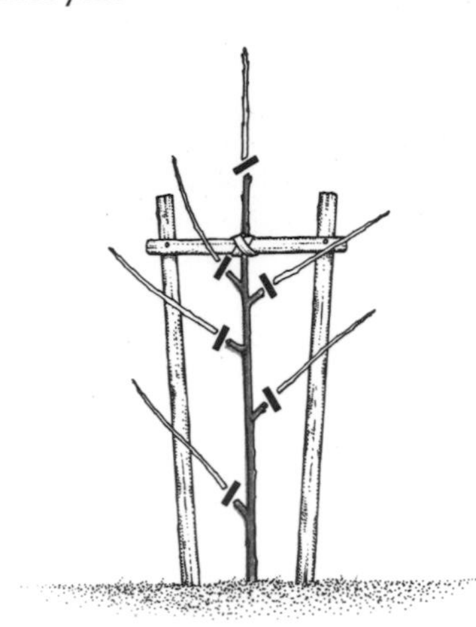

1 November to February. Plant, stake and tie the maiden tree. Cut back to 5 ft from the ground. Shorten all laterals to about 3 in.

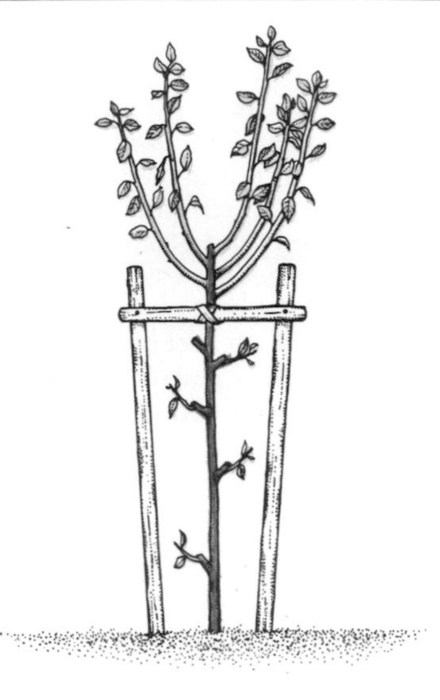

2 July to August. Four or five strong primary branches should develop during the summer. No pruning is required.

The second year

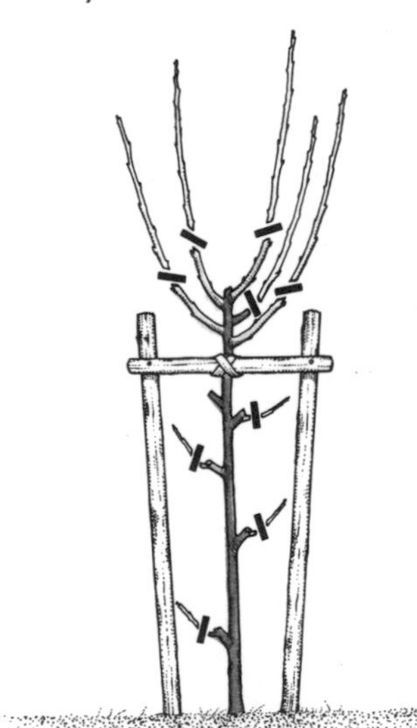

3 November to March. Select four branches that have formed wide angles with the stem. Cut back by one-half to two-thirds, to outward-pointing buds. Cut back laterals to 3 in.

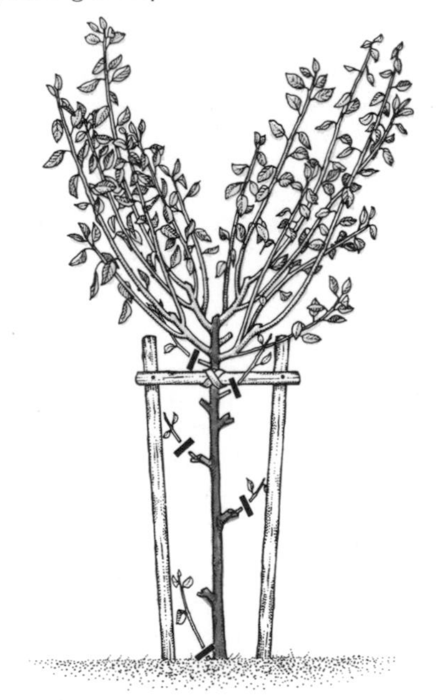

4 July to August. Cut back to 3 in laterals that appear below the first permanent branch. Remove suckers that appear from below ground level.

Bush Tree

The third year
Repeat the procedures adopted last winter, but allow more sublaterals to develop to fill the increased space, allowing up to eight strong, well-spaced and outward-growing branches. Cut these back by one-half to two-thirds of the maiden growth to outward-pointing buds. Shoots on the outer parts of the head, not required for leaders, can be left unpruned if the tree is growing freely. These unpruned laterals will form fruit buds during the following summer. Laterals on the inside of the tree should be pruned back to 3–4 in.

Mature tree
If the tree is growing well, and the branches are strong and in their correct places, leader pruning can now cease. Weaker-growing trees, and the less vigorous varieties such as 'Victoria', should be treated as outlined for the previous winter.

If all has gone well with the development of the head, under a program of careful pruning, good feeding and pest control, then the essential framework of the tree should be formed and the tree is ready for fruiting. From this stage onward the very minimum of pruning should be carried out.

Try to avoid the breakage of branches under the weight of heavy crops by providing temporary branch props or maypole ties. Every broken branch represents a severe loss and a risk of silver leaf entry. If branch removal is unavoidable then the wound must be protected immediately by painting with a proprietary wound paint.

Bird-stripped bare stretches should be removed in March. Trim back laterals on the insides to 3–4 in in summer to avoid crossing tangles. Cut out any overlapping and vigorous growths. All suckers must be removed entirely as soon as they appear. Finally, as soon as the fruit has been picked check the tree for branch breakages.

The third year

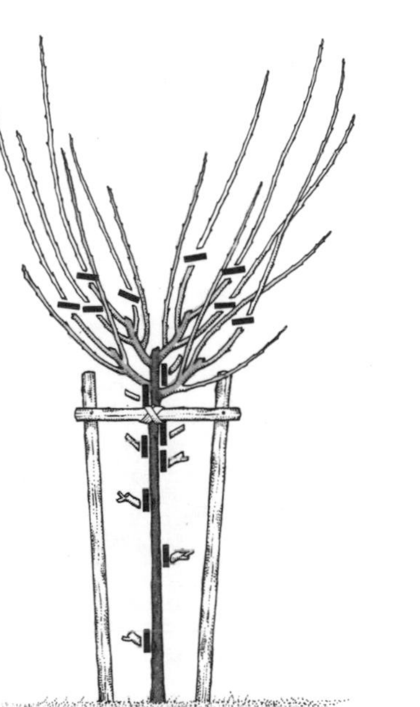

5 November to February. Select four more well-placed branches for the framework. Cut back the eight branch leaders by one-half to two-thirds to outward-pointing buds. Remove all laterals formerly reduced to 3–4 in.

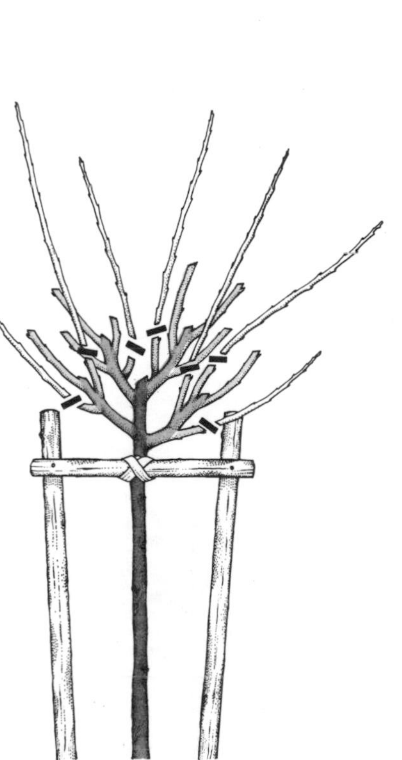

6 At the same time, cut back laterals on the inside of the bush to 3–4in. Leave laterals on the outside of the bush unpruned.

Mature tree

7 July to August. Trim back laterals on the inside of the bush to 3–4in. Cut out any vigorous and overlapping growths. Remove entirely any suckers as they appear. No other pruning is required.

inside lat to 3",

BIRD-STRIPPED BRANCHES

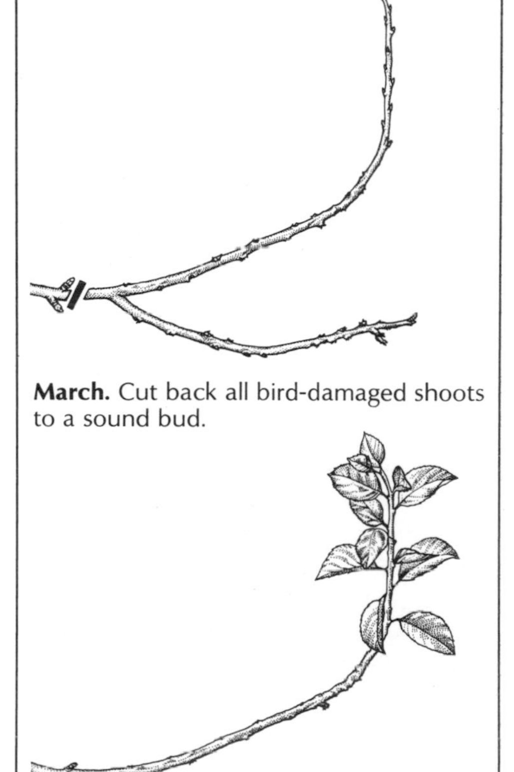

March. Cut back all bird-damaged shoots to a sound bud.

The same branch, if left until July, showing typical bird damage where growth and fruit buds have been stripped during the previous winter.

Dwarf Pyramid

Plums, and particularly gages, can also be grown as fan trees against walls. But wall space is scarce and valuable, and it is well worth growing plums as pyramids.

The first year
Choose St Julien A as the rootstock. Between November and February plant a maiden, preferably one furnished with side-shoots, or feathers, and secure the tree to a tall stake. Leave the initial pruning until March, when the maiden is cut back to a good bud about 5ft from ground level. Clean the stem of laterals up to 18in from the ground. The remainder are kept to furnish the tree, but are pruned back initially by one-half their length. During the first summer, toward the end of July, cut back all laterals that spring direct from the stem to 8in. All laterals from the original feathers should be cut back to 6in choosing a downward-pointing bud. Leave the leader unpruned.

The second year
Start the next season by shortening the central leader in March by two-thirds, cutting to a bud opposite the one from which it originated to retain a straight central leader. In July prune branch leaders to 8in and laterals to 6in, as before, again to downward-pointing buds. Entirely remove any extremely vigorous shoots. Tie down any branches that are too vigorous, using stout twine about mid-way along the branch and tied to the base of the main stem. The aim is to produce branches inclined to the horizontal.

Third and following years
Pruning is now straightforward. Build up a straight central leader in a series of zig-zags until it reaches, say, 9ft, when no further extension is permitted and summer pruning of the main leader takes over, cutting the summer-pruned leader back to base each May. Prune back the laterals to 8in in July, but if a tangle of crossing shoots occurs then they should be disentangled. The real problem, in practice, lies in the top of the tree. The gardener must be stern about this and cut back or cut out any rebellious shoot. Remember always that the intended shape is in outline a broad-based pyramid.

The first year

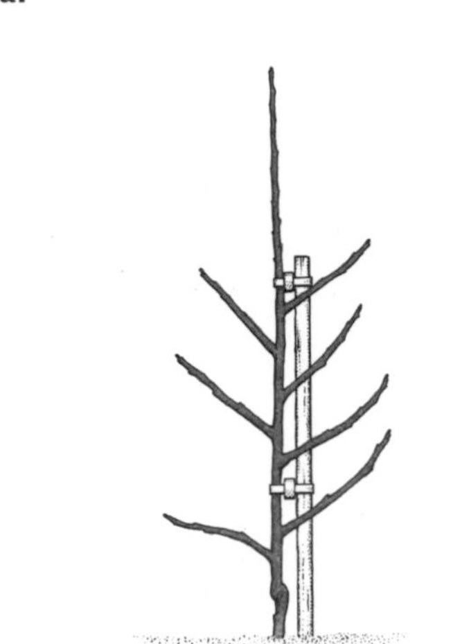

1 November to February. Plant a maiden with side-shoots. Secure the tree to a tall stake using flexible plastic tree ties.

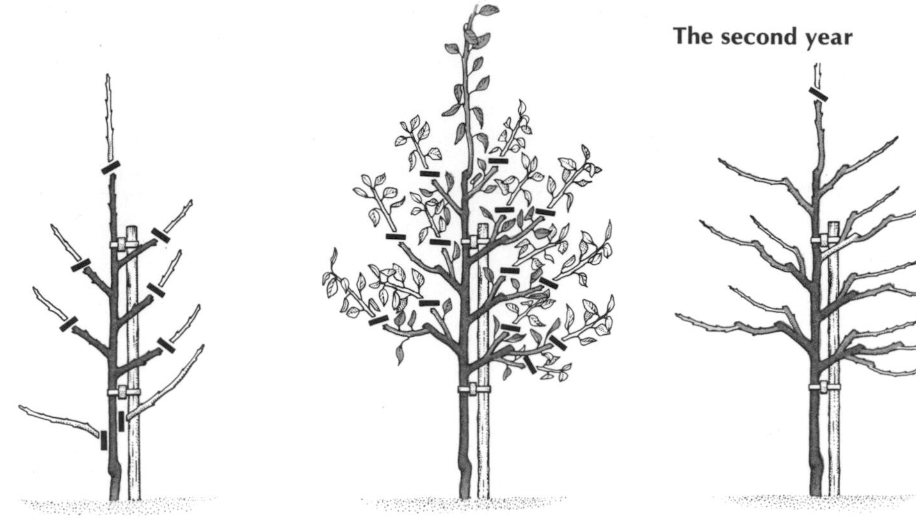

2 March. As buds break cut back the leader to 5 ft. Cut out all laterals up to 18 in from the ground. Cut back the remainder by one-half.

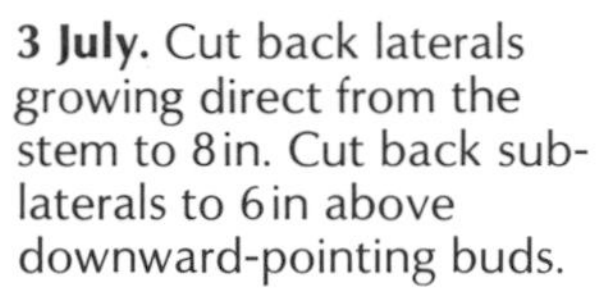

3 July. Cut back laterals growing direct from the stem to 8in. Cut back sub-laterals to 6in above downward-pointing buds.

The second year

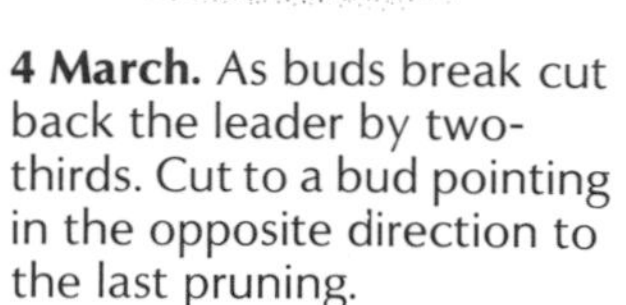

4 March. As buds break cut back the leader by two-thirds. Cut to a bud pointing in the opposite direction to the last pruning.

5 July. Cut back branch leaders to 8in and laterals to 6in to downward-pointing buds. Remove any extremely vigorous shoots. Tie down branches that are too vigorous.

Third and following years

6 March. As buds break prune the leader as before until it reaches, for example, 9 ft, when it can be cut back to base each May. Cut out any crossing laterals and broken shoots.

7 July. Cut back branch leaders to 8in and laterals to 6in. Cut out any crossing laterals. Cut out or cut back severely any vigorous shoots at the top of the tree.

Renovation

Frequently old plum trees, particularly those on vigorous rootstocks, are neglected in gardens and become unkempt and unmanageable. They do not usually take kindly to severe pruning and are even less tolerant of poor growing conditions than apples. Unfortunately they are also prone to the devastating silver leaf disease, as are all *Prunus* spp., including peaches and cherries. Any tree which is badly infected with this disease should be destroyed.

Neglected plums may respond to regular pest- and disease-control measures and to generous feeding, particularly if competing weeds are removed, but in many instances the best advice is to clear out the sick or dying tree and replace it with a young plant on a suitable dwarfing rootstock.

This is, however, a counsel of perfection and many gardeners will be reluctant to remove an old, if neglected, friend without first attempting rejuvenation.

Restoration to reasonable order can be achieved in much the same way as done for a neglected apple tree. The principles of pruning hold good in both cases. The major difference is in the time of pruning which for plums, and all other *Prunus*, is best carried out in summer, preferably between June and August when the danger of infection by silver leaf is minimal.

The aim is to return to a tree with a more or less symmetrical branch system. The diagrams have been drawn without leaves to make the pruning operation easy to follow.

The first year

Initially any large branch that upsets the balance, and any obviously awkwardly placed or crossing branches, should be removed to leave the remaining framework branches as evenly spaced as possible. After cutting off each major branch stand back and view the shape of the tree. Be careful that important framework branches are not cut out by mistake.

This first pruning will usually dispose of a great deal of twiggy growth. The next step is to cut out all dead, diseased and damaged wood while all basal suckers and the twiggy debris that often accumulates on the main stem of a neglected tree are also removed.

The remaining work consists of carefully thinning out all the overcrowded twiggy growth so that an even branchlet system with a balance of young wood and older spur systems remains. If necessary cut back overlong branches to vigorous laterals nearer the trunk, this will encourage a more compact habit.

At each stage it is essential to apply a wound paint to any cut surface.

After rejuvenation the pruned plant will need to be mulched and fed each season and pests and disease controls applied to maintain healthy, vigorous growth.

Second and following years

The season following severe pruning some vigorous shoots are likely to be produced, particularly if large branches have been removed. Sometimes these growths are suitably placed to fill a gap in the framework. If not, they should be cut out between June and August to prevent them spoiling the symmetry of the tree as they develop.

Once a neglected tree has been restored to health little pruning is required except the occasional thinning of overcrowded shoots to maintain a balance of spurs and new wood.

The first year

1 June to August. Cut out any large branches that upset the overall symmetry. Remove crossing or awkwardly placed branches so that a more or less even framework remains. Apply a wound paint to all cut surfaces.

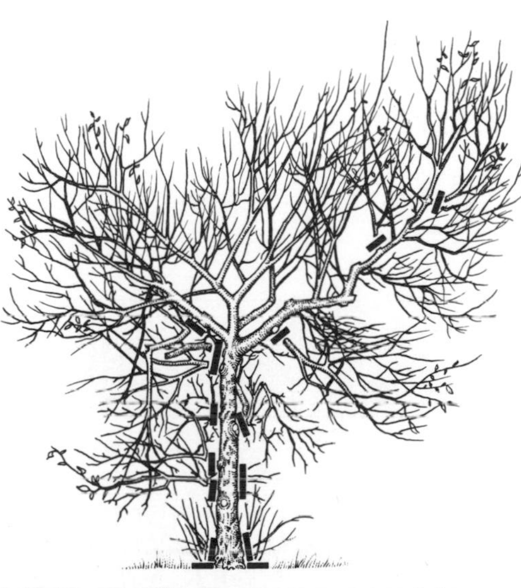

2 At the same time, cut out any remaining dead, diseased or damaged wood. Remove basal suckers and twiggy growths on the main trunk. Apply a wound paint to all cut surfaces.

3 At the same time, thin out any lateral branches and twigs where crowded growth occurs to leave a well-furnished, evenly spaced branch system. Apply a wound paint to all cut surfaces. Mulch the base of the plant well.

Second and following years

4 June to August. Remove any over-vigorous growths that threaten to spoil the overall symmetry. Thin out any remaining overcrowded branch systems. Cut out any further sucker growth and water shoots. Apply a wound paint.

Fan

Two kinds of cherry are grown for their fruit and it is important to distinguish between them because they fruit in different ways and require different pruning techniques.

The sweet cherries (and the slightly less vigorous Duke cherries) form large trees and are slow to begin cropping. They produce their fruit mainly on natural short spurs on two-year-old or older wood.

The Morello, or acid, cherries (see page 72) will begin to flower when only three or four years old and make much smaller trees. The fruit is produced on wood formed the previous season with occasionally a few trusses from spurs on older wood.

Sweet cherries cannot be recommended as trees for the small or even moderately sized garden. A single specimen will reach 40ft or so across and, although attractive flowering trees in their own right, very few gardeners have the room. Another problem is that any fruit produced will be immediately devoured by the local bird population. Yet another problem is that all sweet cherries are entirely self-sterile and to obtain fruit at all it is necessary to plant at least two compatible varieties so that cross-pollination and fertilization can be effective.

There is hope, however, that in the fairly near future a new rootstock, 'Colt,' which is relatively dwarfing, will become available to replace the present vigorous rootstock (F12/1) that is used commercially. The problem of cross-pollination still means that two or more compatible varieties will need to be planted, but at least the plants will be less robust once the new rootstock becomes available.

Standard and bush trees

Those fortunate enough to have garden room available to plant two or more sweet cherries may grow them as standard or half-standard trees or in bush form. Whatever length of clear stem is chosen it is advisable to obtain trees that have been top-worked (high-worked), with the grafts at the height where the primary branches arise. Such trees are less likely to be affected by bacterial canker which can be an extremely troublesome disease.

The training and pruning of standard or bush sweet cherries is very similar to that used for plums (see page 66). The formation of the framework of permanent branches is exactly the same and after the fourth or fifth year no further pruning of the leaders is required. A tree growing well will produce shoots 2–3ft in length and spurs with fruit buds form naturally along their length. Mature trees will require the minimum of pruning, merely the 3 D's (see page 3) plus the removal of crowded or crossing branches that inhibit free air flow through the tree. Any suckers from the rootstock should be removed cleanly and as soon as possible. Pruning should take place in summer to minimize the danger of silver leaf disease and cuts should be painted with a wound paint.

Dwarf pyramids and cordons

Sweet cherries have also been grown as dwarf pyramids and even as oblique cordons, but the vigorous rootstock ensures that constant attention to pruning is needed and after a few years they are liable to get out of hand.

Fan training

Fan-trained sweet cherries grown against a wall, however, can be maintained in the average garden but even then two compatible varieties are required and a span of 15–20ft should be allowed for each. The training is exactly the same as that given to a peach fan to form the basic framework.

As with peaches the basic pruning of fan-trained cherries should be carried out in early spring as growth begins and not in winter as is the case for apples. Sweet cherries will also grow more vigorously than peaches and three or four suitable strong shoots may form in the first year.

Hard pruning may be necessary during the first three years' formative training to establish a neat, evenly spaced framework, but thereafter the leader shoots require very light pruning after they reach to the top of the wall or support structure. They can either be cut back to a weak lateral below if a suitable shoot is available or trained horizontally along a wire if room allows. Horizontal training will slow down growth and encourage laterals to form. In due course the leader can be cut back to one of these laterals.

The first year

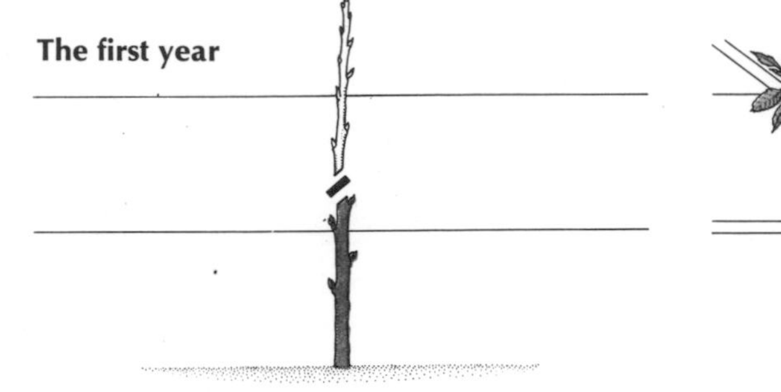

1 February to March. Plant a maiden tree. Cut back to 15in above a suitable bud.

2 May to June. Select two strong shoots close to the tip and tie them to canes set at an angle of about 45 degrees. Remove all other shoots on the main stem.

3 July to September. Tie in the developing shoots. If necessary raise the shoots to increase vigor or depress them to decrease vigor to ensure even growth.

The second year

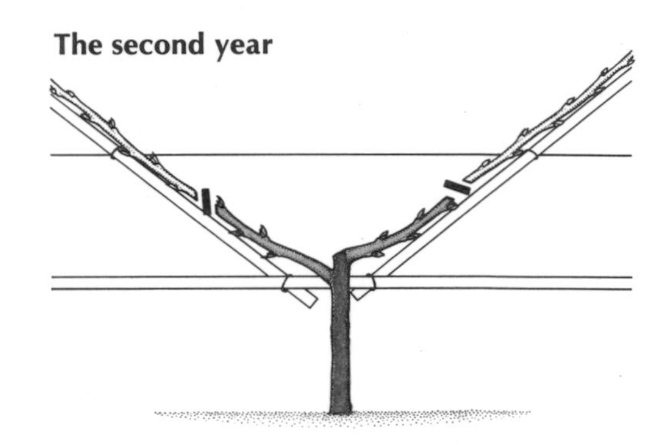

4 February to March. Select suitable buds and shorten each leader to about 12in.

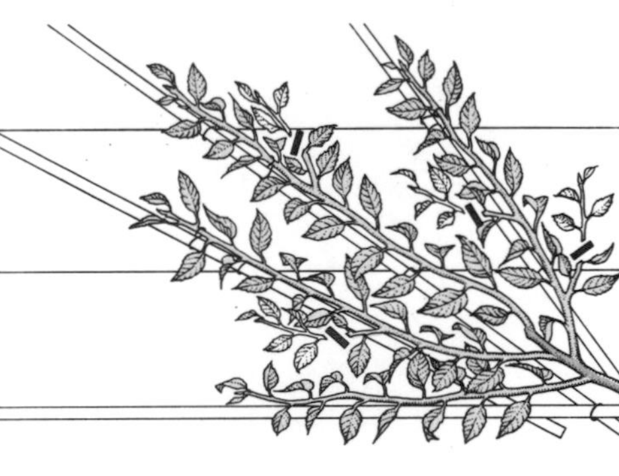

5 June to August. Train 4–6 strong shoots arising from each cut-back leader so that they are evenly spread on both sides of the fan. Tie each shoot to angled canes. Leave the centre of the fan unfilled. Prune back to 3–4in any sublaterals that develop.

Fan

Mature plants
Fruit spurs readily form along the ribs of the fan and relatively few laterals are produced. In summer any excess breastwood or shoots growing toward the wall should be removed completely. If time allows the breastwood or inward-growing shoots can be rubbed out by hand before they develop more than ½in or so. Other laterals, unless required to fill in gaps in the framework, are stopped by pinching out the growing points when they have produced four to six leaves (about 6in) so that fruiting spurs are formed. In September after growth has slowed down cut back the stopped laterals to 3–4in. These spurs will produce buds for fruiting the following year. The 3 D's should be rigorously observed.

Occasionally a rib of the fan may need to be replaced on older plants. A suitable young lateral should be tied in the appropriate position and in late summer the moribund branch can be cut out cleanly flush with the parent stem. Treat the cut surface with a wound paint immediately to avoid the risk of infection.

Root pruning can be practiced if a fan-trained sweet cherry is overvigorous and fruiting sparsely (see page 65). As an alternative it is worth trying to remedy the situation first by bringing down the branches from their angle of 45 degrees to almost horizontal wherever this is practical. This should promote the formation of fruiting spurs by inhibiting terminal growth.

The third year

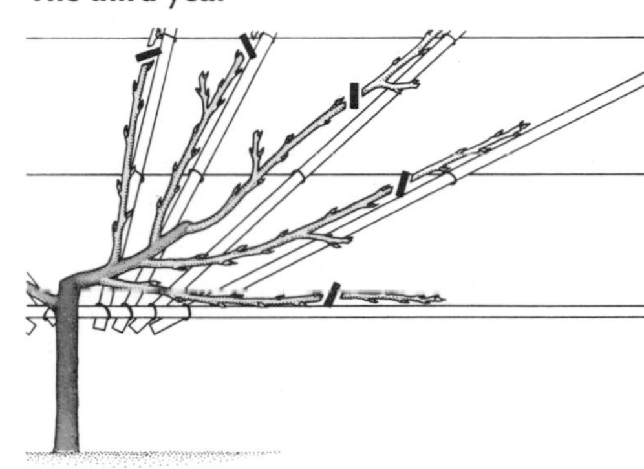

6 February to March. Cut back all leaders to suitable buds, leaving 18–21in of new growth.

7 June to September. Select and evenly tie in 3–6 shoots from each pruned leader, gradually filling the center of the fan. Prune back any sublaterals that develop to 3–4in.

The fourth year

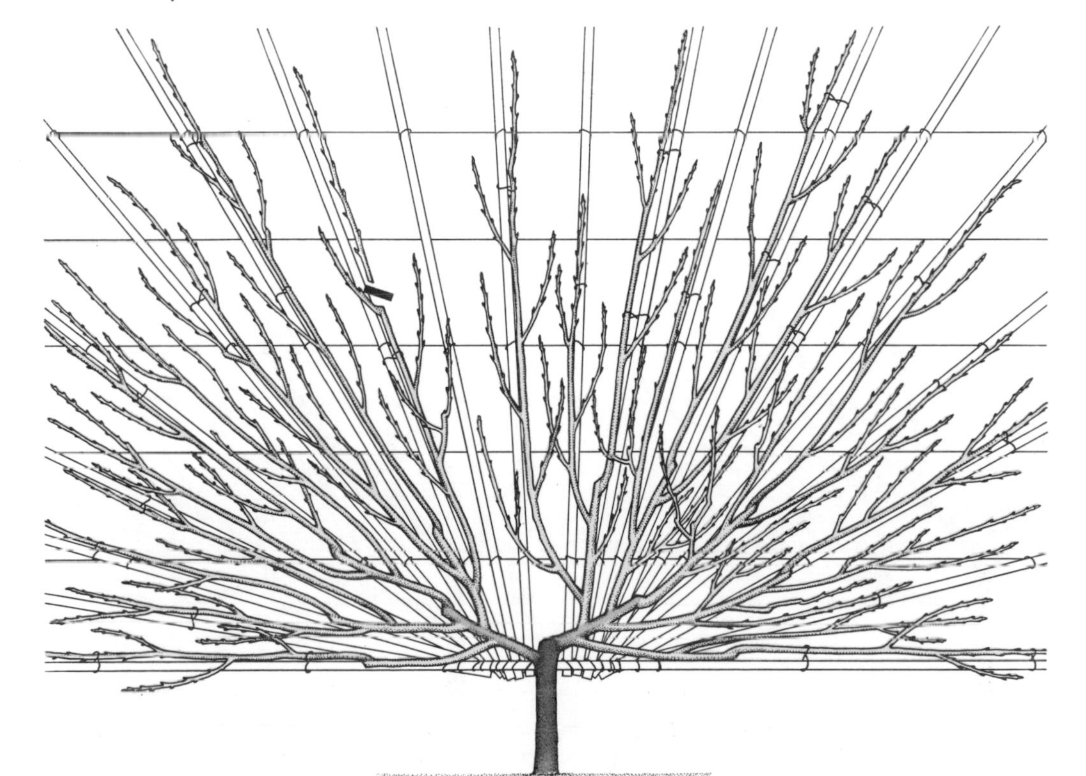

8 February to March. The leaders should now be 12–18in apart at the tips. If spaces remain to be filled on the fan, prune back selected leaders by one-half to stimulate suitable laterals. Leave the remaining leaders unpruned.

FORMING FRUITING SPURS

1 June to August. From the fourth year onwards, rub or cut out all breastwood and inward-growing shoots as they develop. Stop all other sublaterals at 6in or 4–6 leaves to begin the formation of the spur system that will carry fruit in later years.

2 September. Cut back all laterals reduced to 6in in summer to 3–4in to form spurs. These will produce flower buds during the following year. Make sure that all crossing shoots and dead, damaged and diseased wood are removed completely.

Sour – thin older growth to 1 yr laterals
fruit on 1 yr wood.

…ee

Morello, or acid, cherries serve a different culinary purpose to the sweet cherries that are grown for dessert purposes and are mainly used for jams or tarts. If the cherries are left to ripen thoroughly they can also be refreshing as a dessert. They are less vigorous than sweet cherries and most varieties are also self-fertile, which means that only a single plant need be grown if room is restricted.

Morello cherries will also pollinate certain sweet cherries so a single sweet cherry such as 'Bigarreau Napoleon' can be grown close to a Morello and fruit obtained from both. Another point in their favor is their ability to grow and fruit happily on a north wall although, sadly, birds appreciate their fruits as much as they do sweet cherries so protection is still essential.

Flowers and fruit are carried on shoots made the previous year, and pruning of mature Morello cherries is based on the need to provide a regular supply of young renewal shoots to replace the fruiting shoots.

Morello cherries can be grown satisfactorily either as fan-trained plants or as bushes.

Fan-trained

The basic formation is exactly the same as for a peach fan (see pages 74 and 75). Take care to cut the leaders hard back in the first few years of formative training so that a head with plenty of ribs arising close to one another is formed, as with peaches and sweet cherries.

Pruning of the mature fan is again very similar to that given to a fan-trained peach. In both cases a constant supply of young replacement shoots is required for fruiting the following season. These should be tied in when a few inches long while they are still flexible, as they will break once the base has hardened.

Unfortunately some acid cherries are relatively weak growing and the fruiting laterals do not readily produce sublaterals near the base which can be trained in as replacements. If these fruiting laterals are left unpruned and no sublaterals form, they become longer and longer with the base bare and flower and fruit only at the tips on the one-year-old wood.

To obtain a well-clothed fan with young wood it is usually necessary to cut back a few of the longer, older shoots each season in March-April to within 3–4 in of their base. This stimulates the basal growth buds to produce vigorous young shoots to fruit the following season. If the pruned stubs do not produce fresh growth and die back, they should be cut out completely and the wound painted to avoid disease.

Bush tree

The initial training for a bush Morello cherry is very similar to that given to a bush plum with an open-center head (see page 66). The bush is usually trained on a leg of about 30 in and the leaders cut back in early spring as growth begins for the first four to six years to establish the framework.

Mature bushes will bear their fruit along young wood formed the previous season. Pruning consists of cutting a proportion of the older shoots back to one-year-old laterals or young shoots just forming in March to April, so that the older growth is continually being replaced. This thinning of older growth is satisfactory for some years but it is not always easy to maintain the production of young vigorous shoots without cutting back into bare, old wood.

Plants ten or more years old may then require more drastic rejuvenation treatment over a three-year period. Cut back the main branches to within about 3 ft of the head so that vigorous young replacement branches are produced.

Cropping will, of course, be reduced until the replacement wood increases in length and comes into bearing. This rejuvenation operation is best carried out in midsummer to combat silver leaf infection, and all cut surfaces must be covered with a wound paint immediately after pruning.

The third year

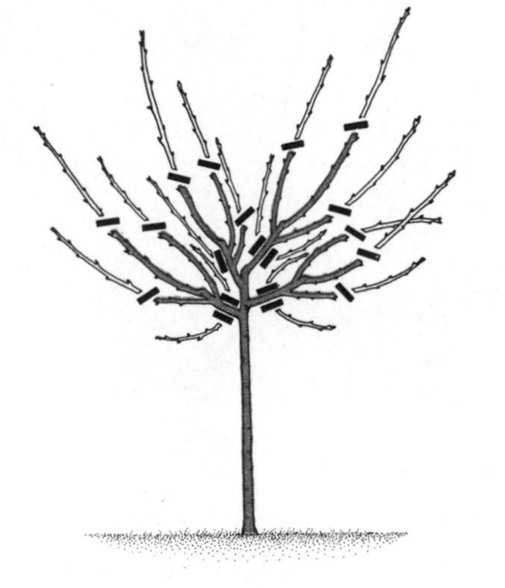

4 February to March. Select 3–4 well-spaced new growths from each primary branch. Cut back all leaders to outward-pointing buds, shortening vigorous ones by about one-half and all others by about two-thirds.

5 November. At the end of the season's growth the main framework has formed and laterals will have developed. No pruning is required.

The fourth year

6 March. As the buds break prune back a few of the older shoots to one-year-old laterals or young shoots just forming. Do not prune the leaders.

Fifth and following years

7 March. As the buds break prune back a few of the older shoots to one-year-old laterals or young shoots just forming to keep a balance of young growth throughout the bush.

Bush Tree

The growing of peaches as bushes has not proved to be a commercial success in many places in the world. But the commercial grower depends on regular and heavy cropping, while the amateur gardener can accept the year of a poor crop philosophically and balance it against the years of profusion. And the bush peach can produce very large crops in the open in favorable years.

The first year

Shorten the maiden to about 24 in on planting between November and February. Any strong feathers can be used to form the first branches. Select four or five well-placed feathers that form wide angles with the stem and shorten each to about 4 in. At the end of the first growing season the branch framework should be clear. Shorten the leaders by one-half to increase and furnish the branches. Always cut leaders to outward-pointing buds. Leave any well-placed laterals unpruned. Remove crossing branches.

Second and following years

Leader pruning should continue for four or five years, after which a switch should be made to a system of periodic shortening of, for example, two branches each year, cutting back into two- or three-year-old wood to a suitably placed lateral or wood bud. The remaining leaders should be left untouched unless they droop too near the ground. If they do, the leaders should be shortened to well-placed laterals or removed completely. The purpose of this branch shortening is to prevent the bush from becoming bare in the center, which results in the crop being carried only on the outside of the plant.

Remove any long lengths of blind wood in April and cut out any tangled and crossing laterals. The aim in pruning an established bush peach is to encourage the constant renewal of well-placed new growths. These new growths are then retained unpruned to provide the following year's crop.

The pinching and de-shooting which is part of the care when growing peaches on walls is not usually practiced, though if it seems a good idea an occasional bout of summer pinching of unwanted shoots is reasonable. Common sense is always a good guide.

The first year / **Second and following years**

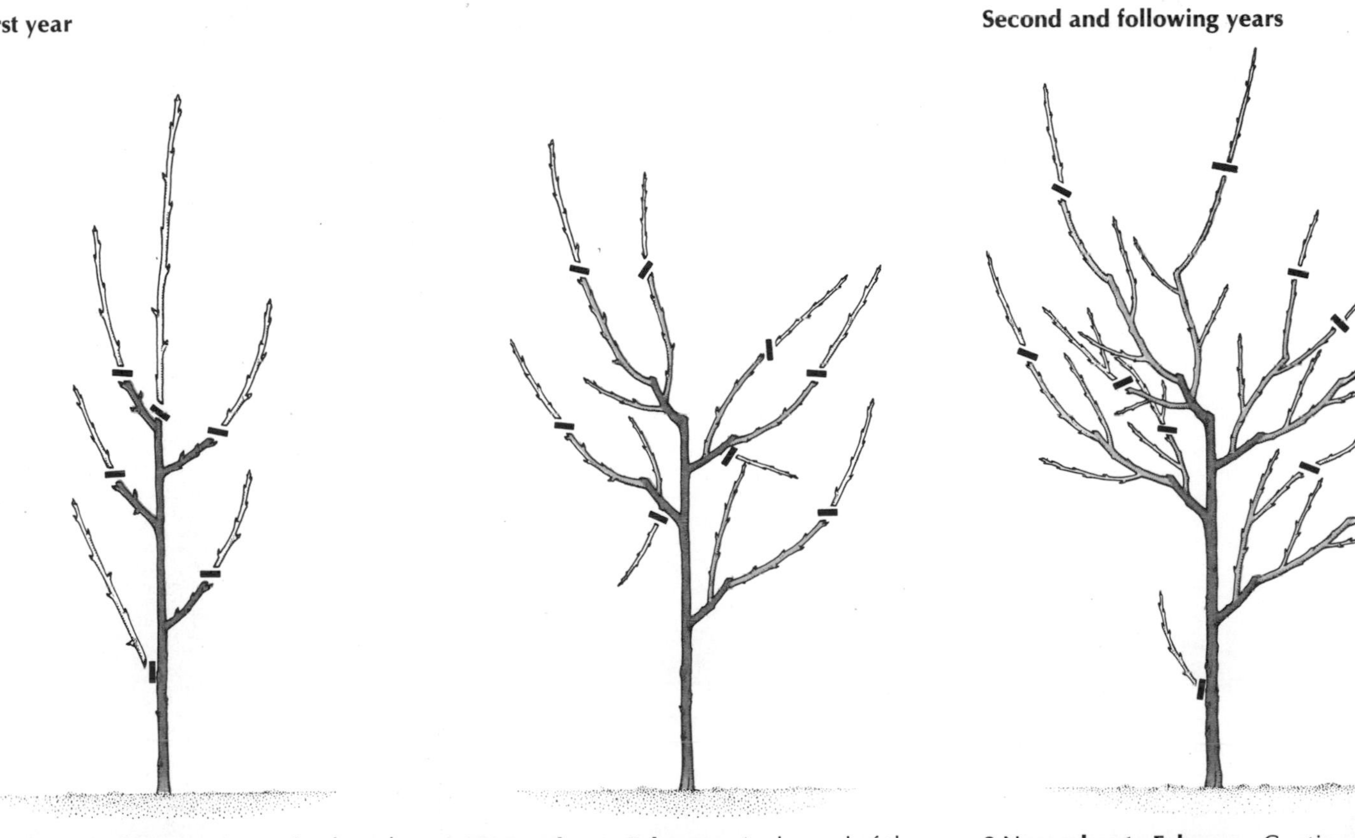

1 November to February. Plant a feathered maiden. Prune back the leader to a suitable side-branch about 24 in from the ground. Remove any lateral below 10 in from the ground, and shorten the remainder to 4 in, to outward-pointing buds.

2 November to February. At the end of the growing season shorten the branch leaders by about one-half cutting to outward-pointing buds. Leave any well-placed and healthy laterals unpruned. Remove any crossing branches.

3 November to February. Continue to cut back the branch leaders by one half to outward-pointing buds. Remove any dead, diseased or damaged growth. Remove any crowded or crossing growth, or any laterals that appear below the lowest branch.

THE FRUITING TREE

November to February. Reduce pruning to the minimum. Remove damaged, diseased and dead shoots. Cut back one or two branches into two- or three-year old wood to encourage new growth.

Fan

Peaches and nectarines are quite hardy, but flower so early that they are particularly susceptible to spring frost damage. For this reason peaches and nectarines are usually given the protection of a wall or fence, or a sheltered part of the garden. The most popular trained forms are the fan and the bush.

Although training against a wall is usual, a fan-trained peach tree can also be grown against a post and wire fence, using canes secured to the wires. In either case the wires must be taut and some 6 in apart.

The first year

Plant a maiden during the dormant period between November and February and cut back to within 15 in of the union. The cut must be made to above a wood or triple bud. The wood buds, from which shoots are produced, are thin and pointed, whereas flower buds are plump and round. A triple bud is composed of two flower buds and a wood bud.

Throughout the first summer shoots will develop from the wood buds. Select three strong shoots, the topmost to grow vertically, and one on each side of the stem to develop laterally. These two shoots should be close together. Remove all other buds or shoots entirely. As the two side-shoots lengthen, tie them to canes at an angle of about 45 degrees. When both these shoots are clearly established and some 18 in long remove the central shoot entirely. Paint the wound with a sealing paint or grafting wax.

At the end of the first season untie the side branches and shorten them by one-half. Lower the canes near to the horizontal. Retie the side branches. Remove any other shoots.

The second year

As a result of the leader pruning, buds will shoot from each arm. In summer, select four healthy shoots on each branch, one at the end to extend the main arm; two others, equally spaced, are chosen on the upper side and the fourth on the lower side, giving the tree a total of eight branches. Carefully train each new shoot to a cane, extending the wings of the fan but leaving the center open. Remove all other shoots as they develop. At the end of the second season's growth no pruning is required.

The first year

1 November to February. Plant a maiden tree. Cut back to a wood bud or triple bud within 15 in of the union.

2 May. Select three strong shoots, one at the tip and two close together on opposite sides. Remove all other shoots as they appear.

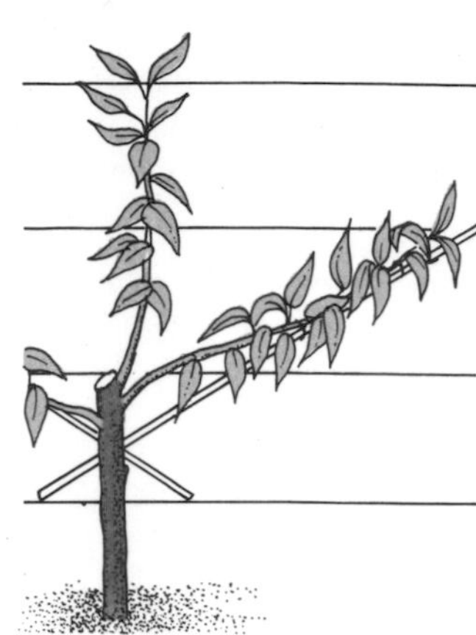

3 June to July. Tie lengthening side-shoots to canes set at an angle of about 45 degrees.

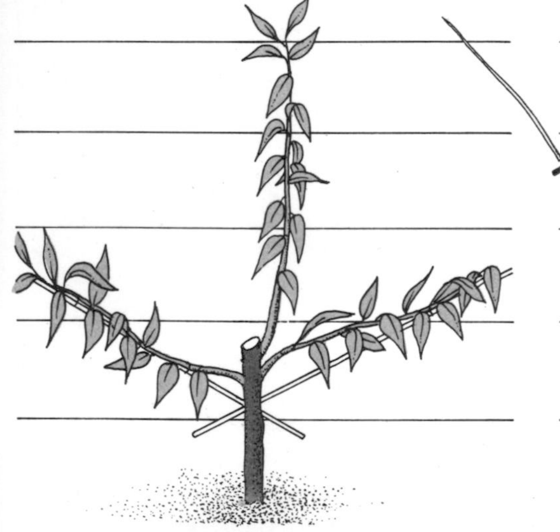

4 August to September. When the shoots are established and about 18 in long, remove the center shoot entirely. Paint the wound with a sealer.

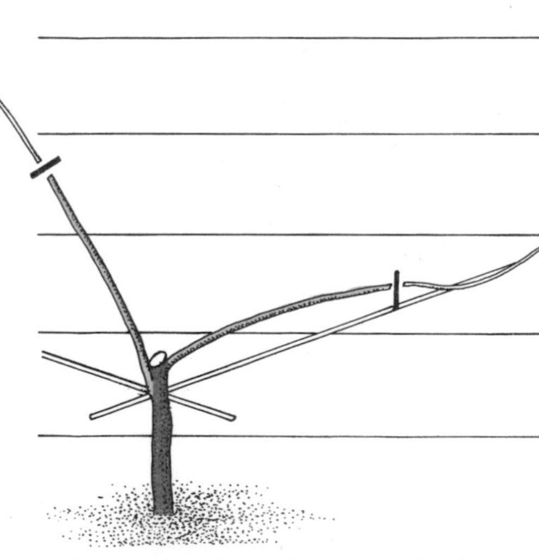

5 October to November. Untie the branches and shorten them by one-half. Lower the canes near to the horizontal and retie the side branches. Remove all other shoots.

The second year

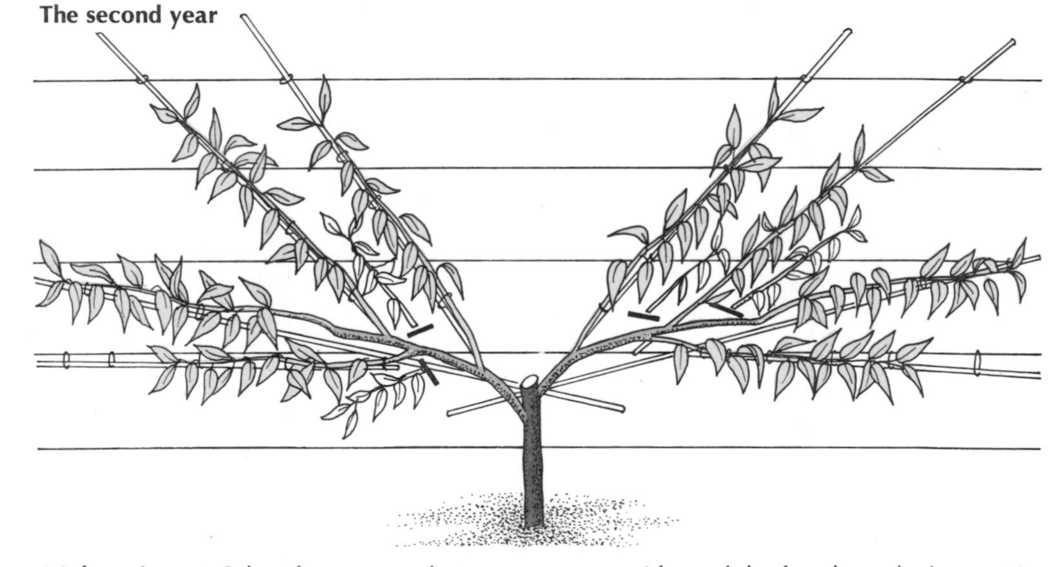

6 July to August. Select four strong shoots on each side branch. One should be at the end to extend the main arm, two on the upper side, and the fourth on the lower side of the branch. Tie them to canes. Remove all other shoots.

Fan

The third year

In February shorten each leader by about one-third, cutting to downward-pointing buds. In summer, choose three equally spaced shoots from each pruned leader and tie them in to the framework. Pinch out all other growths.

During the dormant season from November to February, lightly prune the new growth of the leaders by about one-quarter.

Fourth and following years

Now the center of the fan is being filled out with the added branches and the fruiting laterals can be left in. Confine leader pruning to branches that are not growing vigorously. When the required height and spread have been achieved, pinch back the extension shoots in summer to prevent further growth and, if necessary, at the end of the season's growth, cut them back further to a convenient replacement shoot.

Pinch back to 3 in in summer any misplaced laterals that grow out from or into the wall.

The third year

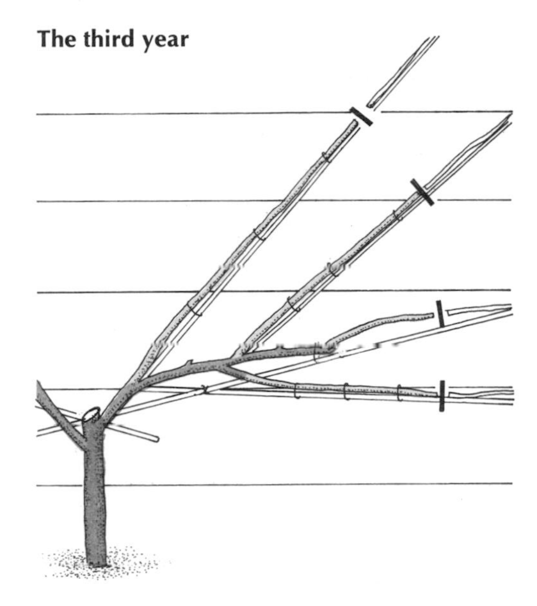

7 February. Shorten each leader by one-third, leaving about 30 in of growth.

8 July to August. Select and tie in three additional shoots from each pruned leader. Pinch out all remaining shoots.

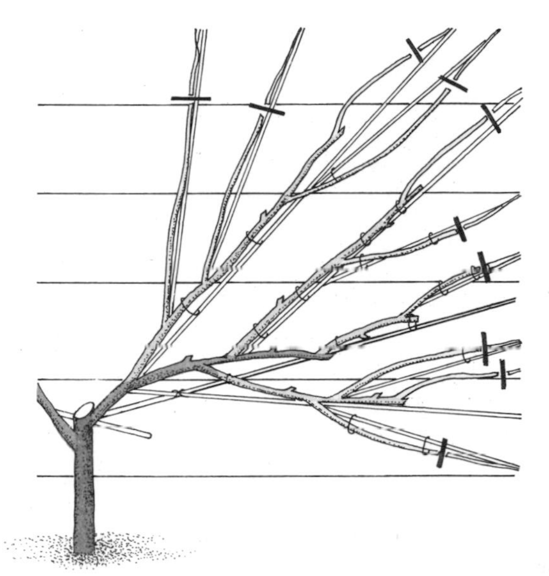

9 November to February. Lightly prune the leaders, removing one-quarter of the growth.

Fourth and following years

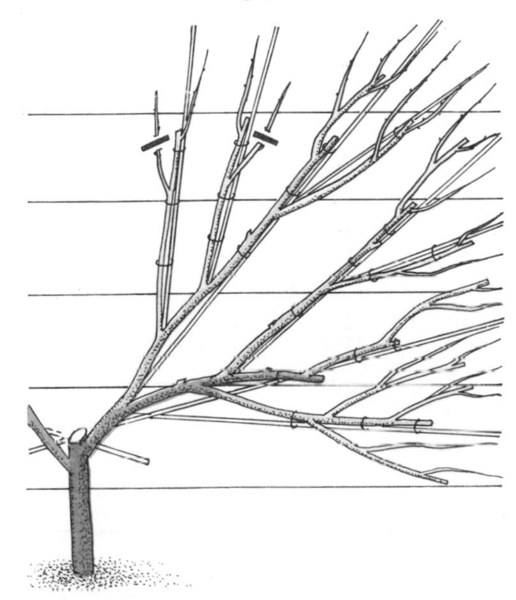

10 November to February. Prune by one-quarter those leaders that need to produce more growth to fill out the framework.

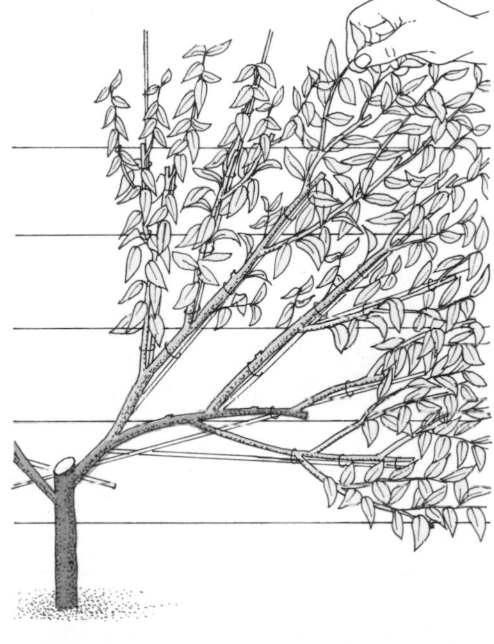

11 July to August. If the tree has occupied all the available height, stop the extension shoots by pinching out the growing tips.

PRUNING FOR FRUIT

The peach carries its fruits on shoots made during the previous summer. Pruning must therefore be aimed at ensuring a constant and annual renewal of well-placed young shoots. It follows also that the system involves the cutting out of the shoots after they have borne fruits to make room for the new young ones. These young shoots are selected annually at an early stage from the bases of the existing fruiting laterals, so they in effect grow side by side.

The fruiting lateral not only carries luscious fruits but also produces side-shoots along its length. Select one at the base as the replacement lateral; allow another to grow from the mid-section of the fruiting lateral, to make sure of a replacement. Finally, the extension growth from each shoot is retained.

The remaining side-shoots are unwanted and wasteful and it is best to pinch them back to two good leaves. If energy is abundant these shoots will push out secondary shoots. Pinch back to 1in as they appear. It may be necessary to completely remove all of the surplus shoots where they are so numerous that it makes more sense than pinching back.

The basal lateral that is selected to form next year's fruiting wood need not be more than 18 in long, so pinch out the tip when it reaches that length.

Harvesting

After harvest tidy up the peach tree, pruning away the laterals that have fruited together with any dead or damaged wood, and bare growths.

The disfiguring disease peach leaf curl is often troublesome. Affected leaves usually fall early and should be burned as soon as possible. Spray the plant in mid-January and two weeks later using Bordeaux mixture or a liquid copper fungicide.

Fan

For many of us figs come in boxes imported from warmer climates. But even in temperate areas it is possible to obtain good-quality figs from plants grown in the open or in a cool greenhouse, where two, or occasionally three, crops can be produced in one growing season.

Figs are said to have originated in western Asia and the eastern Mediterranean countries and are widely grown in southern Europe and northern Africa as well as the south and west of the United States. In these areas they receive the warmth and light required to ripen the fruits and mature the young growth, but in frost-prone regions they are liable to damage from spring frosts or severe winter cold. They are seldom killed outright in temperate winters and, although their growth may be cut back, new shoots quickly break from the base of the tree the following spring. Probably only passionate fig-lovers will be prepared to spare greenhouse space for the 15–18ft spread required for a properly trained specimen grown under glass.

In temperate regions figs can be grown successfully as bushes or standards but seldom fruit satisfactorily when fully in the open. Grown fan-trained against a wall, however, preferably one facing south, the hardiest varieties such as 'Brown Turkey' and 'White Marseilles' will fruit well.

The key to success is meticulous pruning and training so that a supply of young, short, fruiting shoots is maintained. Figs are exuberant growers and it is usually necessary to firmly restrict both root and shoot growth. The roots must be confined, with only a limited soil area and depth available to them if fruiting shoots are to be formed. Elaborate brick pits 3ft square and 3ft deep used to be built for this purpose, but today a pot or concrete drain-pipe of 18–24in diameter with a layer of brick rubble at the base will achieve the same purpose. Root growth and shoot growth is checked in this way, but if the roots do escape from the confined area allotted to them, any excess can be pruned away from the top of the container and also from the base with a little excavation.

An ideal site can sometimes be found between the south wall of a house and a hard path where the soil is well drained but not too rich so that root pruning or artificial confinement is unnecessary. If the plant does bear a heavy crop, however, particularly in a dry year, it may be necessary to water well and feed sparingly to prevent the fruit from dropping prematurely.

It is important to understand how figs bear their fruits because this governs the pruning method. The cultivated fig plants are all female and can develop fruit without the flowers being fertilized, whereas the wild fig undergoes a complicated pollination and fertilization process by the fig-wasp.

Embryo fruits, the size of a pea, form in the leaf axils of short shoots of the current year during late summer, and, providing they survive the winter successfully, will develop into ripe figs by the following August. So from the time that they first form until they finally ripen covers almost a year.

During the summer a further crop of figs will develop in the axils of the leaves of young growth but, although they swell, they very seldom ripen and should be removed by September. By this time further embryo fruits will have formed at the shoot tips. These will pass the winter to form next year's crop each year. So even in the open figs will bear two crops but only one of these will ripen properly in temperate climates.

Early training

The method used to form a fan-trained fig is basically similar to that used for a cherry or a peach (see pages 74 and 75). Alternatively the leading shoots and strong laterals can be trained in to form the basic framework. They are tied in roughly fan-wise to the wall or fence as they extend.

In either case it is important to space these main branches 15–18in apart and the laterals which develop from them should be at least 6–9in away from any neighboring shoot. This ensures that both growth and fruiting shoots are exposed to the maximum sunlight and air. If the shoots are crowded the large fig leaves hinder the ripening process.

Figs often produce an abundance of new growth and only sufficient new shoots should be retained to cover the spaces between the main framework branches. Any surplus or crossing or badly placed shoots should be cut out.

The first year

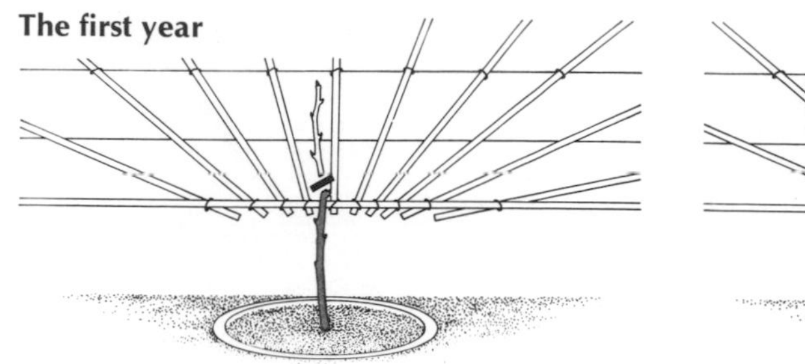

1 March to April. Restrict root growth by planting the young fig in a large container sunk in the ground. Cut back the leader to 15–18in.

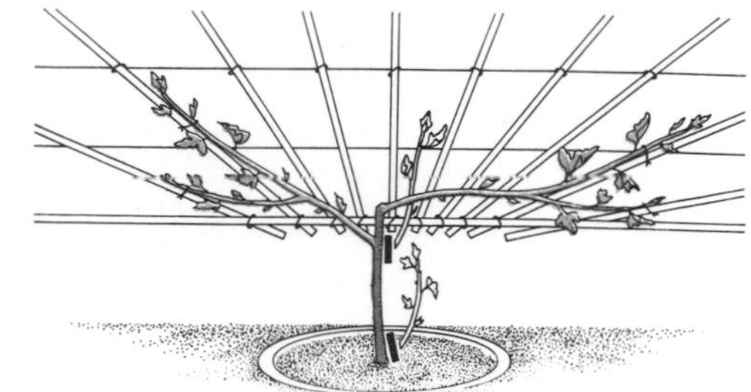

2 May to September. Tie in the developing laterals to form the main framework, spacing them at least 15in apart. Cut out basal growths and misplaced shoots.

The second year

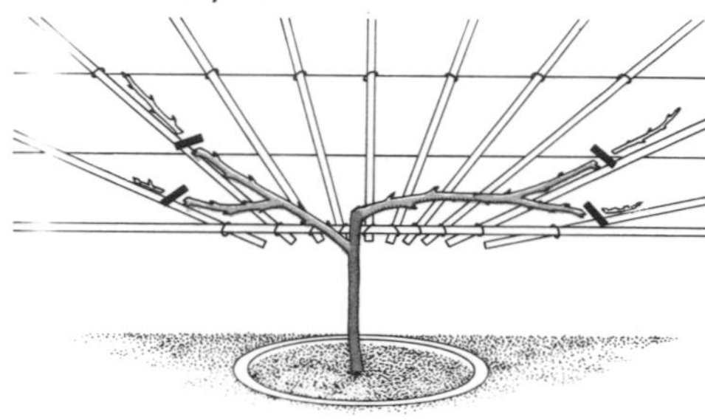

3 March to April. Cut back the framework branches by about one-half of their length.

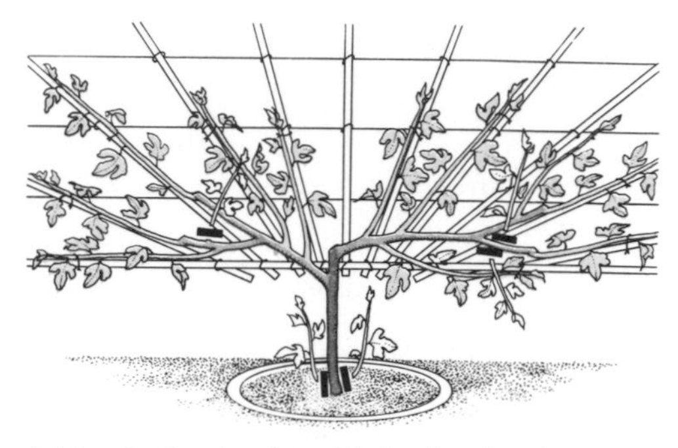

4 May to September. Tie in the developing laterals to the angled canes, spacing them at least 15in apart. Cut out basal growths and misplaced shoots.

The third year

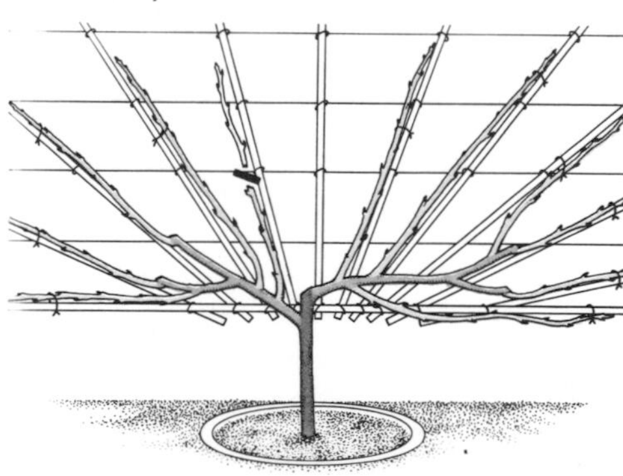

5 March to April. If further framework ribs are needed cut back by one-half framework branches closest to the gaps.

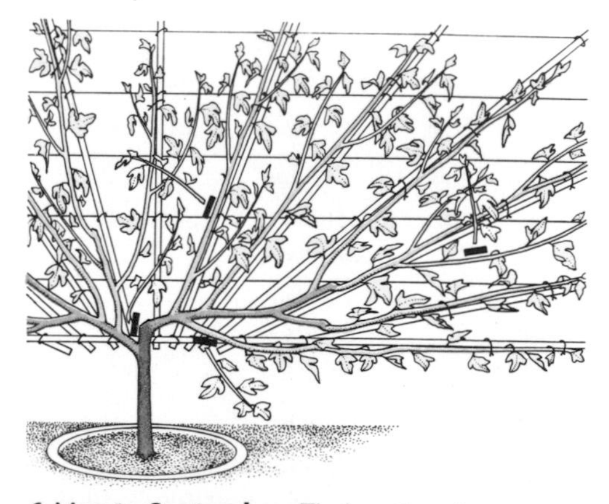

6 May to September. Tie in extension growth of main ribs, and stop them when they have filled the frame. Train in sub-laterals leaving 6–9in between shoots.

Fan

The mature plant

The easiest method is a form of renewal pruning. Figs naturally form extension growth from the terminal bud with only limited formation of laterals. As the fruits are only carried on first- and second-year shoots the older wood gradually becomes bare and unfruitful unless pruned to encourage lateral growth. Pruning, therefore, must be aimed at producing a regular supply of sturdy young laterals each season. The simplest method of doing this is to cut back every alternate lateral on the main branch system to one eye (bud) from its base in autumn after leaf fall. On established plants these will be the laterals that are bearing fruit during the current season. The following spring young growths will develop from these eyes and these are trained to their full length during the summer and will form embryo fruit buds at the tips toward the end of their growth period. After fruiting the next year cut back these shoots to one eye.

The young shoots left after autumn pruning will already have small embryo fruits at their tips. In cold climates it is advisable to protect them during winter by covering the plant with leaves or cloths or a similar material after autumn pruning. The embryo fruits will begin to swell the following spring and young extension shoots will grow from the terminal buds. In late June pinch out the growing points of these extension shoots at the fourth or fifth leaf. This checks growth and diverts food into the expanding fruit rather than into the extension shoot. The extension shoot is unimportant as the whole fruiting branch will be cut back to one eye after leaf fall in autumn. Sometimes a young shoot will form during the growing season near the base of a fruiting branch. It may be convenient to cut back to this point rather than to the basal eye.

This renewal system ensures that each of the main branches is furnished with approximately equal numbers of the current season's shoots alternating with shoots of the previous year which bear fruit.

This renewal principle should not be applied too rigidly and should be varied according to the balance of fruiting and growth shoots needed. The important point is to make sure that both the fruiting shoots and developing young laterals are exposed to the maximum light and warmth. Cut out any surplus shoots to avoid overcrowding.

With older fan-trained figs a complete framework branch which is unfruitful may occasionally need to be cut out and replaced by a suitably placed vigorous shoot from near the base of the plant. Some authorities recommend cutting out about one-third of the main framework branches in this way each season but this is usually only necessary when a fig tree is in poor condition and needs rejuvenation.

Fourth and following years

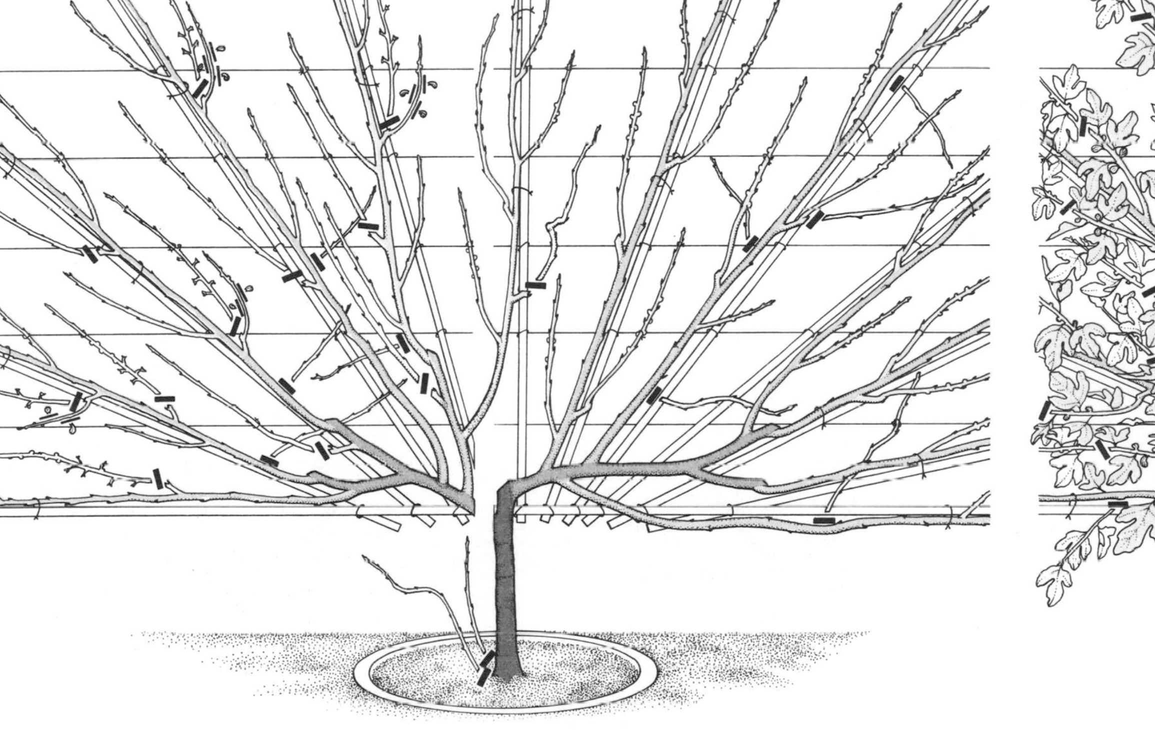

7 October to November. After leaf fall cut back the branches that have fruited to one eye. Tie in all the current season's growth, first removing any immature fruits larger than a pea. Protect the plant in cold areas.

8 March to April. Remove the protective covering. Cut out any winter-damaged shoots. Cut out any surplus shoots if the fruiting branches are overcrowded, leaving at least 6–9in between shoots.

9 Late June. Stop the extension growth on fruiting shoots at 4–5 leaves. Tie in shoots that have developed following pruning. Leave at least 6–9in between each shoot. Cut out any crossing growths or shoots that are not required.

like red curr. July – cut unwanted to 4"
Wi – leaders 1/2 – out. bud.
unwanted to 1-2"

berry

In some ways the gooseberry has the most exact pruning requirements of all the bush fruits, and for this very reason tends to be neglected and left to its own devices in the hope that all will be well. Additionally the gooseberry is equipped with spines, absent from its relatives the currants, and the spines make pruning, picking and weeding all the more difficult. But if the gooseberry is properly trained and pruned much larger fruits and easily handled bushes result. Gooseberry pruning can be divided into two methods, the first dealing with gooseberries tightly pruned similar to the pruning of red currants and the second dealing with a much looser technique of growing similar to that used for black currants. The open-center spur-pruned bush or the cordon form provides larger fruits that are much easier to pick, and bushes which are more pleasant to tend than the specimens which have received a minimum pruning.

First, spur pruning, which can be used for bushes or for cordons, single or multiple. Cordons are treated in the same methodical way as each individual branch of the bush, except that each cordon stem is trained vertically and staked.

Close spur pruning is ideal for the dessert varieties of gooseberry, such as the delicious 'Leveller.' But there are difficulties. Sometimes branches die because of fungus attack, and the loss of a whole branch or branches is a serious matter in a formally trained specimen.

In addition there are fewer fruits to pick, even if the individual ones are larger, and for jam-making and cooking greater numbers of smaller berries are often more acceptable. Bird damage is likely to be more severe on spur-pruned bushes where the fruit buds are closely packed and easier to feed upon.

Propagate gooseberries by hardwood cuttings taken from healthy shoots in November and insert them in the open ground. Remove the weak tip and all but four buds from the upper part of the cutting. The purpose of this is to produce a miniature, open-center bush on a short leg, a form which makes for much easier weeding, picking and spraying. The gooseberry is not as vigorous as the red currant and may require two years in the cutting bed. Alternatively, two-year-old bushes may be bought in. Older bushes are best avoided.

The first year

On planting, from November to February, shorten the four primary branches by about one-half, cutting to upward- and inward-facing buds. This is to reduce the tendency of the gooseberry to produce drooping branches, a bad habit in a spiny plant as it makes weeding difficult and uncomfortable. Subsequent pruning follows the red currant pattern.

At the end of the first autumn, shorten the leaders by one-half of the extension growth, cutting to inward-pointing buds. Select any well-placed secondary shoots suitable for new branches and cut them back by one-half. Ultimately this will create eight or more permanent branches. All other side-shoots should be cut back to 2 in from their bases to form spurs. Remove all dead, diseased or damaged wood and sucker shoots.

Second and following years

During the next summer the branch framework should be clear to see. In July, shorten any unwanted laterals to about 4 in, leaving the leaders unpruned.

In winter, repeat the pruning of the leaders, cutting them back by one-half. Shorten the summer-pruned laterals to about 2 in. Remove all dead, diseased or damaged wood. In summer prune unwanted side-shoots to 4 in, to make picking easier.

If bird damage is likely to be severe defer winter pruning until March, when its extent can be clearly seen and allowed for.

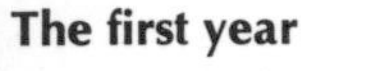

The first year

open center spurs – like red. curr.
easier to pick
larger fruits

1 December. At planting, cut back branches by one-half, cutting to inward- and upward-pointing buds.

2 November. Prune leaders by one-half. Select well-placed shoots to form further permanent branches and cut back by one-half. Cut back all other side-shoots to 2 in. Remove any sucker shoots.

Second and following years

3 July. Cut back unwanted and badly placed laterals to 4 in. The aim is to allow easy access for picking the fruit. Do not prune the leaders.

4 November to February. Cut back leaders by one-half. Cut back to 2 in the laterals that were pruned in summer. Cut out all dead, damaged and diseased wood.

Gooseberry

The gooseberry is an ungrateful subject which really wants to behave like a black currant and is happiest when grown with free-growing shoots. Grown thus more fruits are carried because the gooseberry will fruit readily on two-year-old shoots as well as spurs, and any branches lost through die-back are easily replaced.

The first and second years
Pruning consists of cutting back leaders by one-half in November.

Second and following years
The essential point in pruning these freely grown gooseberries—of which the variety 'Careless' is an excellent and responsive example—lies in a selective thinning out of the shoots each winter, removing any which are crossing, broken, diseased, excessively strong or obviously worn out. Be sure to leave shoots spaced sufficiently far apart to permit the entry of a hand to gather the gooseberries. Neither summer pruning nor leader tipping is usually practiced, but cut back any weeping shoot to an upright existing shoot.

The first year

1 November to February. A one-year-old bush at planting. Cut back leaders by one-half to upward-pointing buds.

2 November. At the end of the growing season select eight branches. Cut them back by one-half to upward-pointing buds.

The second year

3 November to February. Cut back leaders by one-half to upward-pointing buds. Leave laterals unpruned. Cut out crossing, overvigorous and poor shoots.

Third and following years

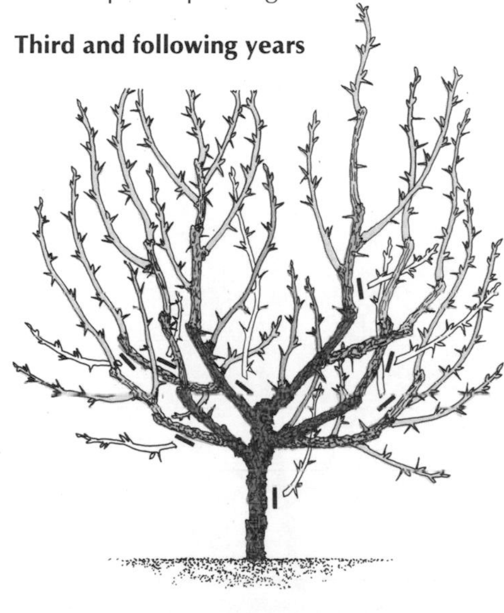

4 November to February. Cease all pruning other than the thinning out of crossing, broken or diseased shoots. Cut out any remaining shoots that make picking difficult.

5 Fruit is carried on two-year-old shoots, and on any spurs that form on the wood that remains after the thinning out of unrequired shoots.

RENOVATION

Occasionally one has to deal with a long-neglected but healthy bush.

Such a bush is overcrowded, with sucker shoots springing from the base and frequently the tips of the weeping branches have not only touched the ground but have actually rooted. In winter cut out any very strong suckers, thin out the competing branches so that picking is made easier, and then shorten any weeping branches.

Treated in this way the bush will fruit profusely on unpruned shoots formed the previous year. Once fruited these shoots should be removed completely to make way for young and eager successors.

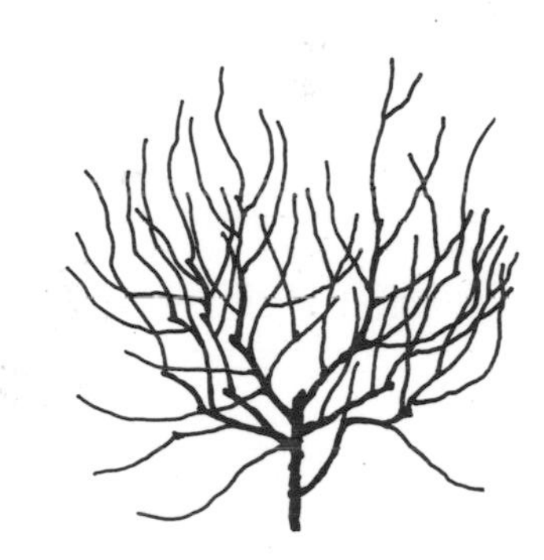

A neglected gooseberry bush. Remove overcrowded, weeping, crossing and sucker shoots.

The renovated bush that allows easy picking and pest and disease control.

summer — shorten unwanted lat to 4"
wh - cut leaders ½ to out bud
cut 4" lat to 1"

Red currant

Red and white currants are easy to grow and very fruitful; it is sad that they are not grown more widely in gardens. The major problem with red currants is that birds find both buds and fruit very tasty and must be prevented from stripping branches bare by using nets, scaring devices or a permanent fruit cage. If bird damage occurs, defer pruning until spring so that you can assess accurately and allow for the extent of the damage.

The white varieties of currant—typified by 'White Dutch'—are treated in the same way as the red currants. The red currant is usually grown as a miniature open-center bush, with a short leg and some eight radiating permanent branches. The leg is formed at the cutting stage.

The first year

One-year-old or two-year-old bushes are best for planting. At planting in November, shorten the branches by one-half, cutting back to outward-pointing buds. This pruning stiffens the branches, ensures that the extension growth is in the correct direction and stimulates laterals to form. Any shoots from the leg or suckers from below ground should be removed as they appear.

At the end of the first autumn, shorten the leaders by one-half of the extension growth, cutting to outward-pointing buds. Select any well-placed secondary shoots suitable for new branches and cut them back by one-half to outward-pointing buds. Ultimately this will create eight or more permanent branches. All other side-shoots should be cut back to 2 in from their bases to form spurs. Remove all dead, diseased or damaged wood.

Second and following years

During the next summer the branch framework should be clear to see. In July, shorten any unwanted laterals to about 4 in, leaving the leaders untouched.

In winter, repeat the pruning of the leaders, cutting them back by one-half to outward-pointing buds. Shorten the summer-pruned laterals to about 1 in. Remove all dead, diseased or damaged wood. In summer prune unwanted side-shoots to 4 in as soon as the fruit begins to colour. This allows the fruits to color more easily and makes picking easier.

The first year

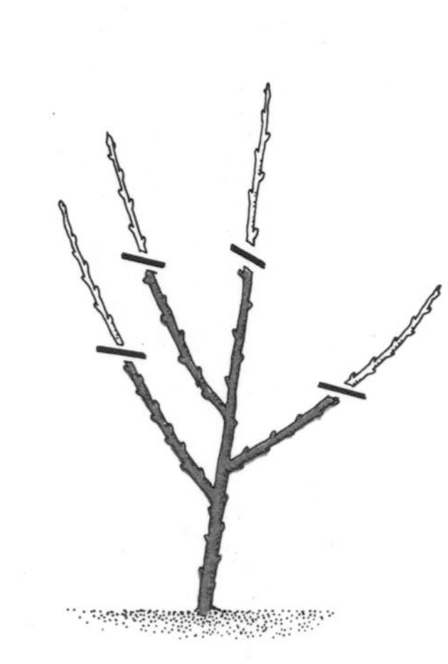

1 December. A one-year-old bush at planting. Cut back branches by one-half to outward-pointing buds.

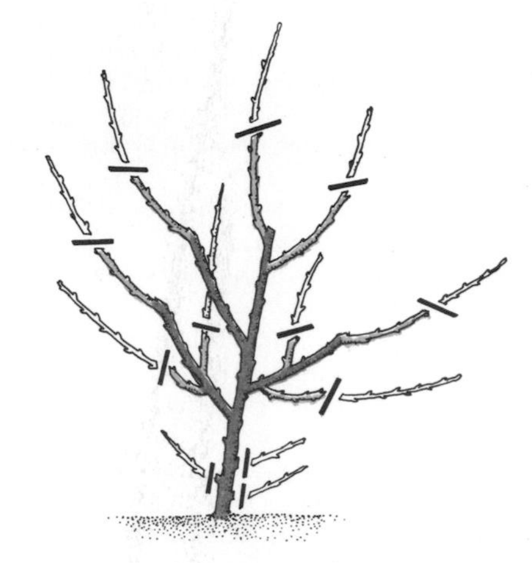

2 November. Prune leaders by one-half to outward-pointing buds. Select any well-placed shoots to form permanent branches and cut back by one-half to outward-pointing buds. Cut back all other side-shoots to 2 in. Remove any sucker shoots.

Second and following years

3 July. Cut back unwanted laterals to 4 in to allow light to reach the fruits. No leader pruning is required.

4 November to February. Cut back leaders by one-half to outward-pointing buds. Cut to 1 in the laterals that were pruned to 4 in.

PROPAGATION

The gardener who would like to propagate his own red currant bushes can easily do so by taking cuttings in October, choosing healthy young wood of the new season's growth. Each cutting should be straight and as thick as the average ball-point pen, no thinner. The tip of the shoot should be removed and cuts made just above a bud at the top and just below a bud at the base, the resulting cutting being some 12 in long.

This has a direct bearing on pruning, because the next step is to select four prominent and well-placed buds at the top, and then to remove all the others. The intention is to start the rooted cutting with four good branches and a short leg of about 4 in between the lowest branch and ground level. The cuttings are inserted in the open ground and should be ready for planting in one year's time.

Red currant

Red and white currants are very accommodating and can be easily trained in a variety of forms in addition to the more usual open-center bush on a short leg. The trained forms, which include cordons, espaliers and occasionally fans, are particularly useful for north-facing situations although fan-trained plants ideally need a wall or fence.

The first year

On planting shorten the central leader by half (usually about 6in) and cut back all other laterals to 1in to form spurs.

Second and following years

During the following and subsequent years the leader is reduced to about 6in of the maiden wood each winter, taking care to cut to a bud on the opposite side to last year's cut. This keeps the more or less straight central stem with a series of slight zig-zags. When the central leader of each cordon stem reaches a height of 5 or 6ft it is stopped by summer pruning to 4–5 leaves. Each summer the laterals that form along the cordon stem are pruned to about 4in (3–5 leaves). Do this in late June or July, not earlier, as secondary growth will be stimulated if summer pruning is carried out earlier. In winter these laterals (which eventually form fruiting spurs) are cut back to about 1in. Once the cordon has been trained to the required height of 5–6ft, the leading shoot is also cut back in winter to leave one bud of the previous summer's growth. The removal of most of the previous summer's growth from the leader shoot helps to maintain the cordon at approximately the same height for some years.

The first year

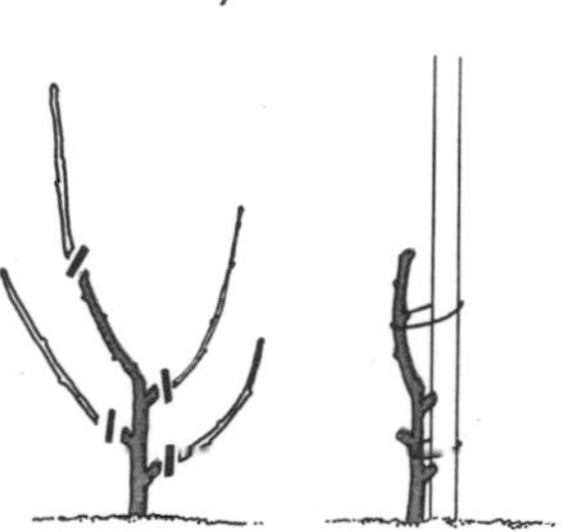

1 November to February. Cut back to 6in the strongest shoot to form the main stem. Tie it to the vertical support. Reduce other laterals to 1in.

2 July. Train in the leader vertically and tie it to the support. Leave it unpruned. Shorten all laterals to 4in (3–5 leaves).

The second year

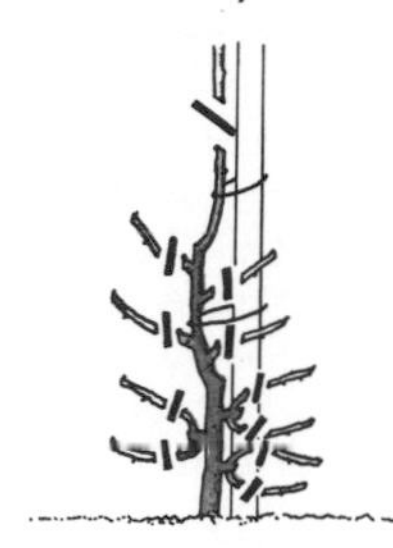

3 November to February. Shorten the leader to leave about 6in of the previous summer's growth. Prune all laterals back to 1in.

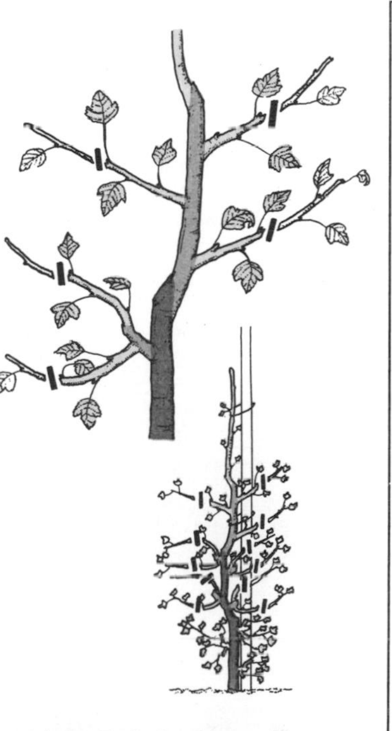

4 July. Train in the leader vertically and tie it to the support. Leave it unpruned. Shorten all laterals to 4in (3–5 leaves).

The third and following years

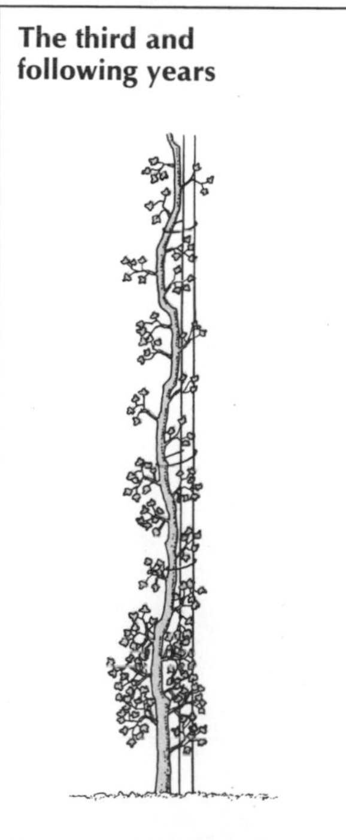

Repeat second-year instructions until the vertical cordon stem has reached the required height of 5–6ft.

Mature cordon

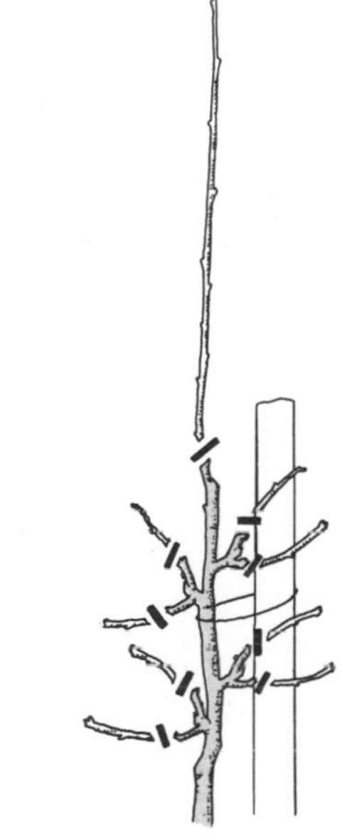

5 November to February. Shorten the leader to leave one bud of the previous summer's growth. Prune all laterals back to 1in.

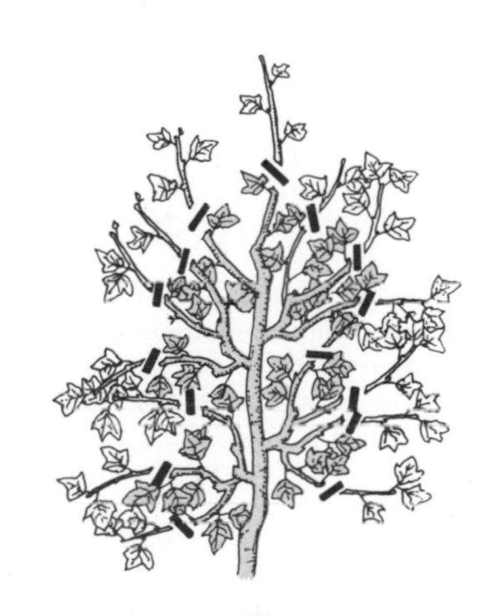

6 July. Shorten the leader and all laterals to 4in (3–5 leaves).

ESPALIERS

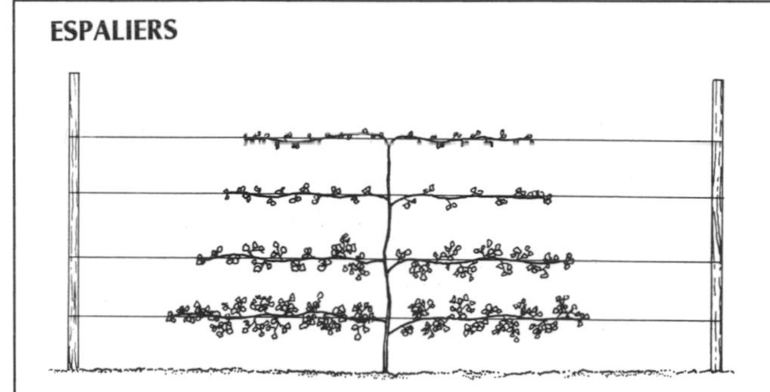

Espaliered red or white currants are really multiple cordons fairly evenly spaced on a central vertical stem. They can be grown free-standing, or on walls or fences. A one-year-old plant with three or more strong shoots should be used to train an espalier. Ideally there should be one strong shoot which can be trained vertically as a central stem, and two of roughly equal vigor on opposite sides to form the first pair of espalier arms. The espalier is formed in much the same way as with apples (see pp 60–61) and the aim should be to obtain a plant about 5ft high with four pairs of horizontal espalier arms. These should eventually extend $2\frac{1}{2}$–3ft on either side. The lowest arm should be about 12in from the ground. Once the espalier has been formed the pruning is identical with the program used for cordon red or white currants. In winter shorten the leader to leave one bud of the previous summer's growth. Prune all laterals back to 1in. In July shorten the leader and all laterals to 4in.

Black currant

The black currant carries the best fruits on wood produced the previous year, but it will also crop on older wood. It follows that the aim of the gardener is to ensure a regular supply of young wood from the base of the stock while the bush is young, and to encourage vigorous side branches from the older wood as the bush enters into middle age. A start should be made with healthy certified bushes, one or two years old but no older.

The first year

Cut down the newly planted bushes to within 2 in of ground level. This drastic decapitation calls for courage, but it is essential to ensure that the transplanted bush makes a good start. Growth will be poor if this hard initial pruning is not carried out. If the plants are healthy, from certified stock, then the pruned shoots can be used as cuttings, so the gardener need only buy in half the number of bushes he requires, filling the vacant positions with three cuttings to each station.

As a result of the hard initial pruning the young bush should produce three or four strong shoots from the base, each shoot being 18 in or more in length. No pruning is required at the end of the first year, the strong young shoots should be left to fruit the next summer.

Second, third and following years

The second season will see the bush engaged in two distinct activities. On the one hand it will produce fruit on last year's wood, and on the other it will produce strong new shoots from the base.

In November, at the end of the second year, some thinning out of weak and overcrowded shoots may be necessary, together with any branches that are too close to the ground, are broken, or obviously mildewed. Remove these entirely, as close to the point of origin as possible.

From this stage onward it is necessary for the gardener to be able to distinguish the young wood from the old. This is fairly easy, in that the bark of the young shoot is much lighter in color than that of the wood that is three-years or older.

The annual winter pruning is now straightforward. A simple formula is to remove entirely three old branches each year.

The first year

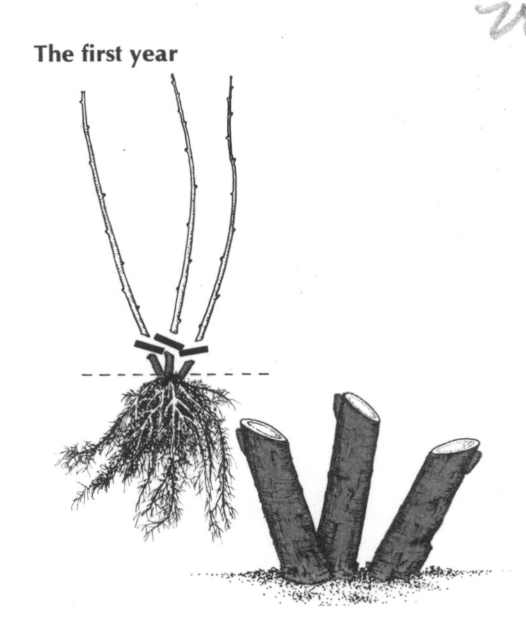

1 November to February. A one-year-old plant suitable for planting. Cut down all shoots to within 2 in of ground level.

The second year

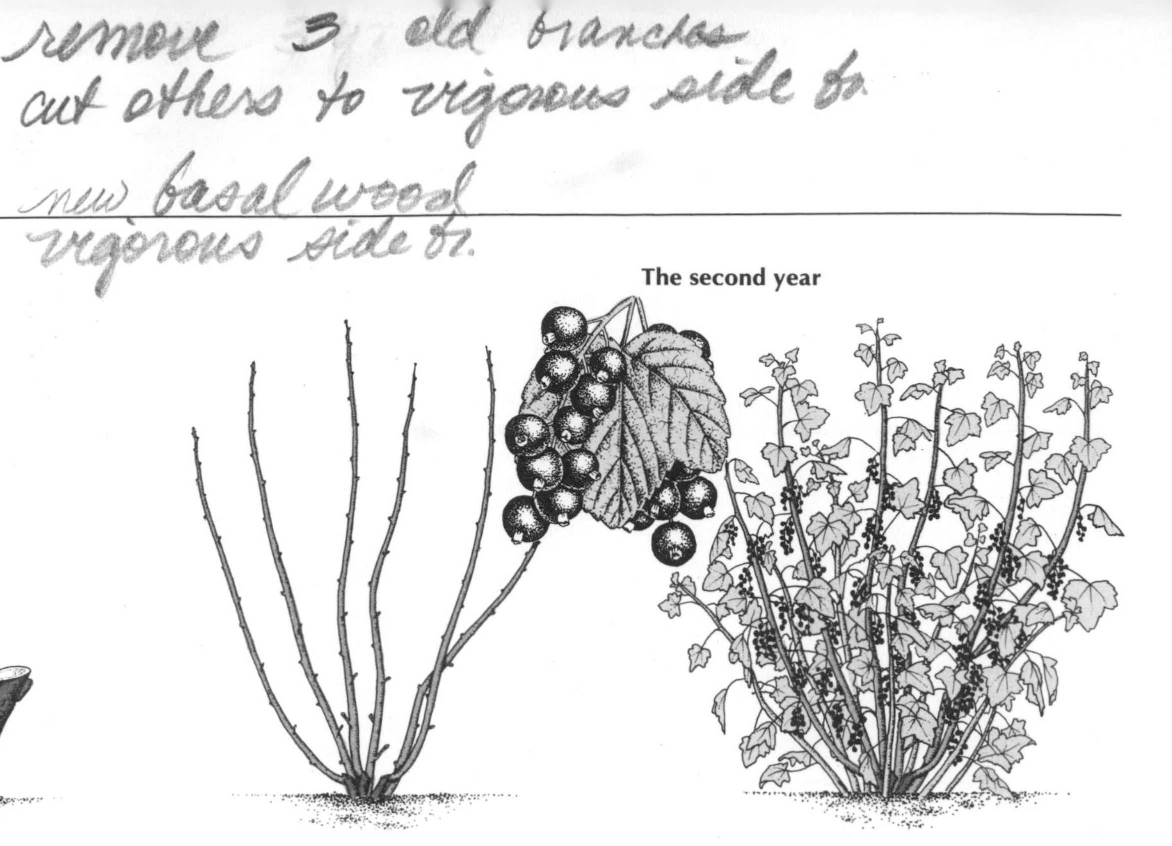

2 November. The severe pruning has resulted in strong new shoots appearing from the base. These will fruit the following year. No pruning is required.

3 July. The bush fruits on last year's wood. New basal growths develop.

Third and following years

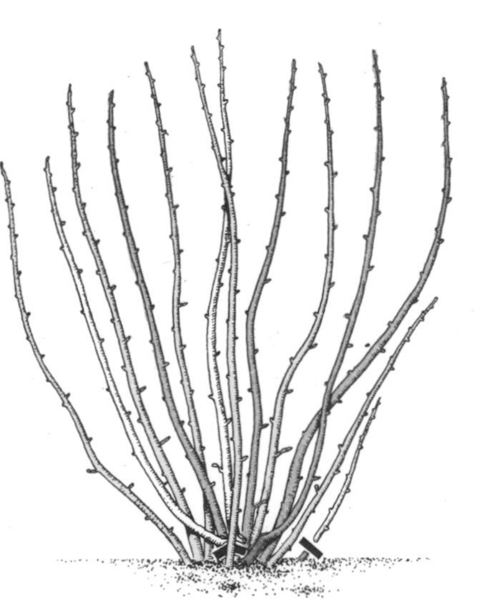

4 November to February. Cut out about one-third of the fruited branches to base. Cut out damaged and weak growths.

5 July. The bush fruits mainly on last year's stems. New basal growths and side branches are produced.

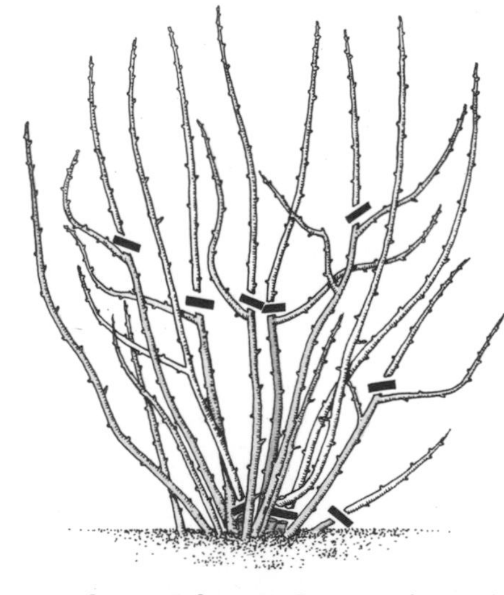

6 November to February. Remove three of the old branches entirely. Cut other fruited branches to vigorous new side branches. Remove damaged branches.

Loganberry

The loganberry grows rather weakly compared with its vigorous cousin the blackberry. Loganberries can therefore be planted more closely together and are very suitable for small gardens.

Make certain you plant the heavy cropping variety distributed as LY59. Most other stocks available are poor croppers or maybe virus-ridden. A healthy, heavy-cropping thornless loganberry (L 654) is also on the market.

The first year

Plant canes 8ft apart in November, taking care to spread the roots out. Shorten the canes to within 10in of ground level. Always plant healthy, disease-free plants because, unfortunately, the loganberry is very susceptible to attack by a fungus disease called cane spot. This is carried over from year to year by transmission from the old cane to the new, the fungus spores falling in rain drops from the diseased canes land on the young growths arising from the base. It is important, therefore, to train the loganberry so that the new growths are, as far as is possible, kept above or to one side of the old canes.

A fan system of training allows this to be done. The loganberry does not fruit the first year and the rods that appear during the first summer should be trained into a fan shape as they develop.

Second and following years

In spring, prune back the tips to leave canes about 5ft long. Take the new canes as they appear from the base up through the center "V" of the fan and then along the top wire. In the autumn, cut out the old fruited canes completely and consign them to the bonfire. Release the young new canes from the center "V" and the top wire and fan them out in their fruiting places. In spring, remove the weak tips to encourage fruiting laterals to break freely during the summer.

The most effective way to keep loganberries fruitful is to keep down the disease which causes cane spot. Pruning and training, coupled with healthy plants to start with, go a long way to achieving this.

It is helpful to spray with Bordeaux mixture or a liquid copper fungicide immediately before flowering and again once the fruit has set.

The first year

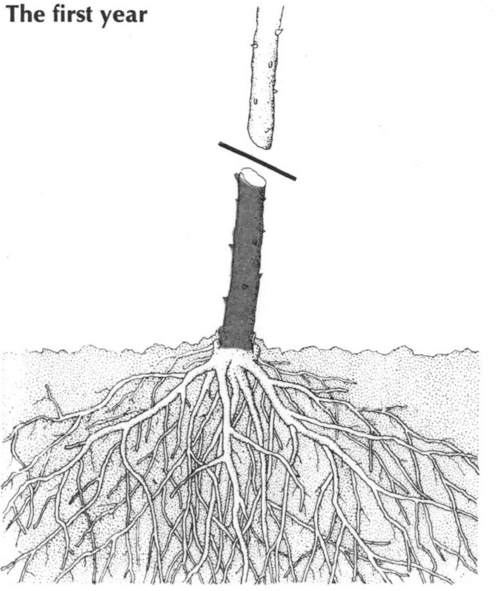

1 November. A well-rooted young loganberry plant shortened to about 10in ready for planting. Plant the canes 8ft apart.

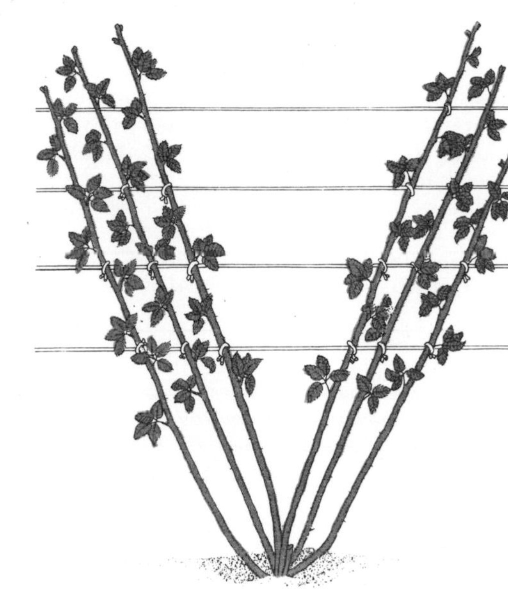

2 June to September. Train the new rods as they appear into a fan shape.

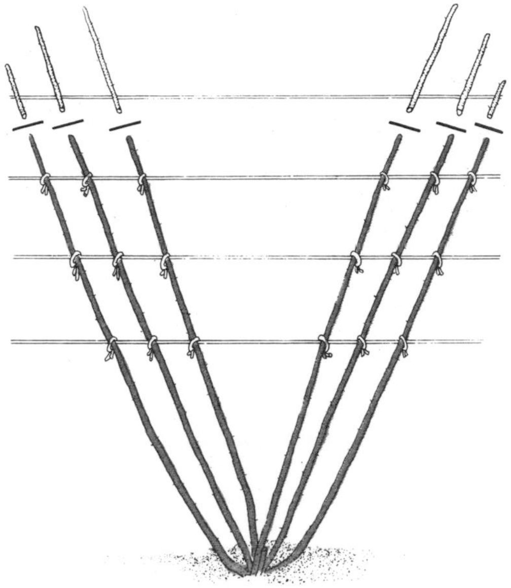

3 February to March. Prune back the weak tips to leave canes approximately 5ft long.

Second and following years

4 July to August. Last year's rods fruit on side-shoots. Train the young rods up the central space and along the top wire, thus keeping young and old separate.

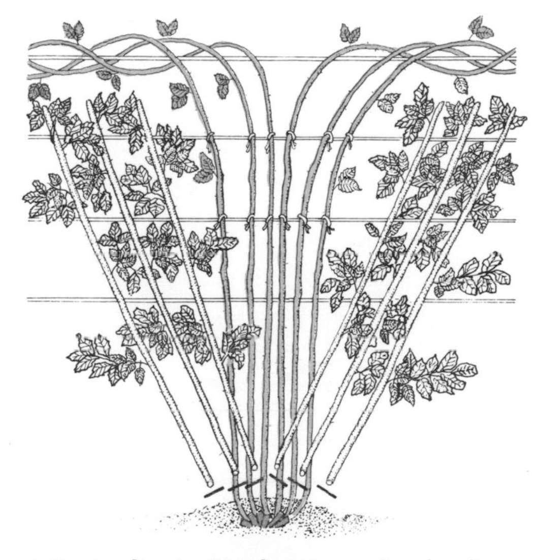

5 September to October. Immediately after harvest cut out the fruited rods completely.

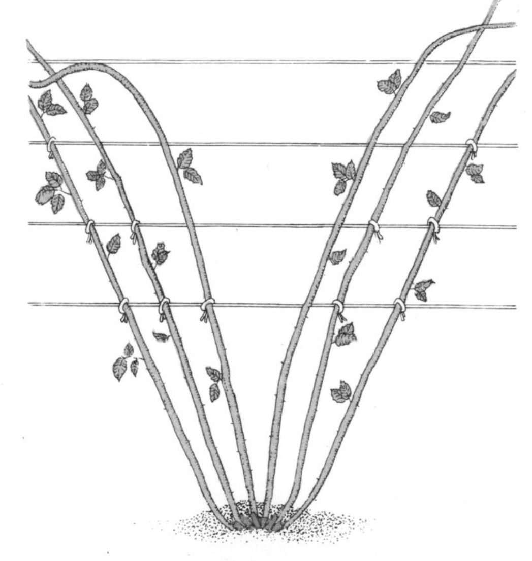

6 At the same time, release the young rods from the center, spread them out and tie them into their fruiting positions. Leave a wide "V" in the center for next year's rods.

Raspberry

The raspberry is a perennial plant with biennial stems. The aim of pruning is to encourage enough, but not too many, new canes to replace the old ones as they fruit and die. There are, however, differences between summer- and autumn-fruiting varieties.

The summer-fruiting varieties are more popular and have heavier crops. The modern range bearing the prefix Malling—'M. Promise' and 'M. Jewel', for example—are in the summer-fruiting group. The fruit is carried on laterals, or side shoots, produced from the canes which grew directly from the root system the previous summer. It follows that the greater the length of cane the greater the number of fruiting laterals, always providing the growth has not been so lush that there is an unusually wide spacing between the buds.

To accommodate the length of cane that modern varieties can produce, the tips of the canes can be bent over so that the upper bearing laterals can still be reached from the ground. This is much better than cutting the canes back to an even height of 5ft, which used to be the routine approach. If the cane growth is weak, perhaps because of poor soil or advanced years, then it is necessary to shorten the canes by the removal of the weak tips.

The autumn-fruiting varieties such as 'September' and 'Zeva' have the knack of fruiting on the new wood. For those who find particular pleasure in eating fresh raspberries in autumn, these varieties are well worth growing, although the crop is not as heavy as that borne by the summer-fruiting kind. The autumn-fruiting varieties spend their energy on the production of annual rather than biennial canes. The annual canes are produced by cutting down all canes in the winter.

The first year

Healthy canes of the summer varieties should be planted in the autumn or winter. Cut these canes back to within 10in of ground level. Do not cut any shorter at this stage or there is a risk of the plant dying.

There will be no fruit the first season. If any flowers appear on the cut-down stumps they should be removed. New canes will emerge from below ground. If there are too many produced, something much more likely to occur in later years, the surplus young canes—collectively called spawn—are thinned out to leave the strongest survivors about 4in apart. Some varieties are prickly and you should use a glove when pulling out the young spawn. Once the new canes are growing well, the 10in stubs should be cut to ground level.

In autumn, twelve months or so after planting, a series of strong canes should have appeared. Tie them into a post and wire support, with the top wire 6ft from the ground. Each cane should stand separate from its neighbors, approximately 4in apart. At this stage, if growth has been strong, loop the tips over to form a series of arches.

The first year

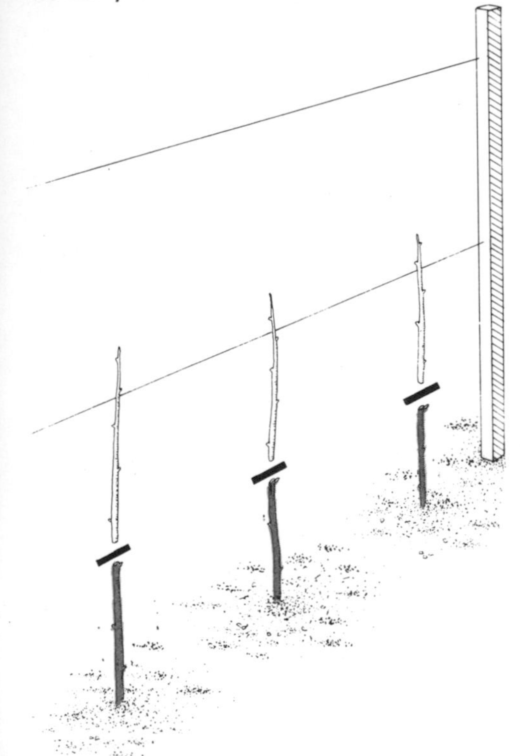

1 November to February. Plant canes 24in apart. Cut back each cane to within 10in of ground level.

2 Spring. New canes appear. Cut down old stumps to ground level.

3 June to September. New canes develop. As they appear, tie each cane 4in apart on to a post or wire support. No fruit is produced this year.

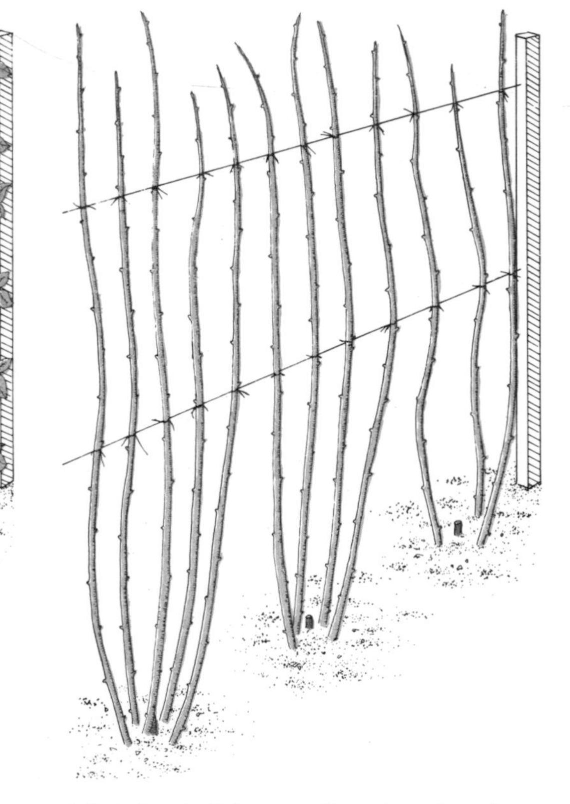

4 October to February. Complete the tying in of canes, 4in apart.

Raspberry

Second and following years
In the early spring—around February—any tips that are either obviously weak or have been damaged by the winter's blasts should be cut back into strong, sound tissue. If this tipping is done in autumn there is the risk of further die-back during winter. After this, the pattern is straightforward: the canes of summer-fruiting varieties that have borne fruit are cut down to ground level as soon as possible after harvest, and the thrusting young canes are tied into the wire to take their place.

Surplus spawn—the excess of the required number is to give a final 4in spacing—should be removed completely during the growing season.

AUTUMN FRUITING

These varieties produce fruits on laterals carried toward the ends of canes grown in the current year.

The first year
The newly planted cane is treated in the same way as the summer-fruiting varieties. A few fruits can be gathered in autumn.

Second and following years
All the cane is cut down to ground level in the early spring so that the new cane is encouraged to grow rapidly, to fruit in September. After fruiting remove the cane.

Second and following years

5 February. Cut back dead and weak tips to about 5ft to encourage fruiting laterals.

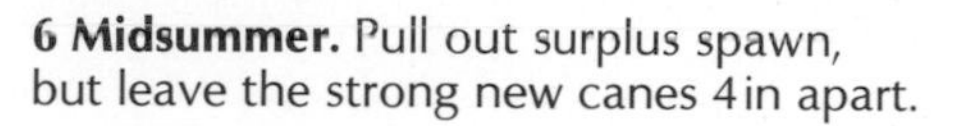

6 Midsummer. Pull out surplus spawn, but leave the strong new canes 4in apart.

7 July to August. Fruit is carried on laterals from last year's canes. New canes continue to develop.

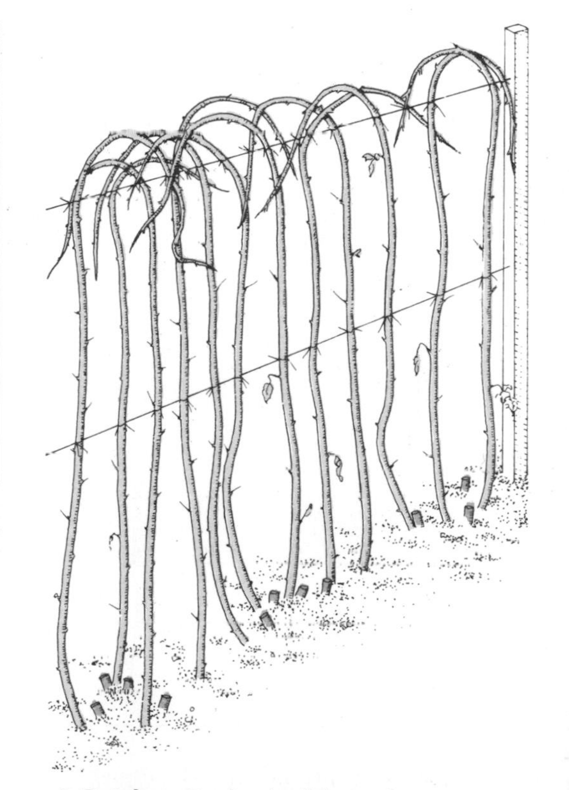

8 October. Cut back all fruited canes to ground level. Tie in new canes 4in apart. If growth is vigorous loop the new canes over to form a series of arches.

Blackberry

The blackberry is often confused with its close relative the loganberry, but the two are best treated separately because the blackberry is much more vigorous and unruly in habit and ideally the training should be slightly different.

Most blackberry varieties are armed with formidable thorns and gloves and old clothes that will cover your arms are necessary when pruning. Because the task of pruning a blackberry can be difficult it is best to train the plants in such a way so that the rods are handled the minimum number of times.

Two methods are illustrated. The one-way system has the advantage of keeping handling to the minimum but wastes space (see page 87). It is not particularly suitable for small gardens. The weaving system is designed to take advantage of extremely long rods. Another approach is to use the neat variety 'Oregon Thornless,' which has the virtue of being easier to handle.

Blackberries fruit on laterals that grow from the rods produced the pervious year. The pruning is relatively simple: all that is necessary is the annual removal of the rods that have fruited and the training-in of new young rods from the base of the plant. Sometimes, however, the new rods are sparsely produced. When this occurs any healthy rods can be retained for a second season of cropping, merely shortening the laterals to 1in or so.

The first year

Plant the canes 10–12ft apart or up to 15ft apart for the more vigorous varieties and shorten them to within 10in of ground level. Train the young rods on wires or up poles as they appear. It is not good to allow them to grow freely; it is important to establish their direction from the beginning.

At the end of the growing season remove the weak tips from the carefully tied-in young rods.

Second and following years

The following summer fruit will be carried on laterals growing from the rods. At the same time new vigorous growths will spring from the base of the plant. These young growths should be secured and directed to a safe place at an early stage, either to one side or straight up and then along the top wire, aiming to keep the fruiting rods separate from the new ones. After fruiting cut out the old rods entirely and train in the new growths to take their place, removing only weak tips from the latter. Subsequent pruning consists of cutting out the fruited rods each year and replacing them with young rods.

The first year

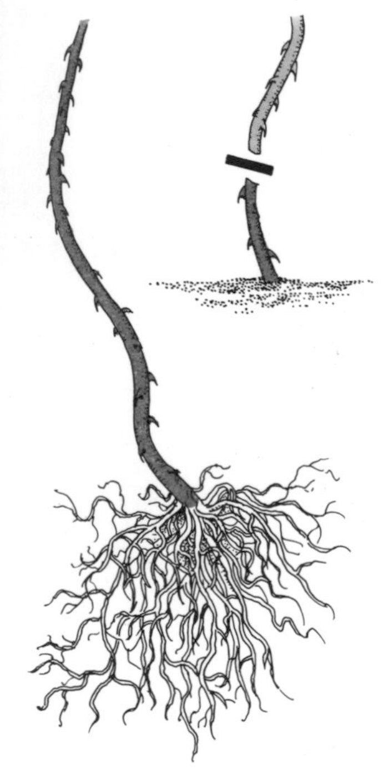

1 November. A well-rooted young blackberry plant. At planting cut back stem to within 10in of ground level. Plant canes 10–15ft apart.

2 Summer. As the young rods appear tie them to a strong wire support. Weave them in and out of the bottom three wires.

Second and following years

3 Summer. Train the new rods up through the centre of the bush and along the top wire. Fruit is carried on laterals of last year's rods.

4 October. After fruiting cut out all fruited rods to base.

5 At the same time, untie the current season's rods and weave them in the lower three wires. At the end of the growing season remove the weak tips from the young rods.

Blackberry

THE ONE-WAY SYSTEM

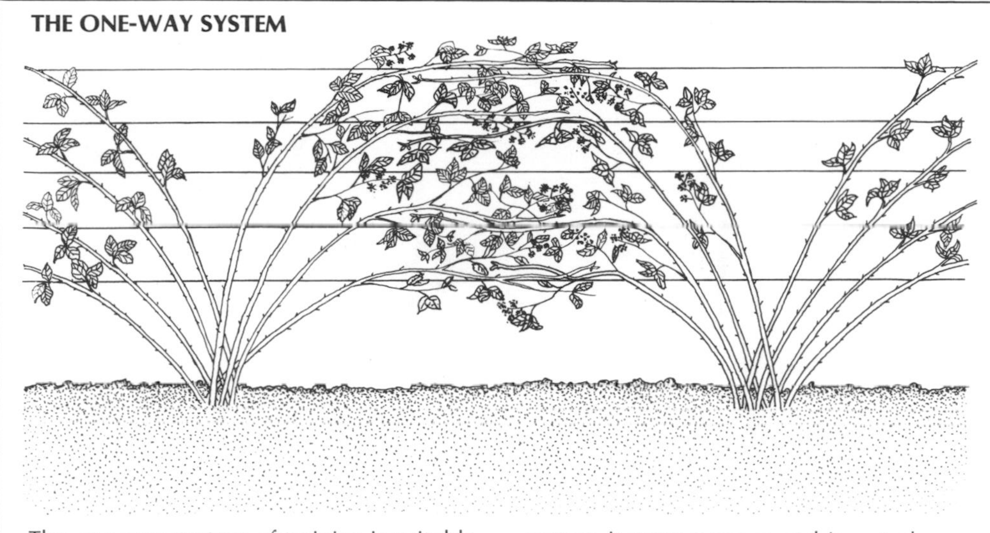

The one-way system of training is suitable for such vigorous varieties as 'Himalaya Giant' and 'Bedford Giant' as the canes need only be handled once. Although it is more straightforward than the weaving system it wastes space and is not always suitable for a small garden.
At planting in November the young plant should be treated as for the "weaving system".

The first year

1 Summer. As young rods appear tie them to a strong wire support. Tie them along the wires to one side of the plant. No fruit is produced this year.

The second year

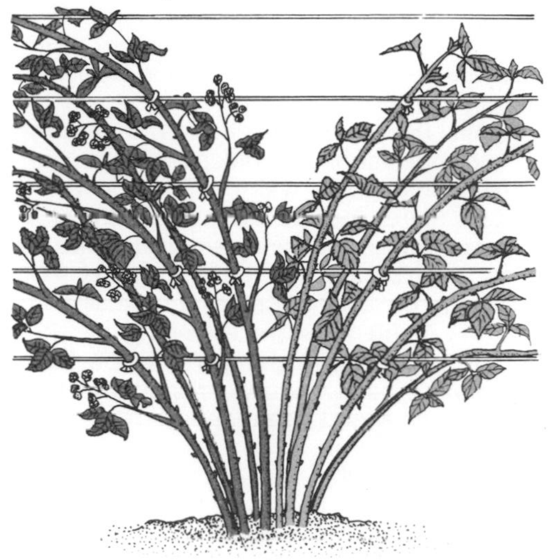

2 Summer. As new rods appear, train them along the wires in the opposite direction to the previous year's growth. Fruit is carried on laterals of last year's rods.

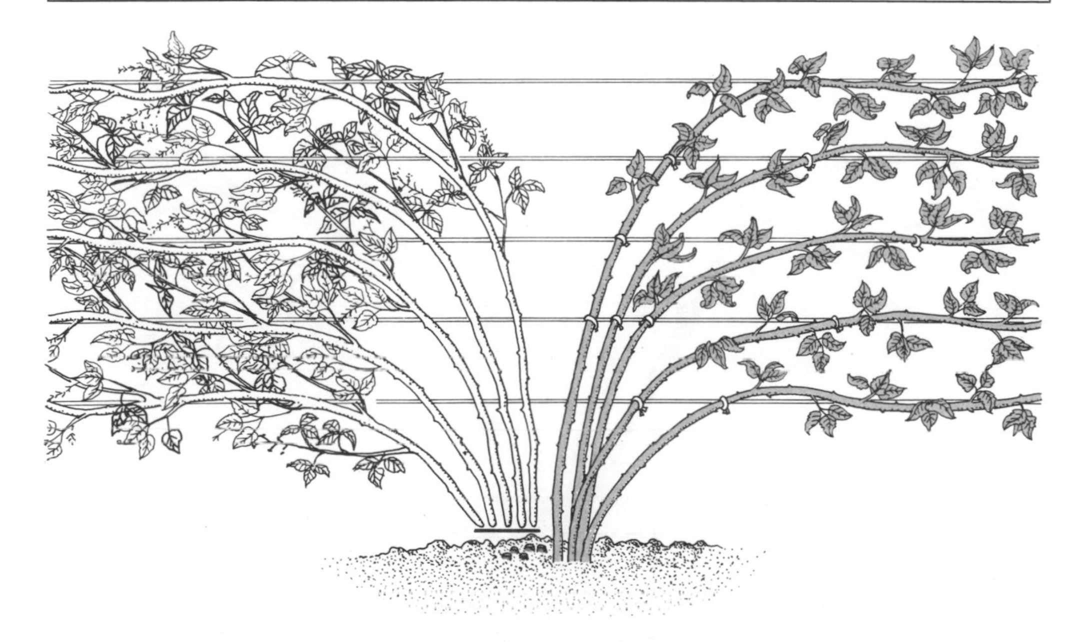

3 October. After fruiting and harvesting untie the fruited rods from the wire and cut them out completely. It is wise to wear stout gloves to protect your hands.

The third year

4 Summer. As new rods appear train them along the wires in the opposite direction to the previous year's growth. Fruit is carried on laterals of last year's rods.

remove 2-3 twiggy old branches - cut to ground or vigorous shoot.

Blueberry

The blueberry is sometimes also referred to loosely as blackberry, whortleberry or bilberry, and is related to the cranberry. With this plant pruning is reduced to a commonsense minimum.

A new impetus has been given to interest in the cultivation of blueberries through increased familiarity with the life style of the United States, where the blueberry is a popular fruit, grown on many thousands of acres of acid land unsuitable for other fruit crops. Some of the American species are highly variable, and interbreeding has occurred, producing high-bush and low-bush blueberries, and a number of named varieties. It is the high-bush kinds that have responded best to cultivation.

Any garden that grows good rhododendrons can also be used for blueberries. Bushes grow quite tall under favourable, acid soil conditions, and may reach 12ft in height but are more likely to be about half as tall.

Vigorous shoots grow from the base of the stock or close to the ground. The fruit is carried on side-shoots, the flower buds appearing on the previous year's growth.

Fruiting becomes irregular and the individual fruits become smaller unless the bush is stimulated by manuring or fertilizing and pruning. Pruning essentially consists of thinning out the crowded and worn-out shoots and branches. The usual approach is to leave the bushes largely untouched for the first three years after planting. In subsequent winters cut back to a vigorous young shoot or to ground level two or three of the previously fruited branches that have become markedly twiggy and thus likely to overcrop. Broken branches, dead shoots and branches that have become too close to the ground because of the weight of cropping are also removed. And that is all there is to the pruning of blueberries—common, garden sense.

Fruits are carried on side-shoots. Detailed pruning is not required.

Well-furnished young shoot carrying large fruits.

Fruiting unit showing signs of age. Cut back in winter to a vigorous shoot or to ground level.

Third and subsequent years

November to February. Cut back two or three of the fruited branches that have become twiggy to a vigorous young shoot or to ground level. Cut out close to the base any broken or dead branches, dead shoots and branches that have grown too close to the ground from the weight of the fruit they carry.

Trees: introduction

Although many gardeners will prune roses and shrubs regularly each season few consider it necessary to train or prune the trees they grow. Training and pruning during the early years of a tree's life, however, are essential to obtain shapely, well-furnished and healthy specimens.

Usually nurseries can be relied upon to provide well trained young trees that have been correctly tended from the propagation stage. In most cases only relatively minor pruning is required to continue to build on this early training and produce an attractive tree with a symmetrical, well-balanced crown.

The aim is to obtain a plant with evenly spaced branches that form a strong framework. Crossing or misplaced branches should be cut out wherever possible at this early stage, but care must be taken not to spoil the natural habit of the tree. The weight of the branches on a mature tree is considerable and it is essential for the stem and main branch system to be able to support them. Good early training reduces the risk of wind or storm damage in later years.

Once trees are well established the need for more than cosmetic pruning involving the 3 D's is minimal (see page 3). Most gardeners will not find it practical to do more than cut out the odd branch once the tree has approached a good size. Any major pruning or thinning of the crown of large trees is best dealt with by a competent tree surgeon approved by your state or local nurserymen's society; he is a specialist and has the equipment to carry out the work safely and correctly. Be warned. Avoid unknown "tree surgeons." They may be cheaper but are liable to mutilate trees and may leave them in a far more dangerous condition than before they started the renovation pruning.

Seedlings or rooted cuttings
The terminal bud of a seedling, or the uppermost bud in the case of a rooted cutting, produces a vigorous upright extension shoot, the leader, which at intervals during the growing season should be tied to a suitably strong stake to form the main stem. Usually, although not invariably, lateral shoots grow from buds lower down the stem. If a tree with a length of clear stem—a "leg"—is required, all the laterals produced during the first growing season are cut back by half their length when they reach 9–12in. A few of the upper laterals produced later in the season may be left unpruned until the following year. The pruning of laterals channels much of the food supply towards the leader so that the maximum length and thickness of the stem is achieved in the shortest time. Cut back the stubs of the pruned laterals flush with the stem in late autumn or early winter.

This training process, the removal of the current season's laterals in two stages, is repeated each year until the desired length of clear stem has been produced.

If the aim is to produce a tree with a single main stem and branches almost to ground level—a feathered tree—then only a few of the smaller and weaker near-basal laterals need to be removed during the second or third year. With feathered trees no further pruning of laterals is normally needed during the initial training.

Grafted or budded plants
Few gardeners attempt to bud or graft trees themselves, but sometimes nurseries offer one-year grafted or budded plants. If these have been grown with a clean stem they are known as maiden trees; if lateral growth is present they are called feathered maidens.

If a clear stem is required the two-stage pruning of laterals is carried out in exactly the same way as described previously.

SUCKER GROWTHS

Many garden trees are propagated by budding or grafting on to a stock of a related species and, even on established vigorous trees, suckers may grow from the stock. These should be removed as they appear or they will gradually weaken the tree. Suckers that appear below the budding or grafting point or on the stems of top-worked plants should be carefully pulled or cut away and the cut surface pared over with a knife. If the pared surface is fairly large a wound paint should be applied. If suckers are simply cut back, dormant buds may be present on the snags and more suckers will grow.

EPICORMIC OR WATER SHOOTS

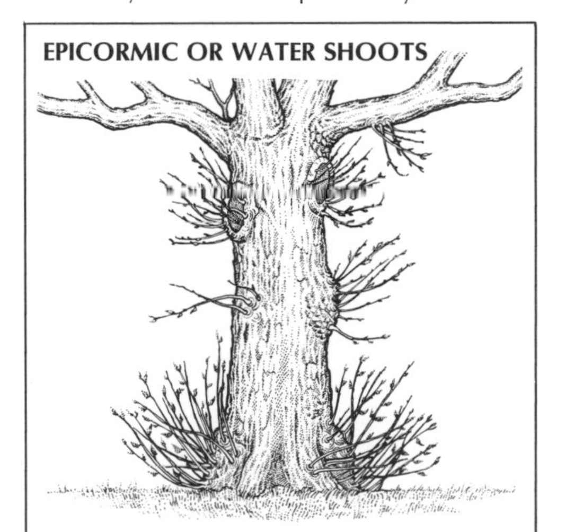

Clusters of strong shoots may arise from dormant or adventitious buds on the trunks or main branches of trees, from the edges of a wound where a branch has been removed, or directly through the bark on the trunk or from its base. The water shoots seen on apple trees subjected to "haircut" pruning are of similar origin.

They should be cut out to the base every year preferably during the dormant season (October to February) wherever it is practical to do so. If left they may contribute to the weakening of branches higher up in the crown of the tree by using up part of the food supply.

Leader shoots
The terminal bud of the main shoot or leader of a young tree is normally dominant in growth and generally controls the development and growth of lateral buds and shoots. If the leader is broken or damaged, or is very weak, it is important to train in a replacement to take over its functions as soon as possible. Uneven growth is then avoided.

Select a strong, conveniently placed lateral and train it as near to the vertical as possible; or if the damage occurs in late autumn or winter cut back the leader to a strong growth bud and train in vertically the shoot which develops from this bud. A long bamboo cane should be tied firmly to the stake to extend the length of the support.

In the case of taller, more mature trees, no longer staked, the cane may be tied to the main stem itself. Care must be taken to ensure that the ties holding the cane never cause constriction of the main stem as this will retard its growth.

Once the leader is well established after one or two seasons the cane should be removed and after a few years it will be difficult to see where the replacement treatment occurred.

If one or more of the lateral shoots begin to overtake and dominate the leader, cut back the overenthusiastic growth slightly to re-stimulate the terminal shoot.

Forked or competing leaders
Trees sometimes develop two rival leaders, either naturally or through damage to the main shoot. If both are allowed to develop they may eventually form main branches which are the equivalent of large tree-trunks in size.

Gradually the angled, forked leaders will be pulled apart by the weight of the branches and cracks or weakness will develop at the angle where they join (crotch). Water lodging in the crotch will cause decay. In severe gales a large part of the tree is liable to tear away at the weak point, leaving an ugly tree which is still a source of danger. At the earliest stage possible, the better placed of the two leaders should be left and staked, and trained vertically as previously described, while the rival leader should be cut out completely.

Trees: introduction

The natural habit and growth of trees inevitably affects the ways in which they can be trained and pruned. It cannot be emphasized too strongly that the individual growth characteristics of the tree can be spoiled by rigorous training and overenthusiastic pruning. Some trees such as *Parrotia persica* naturally produce, from the base, a number of gently twisting stems with attractive flaking bark. These should be left virtually untrained, with pruning restricted to the removal of the occasional wayward branch that upsets the symmetry of the tree.

In some gardens the formality of the single-stemmed tree may not be suitable. Birches, alders and a number of other trees will form multi-stemmed plants of slightly informal growth which may be more in keeping.

With these exceptions in mind the habit of trees for garden purposes can roughly be divided into two main categories. The first contains those trees that are grown with a single central leader. The laterals are spaced at fairly regular intervals along the length of the leader and may or may not have a length of clear stem at the base. Their ultimate shape is pyramidal or conical.

The second group contains trees with branched, balanced heads lacking a central leader but usually on clear stems of 5–7ft. Generally they have a more bushy, rounded appearance and differ in their method of training and to some extent in their later pruning treatment.

Variations on these two themes occur and those divisions must not be regarded as rigid.

Staking

Although it may not appear directly relevant to pruning, correct staking of young trees is very important. Trees that are given inadequate stakes, or no stake at all, are vulnerable to wind damage and the breaking of branches or may produce uneven, one-sided growth. This almost always complicates training and pruning. A strong, correctly positioned stake preferably with adjustable, flexible tree ties, is essential for a well-balanced tree.

After a few years, when the tree is fully established, the stake can be removed, but in the meantime a periodic check is needed to make sure that the stem is not being constricted by the tree ties. Adjustable, flexible, plastic tree ties should be used rather than rope. Wire should never be used.

Feeding and watering

Feeding and watering may not at first appear relevant to training or pruning but a young tree that lacks adequate food or water will grow slowly and unevenly. If insufficient vigorous young growth is produced then early training is much more difficult. Make sure that the soil in the planting hole is mixed with well-rotted manure or compost prior to planting and also give a dressing of a balanced fertilizer following planting. Finish off by mulching the base of the tree well, a process that should be carried out each spring during the early years of the tree's life to help to maintain vigor.

Water the young tree during any dry periods for the first season or two after planting—it may seem unnecessary but it pays.

LIMB OR BRANCH REMOVAL

Heavy and awkwardly placed branches on large trees should always be dealt with by a reliable, qualified tree surgeon. Most gardeners can remove smaller branches from their trees when this is needed.

The old practice of leaving stubs of cut branches on the trunk is both unsightly and dangerous. The stub or peg almost always dies and provides an entry point for disease spores. The branch should always be removed flush with the trunk or parent branch while exposing the smallest area of cut surface possible without leaving an unnecessary stub.

The method is simple. If the branch is fairly long and too thick to cut easily it should first be cut back to leave a stub of about 12–18in. If necessary cut a long, heavy branch into several convenient, manageable lengths to reduce the weight in easy stages.

A final cut from above will remove the stub of small branches cleanly, but branches of any size should be undercut slightly, close to the point of origin, before the final cut is made from above. This undercut prevents any possible tearing of the bark below the branch. All wounds should be carefully pared over with a sharp knife and covered with a wound paint.

1 Cut the branch into convenient lengths at the points shown to reduce the weight. Leave a stub of 12–18in.

Heavy branch

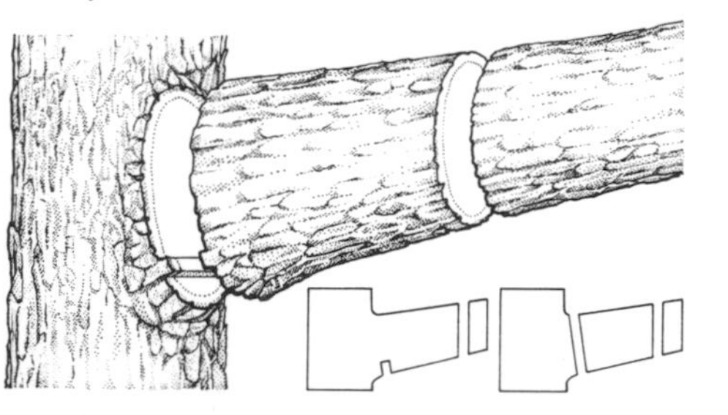

3 Undercut the stub slightly, close to the trunk, to prevent the bark being torn. Cut the stub through from above.

Medium branch

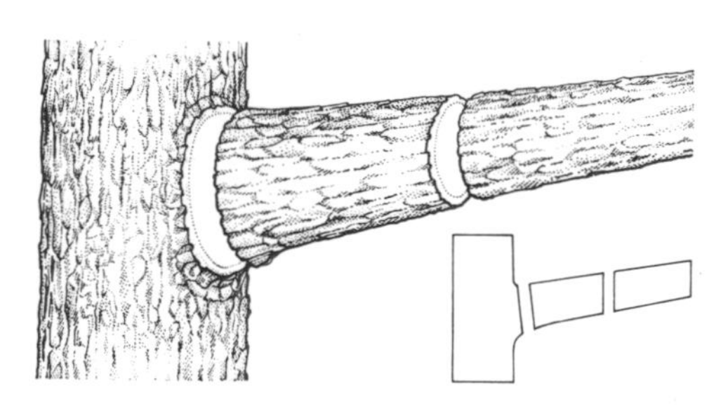

2 Cut the stub from above. Angle the cut very slightly away from the trunk to avoid creating too large a wound.

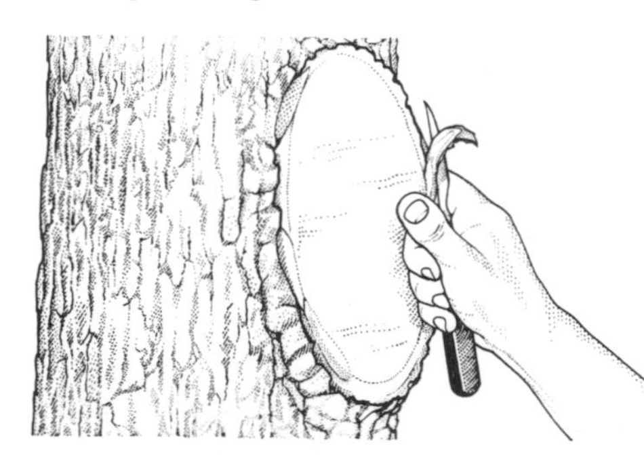

4 Pare the edges of the cut surface to make them smooth. Apply a wound paint to protect the entire cut surface.

INCORRECT PROCEDURE

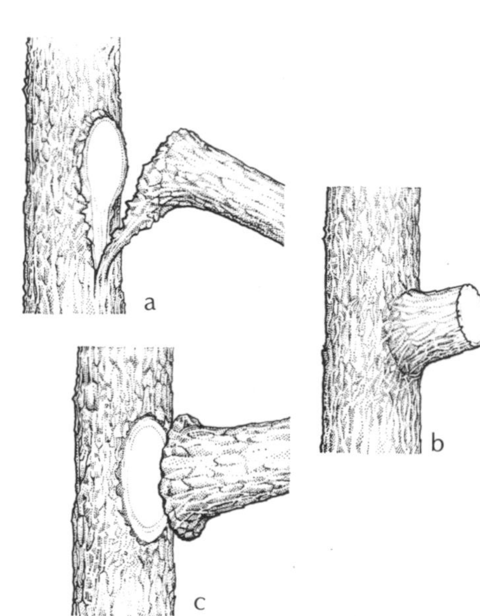

Unless undercut, the weight of a heavy branch will tear the bark of the trunk (a). An ugly stub left behind will almost certainly die back, and is an entry point for disease (b). A dangerously large and vulnerable wound results from a cut made too close to the trunk (c).

Feathered Tree

Stake tree init
remove basal shoots
maintain strong central leader
remove competing laterals
remove damaged wood
remove weak, poorly placed laterals

The feathered tree is the most natural form of deciduous tree, with a single main stem well furnished with lateral shoots almost to the base. This is the typical growth pattern for the silver birches, poplars, rowans, alders and many other common trees.

Early training is simple. The most important point is to make sure the prominent leader remains dominant and that a forked or double leader is not allowed to develop. Similarly, any basal stems that grow and may rival the leader should be removed as soon as possible, unless a multi-stemmed tree is required.

A feathered tree will branch naturally and roughly symmetrical on its own. Only if a lateral is badly placed or likely to unbalance the overall shape is any pruning needed. Any lateral that is poorly placed should be cut out entirely in October or November.

The first few lateral branches are usually small and do not develop well, but later the laterals increase in size and vigor, keeping pace with the leader. As the tree develops the smaller near-basal laterals are removed, leaving a short, clear stem at the base of the tree. With vigorous trees they may be cut back to the stem at the end of the season or, if preferred, they may be removed in two stages as described on page 89.

As the tree matures it may be necessary to remove a few laterals if they are crowded, or to completely prune away some of the lower branches if they interfere with mowing or other necessary cultivation. Otherwise, apart from cutting out any rival leaders which appear and removing damaged, diseased or dead wood, no further pruning is usually necessary.

As will be realized, a feathered tree can readily be trained as a standard with a central leader by cutting back the laterals flush with the stem each autumn until the required height is reached.

The first year

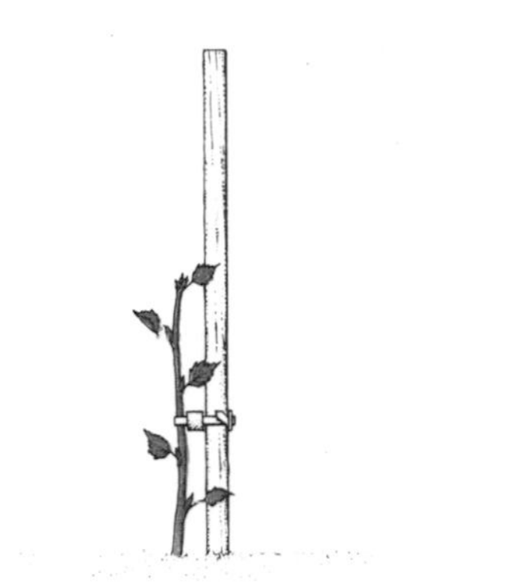

1 April to July. Stake and tie in the central leader shoot as it develops.

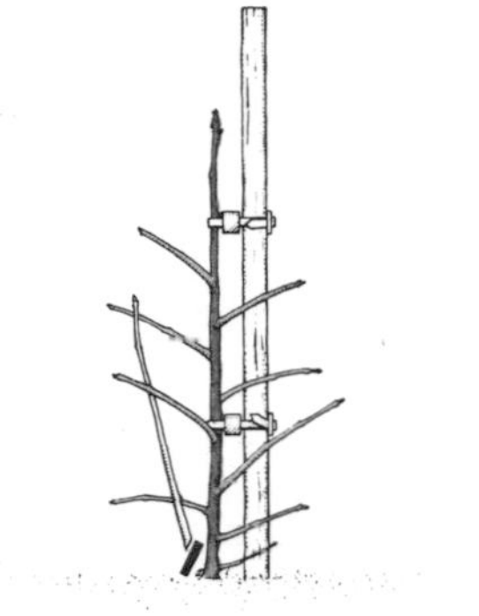

2 October to November. Laterals have developed. Cut out any basal shoots.

The second year

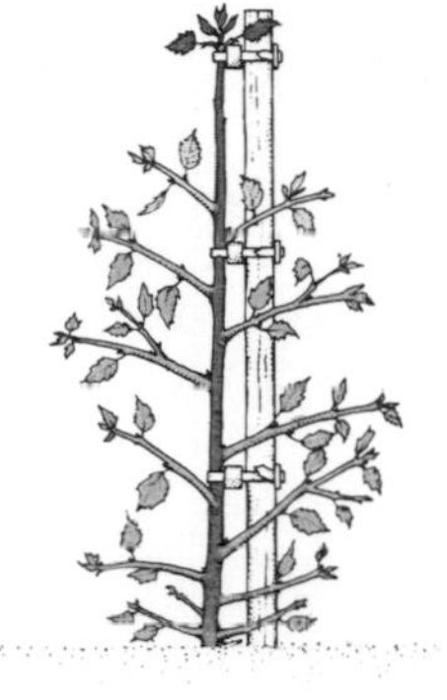

3 April to July. Tie in the central leader as it grows during spring and summer.

The third year

4 October to November. Carefully remove weak basal laterals flush with the main stem. Cut out dead, damaged and diseased wood.

5 April to July. Further extension growth of the leader occurs. Cut out the lateral that is competing with the leader.

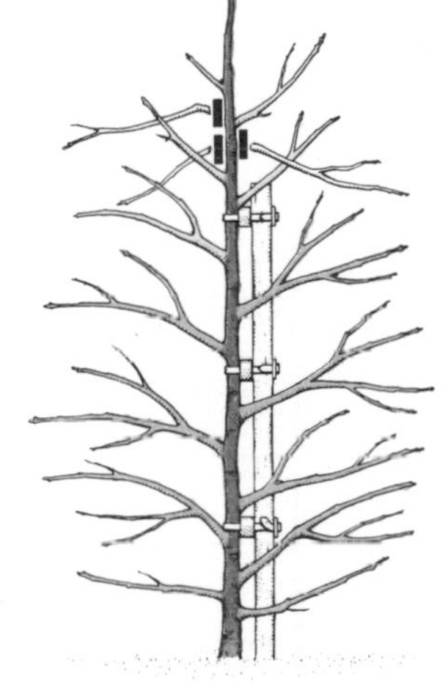

6 October to November. Cut out any badly placed and weak laterals or sublaterals that spoil the symmetry and balance of the young tree. Cut out dead, damaged or diseased wood.

Fourth and following years

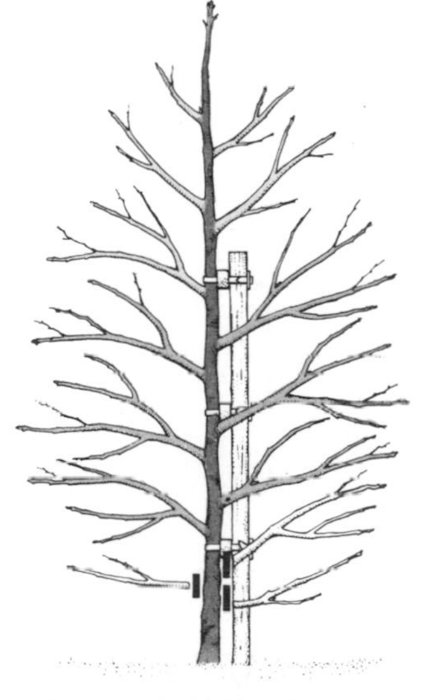

7 October to November. If a cl[...] the stem is required, cut out a [...] lowest laterals flush with the st[...] this in the following autumns u[...] desired height of clear stem is [...]

92

Branched-head Standard Tree

Standard tree

The standard is the commonest form used for ornamental trees. The main stem is clear of branches for the first $5\frac{1}{2}$–6ft from ground level. The formation of the crown of the tree will differ, depending on the natural growth of the plant and the kind of tree required.

Branched-head standard

The lowest branches of a mature tree are $5\frac{1}{2}$–6ft from the ground, but there is no central leader. A branched but balanced head is formed, either naturally or by artificial training. This growth habit is suitable for such small trees as ornamental cherries and crab apples but is not recommended for very large trees. Oaks, elms and a number of other trees sometimes form branched heads naturally, but mechanically this kind of branch formation is less sound than the central-leader growth habit.

Initial training is exactly the same as for a central-leader standard. Once the appropriate length of clear stem has been formed, cut back the leader so that the buds below are stimulated into forming laterals that act as the main framework of the branched head. With many trees these laterals will have formed naturally and if present should be cut back by one-half their length when the leader is pruned. The lowest of these laterals should be $5\frac{1}{2}$–6ft from the ground if the conventional standard tree is required. Allowance must be made for this when cutting the leader back to form the branched head, the laterals forming on the first foot or so above the clear leg.

The framework branches should be as evenly spaced as possible and any crowded or crossing branches should be cut out at this stage. Thereafter the framework branches are allowed to develop naturally, further pruning being confined to maintaining a balanced, even shape.

Vigorous, upright shoots may develop within the framework on young trees for a few years and, if left, will quickly develop into new leaders. Remove them immediately if an open-center tree is to be maintained.

CENTRAL-LEADER STANDARD

This is similar to a feathered tree but with the lowest branches $5\frac{1}{2}$–6ft from the ground.

Early training

Stake and tie the vigorous extension leader of a young seedling or root cutting.

Usually, although not always, the lateral shoots grow from buds lower down the stem. All the laterals produced during the first growing season are cut back by one-half their length when they reach 9–12in. A few of the upper laterals produced later in the season may be left unpruned.

The pruning of laterals channels much of the food supply toward the leader. Cut back the pruned laterals flush with the stem in late autumn or early winter.

This training process is repeated each year until the desired length of clear stem has been produced.

The third year

1 October to November. Cut back the leader to a strong bud or lateral 12–18in above the length of clear stem required.

The fourth year

2 April to July. Further laterals and sublaterals develop. No pruning is required.

3 October to November. A framework of 3–5 evenly spaced laterals is required. Remove crossing or crowded laterals and sublaterals. Remove any vigorous, upright shoots which may form a new leader.

Fifth and following years

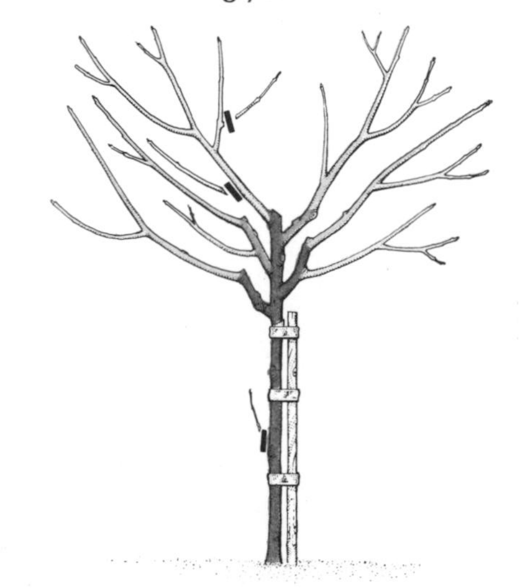

4 October to November. Cut out any young branches that threaten the symmetry or the open center of the tree. Remove any feathers that develop on the clean stem and main branches.

Renovation

Trees that have been neglected or mutilated by improper pruning are all too common in gardens. They may be overgrown large trees such as oaks or cedars that have received no attention since they were planted and are full of dead wood and damaged branches; sometimes they may be ornamental crabs or cherries choked in the center with thin, weak growth. Or they may have been brutally and unskillfully chopped each winter until their shorn branches resemble an army haircut.

In all cases some remedial treatment is required. The first essential is to remove all dead, damaged and diseased wood completely and survey what is left. With large trees treatment by a competent tree surgeon will almost certainly be necessary. The removal of large tree limbs is a skilled job and it is extremely dangerous to attempt to cut off large branches without the correct equipment and knowledge.

When working with neglected small trees, such as crab apples and flowering cherries, the aim, once the 3 D's have been carried out, is to re-create the original balance of branches and an open-center habit. Remove crossing or rubbing branches and the jumble of upright or inward-growing shoots usually to be found in the center. If necessary one or two larger branches that spoil the overall balance of the framework can be removed completely.

Water shoots will probably appear after major pruning and should be removed as they appear, preferably by rubbing away.

The knobby spurs of the "haircut" pruned tree need drastic thinning in order to reestablish normal growth.

Each of the main branches should then be thinned if the side-shoots are overcrowded, taking care to keep the growth evenly distributed. But be careful not to end up with a skeleton of stubby branches by overenthusiastic pruning.

This rejuvenation treatment will probably stimulate a burst of water shoots for a season or two after major pruning has occurred and those should be removed as previously described (see page 89).

The "haircut" pruned tree has suffered from the annual winter trimming of all new growth, which results in a framework of knobby branches, each similar to a stump, and producing a congested cluster of growth shoots every season. Apart from its extreme ugliness this treatment actively discourages flower and fruit production, so it is essential either to replace the tree if it is beyond treatment or to prune it carefully to produce a balanced, attractive specimen once again.

The treatment is much the same as described before, differing only in the pruning of the knobbly stumps at the ends of the main branches. These need drastic thinning so that the "knobs" are reduced to one or two at the ends of the branches. The cluster of one-year-old growths on the retained "knobs" is also reduced to one or two shoots, the remainder being cut out completely. Cut back the remaining one-year-old shoots by about one-third of their length.

With this treatment a reasonably balanced growth pattern can be developed and within a few seasons the tree will resume its normal habit and shape.

Rejuvenation treatment is best carried out in late autumn or early winter, particularly for those trees that produce large quantities of sap and are liable to "bleed" profusely if they are pruned during the growing season or just before the growing season in winter.

Conifers, birches, walnuts, maples and horsechestnuts all come into this category and are best pruned during October and November. With oaks, beeches, limes, hornbeams and other "dry" wood trees pruning can be carried out at any season, although it is best to avoid spring. The major exceptions to pruning in the dormant season are the cherries (and other members of the genus *Prunus*), which should be dealt with during the summer before the end of July as this minimizes problems with silver leaf disease.

All pruning cuts of more than ¼–½in in diameter should be pared over and covered with a wound paint as soon as possible.

In addition to the two main kinds of standard tree described, tall standards with clear stems of 6–7ft, three-quarter standards (4½–5½ft), half standards (3½–4ft) and bush trees (1–2½ft) are sometimes produced. The training method does not differ from that of the conventional standard (see page 92).

Some trees produce weeping variants and these are usually propagated by topworking on to stocks with 5½–6ft stems to produce weeping standards. Again pruning should be restricted to removing shoots that threaten to spoil the overall balance of the tree. Some weeping variants such as *Fagus sylvatica* 'Pendula' the weeping beech, tend to throw up a series of semi-upright stems that produce long, weeping growths and create a flowing, unevenly mounded plant. These stems should not be cut out but allowed to develop normally as this is the natural growth form.

Broadleaved evergreen trees

Relatively few broadleaved evergreen trees are grown in gardens. They usually require only a minimum of training as young plants are best treated as feathered trees (see page 91). A strong central leader should be established and any badly placed laterals or competing leaders cut out during the early years of growth. As the tree develops further pruning (apart from the 3 D's) is seldom necessary and often undesirable. The attractive, billowing outlines of trees such as *Quercus ilex*, the Holm or evergreen oak, can be ruined by attempts to prune them formally and they are best left alone to develop naturally.

Conifers

The feathered tree technique can also be used on most conifers. The basic growth pattern of pines and firs is for a single central leader to grow with whorls of branches developing at fairly regular intervals along its length. They should be left to grow naturally and only if the shoots are damaged is any pruning or training (apart from staking) necessary. Sometimes the leader or the terminal bud dies and one or more shoots from the uppermost whorl will usually begin to replace it naturally. As soon as the need for a replacement leader is seen the best-placed shoot of the upper whorl should be trained vertically as described on page 89. Any competing shoots should be cut out completely.

Several conifers such as yew, *Chamaecyparis* and *Thuja* make excellent hedge plants and withstand clipping as young plants. Unlike broadleaved trees, however, conifers (with the exception of yew) do not regenerate readily from mature wood as there are few or no dormant buds present in the older woody branches and stems. Any pruning of mature conifers should be restricted to removing entirely dead or moribund branches. Attempts to reduce them in height normally prove unsatisfactory and frequently leave ugly, mutilated plants that are best removed.

Index

This index refers to the appropriate pruning group and the page for the genera listed. Where there is a slight variation from the pruning suggested for a particular group, this is briefly described. Some genera such as *Buddleia* contain several groups of species, each requiring different pruning methods and these are listed separately.

Occasionally one or two species require a pruning technique different from the remainder of the genus. It is not possible to deal with these in detail but common sense dictates that low-growing birches such as *Betula medwediewii* and *B. nana* and the dwarf mountain ashes *Sorbus reducta* and *S. pygmaea* are treated as shrubs and not as feathered trees or central-leader standards as would apply to most other species in these genera.

Not every plant will fit neatly into the groups described. Not all the shrubs listed as Shrubs group 2, for example, will require pruning exactly as *Buddleia davidii*, which is illustrated. The principles are correct but most *Sorbaria* species, which come into this group, produce basal growths annually unlike *B. davidii*. A more substantial well-spaced framework is required for *Sorbaria* species and the basal growths can be used to renew old and weak framework shoots in mature plants. It is therefore important to take into account the natural habit of a plant and its position in the garden before applying the pruning techniques described.

A

B

C

D

E

Index

Index 3/Acknowledgments

ACKNOWLEDGMENTS
Artists: Tony Graham, Chris Forsey, Mike Saunders, William Giles, Terri Lawlor, Paul Buckle, Ray Burrows, Bob Scott, Roger Hughes, Harry Chlow, Venner Artists, Cynthia Swaby, Alan White.

All artwork in this book has been based on photographs specially commissioned from R. Robinson of the Harry Smith Horticultural Photographic Collection.